MORE DINERS, DRIVE-INS AND DIVES

MORE

Diners

DRIVE-INS.

DIVES

A DROP-TOP
CULINARY CRUISE
THROUGH AMERICA'S
FINEST AND FUNKIEST
JOINTS

food network

guy fieri

WITH ANN
VOLKWEIN

WILLIAM MORROW
An Imprint of HarperCollins*Publishers*

HarperCollins books may be purchased for educational, business, or sales promotional use. For information please write: Special Markets Department, HarperCollins Publishers, 10 East 53rd Street, New York, NY 10022.

FIRST EDITION

Designed by Kris Tobiassen

Library of Congress Cataloging-in-Publication Data has been applied for.

ISBN 978-0-06-189456-5

09   10   11   12   13   ID/RRD   10   9   8   7   6   5   4   3   2   1

To all the road-trippin', off-da-hook eatin'
fans of Triple D—that's money!

Guy!

Contents

NORTHEAST AND MID-ATLANTIC

SOUTH

MIDWEST

WEST AND SOUTHWEST

Foreword

by Emeril Lagasse

How fascinating are American diners, drive-ins, and dives? I remember eating some of my first family meals with my parents at Al Mac's Diner in my hometown of Fall River, Massachussetts. It was a proud moment for them, and it's a special food memory for me. Then I realized that my hometown had lots of great diners and drive-ins, especially between Memorial Day and Labor Day. I cherish the memories of clam rolls and buckets of fried clams, hot dogs from Nick's, cheeseburgers from King Phillip, chow mein sandwiches from MeeSums. Wow—what memories! My mouth is watering just thinking about it.

It's so refreshing to know that America has so many of these special places from pizza to cheese steaks and po-boys to pulled pork sandwiches. From the East to the West, from the Midwest to the South, we are so blessed with these American treasures each serving their own "food of love." And that, my friends, is what Guy Fieri brings to you in this book: an American journey of very special food, people, and places that he and his amazing team discover and share with you. It's a journey of some of America's finest people, places, and stories—and great food.

Oh, and did I forget to mention that the book has great recipes? So take an adventure with Guy across America with a true gem of a book. Hold on tight as Guy puts you in the zone. The American food zone!

BAM!

I'M CONCENTRATING REALLY HARD . . . TRYING TO RETRIEVE MY BLING!

Introduction

All I wanted was to be a great dad and a chef—to own a restaurant, cook what I want, feed people, make them happy—okay, maybe I wanted to be a rock star, but I can't play a thing, so that wasn't going to happen.

But I gotta tell you, I totally dig what I've got goin' on now. It's taken on a whole new life, and the relationships that I have with the locations we cover is indescribable. I get to shine a light on a real group of people—not the high-end joints with the seventy-five-dollar filet and such-and-such. I get to bring out the kid and adventurer in all of us, and it benefits families, communities, and our country. We're reminding people to get back to the basics: real food from real people. When I'm on the road, missing my family, I can always bring myself back around because the show has such an amazing impact on the people profiled through more business and expanded opportunities.

Hopefully my industry will say I carried the torch for the mom-and-pop joints. Helping rebuild American culture, one funky joint at a time.

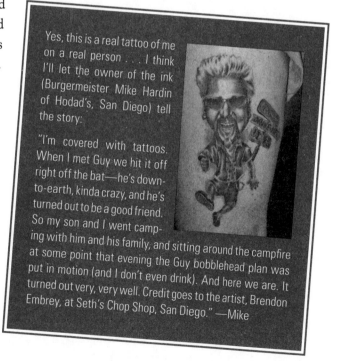

Yes, this is a real tattoo of me on a real person . . . I think I'll let the owner of the ink (Burgermeister Mike Hardin of Hodad's, San Diego) tell the story:

"I'm covered with tattoos. When I met Guy we hit it off right off the bat—he's down-to-earth, kinda crazy, and he's turned out to be a good friend. So my son and I went camping with him and his family, and sitting around the campfire at some point that evening the Guy bobblehead plan was put in motion (and I don't even drink). And here we are. It turned out very, very well. Credit goes to the artist, Brendon Embrey, at Seth's Chop Shop, San Diego." —Mike

A Q&A WITH "GUIDO" FIERI

I'm a Letterman fan, so in honor of Dave and the Top 10 . . .

TOP TEN QUESTIONS I'M ASKED ABOUT TRIPLE D

10) Do you like everything? Uh, no—do you? If I don't like it, I won't lie and tell you I do.

9) Funkiest thing you've eaten? See page 5.

8) Is the car yours? No. Thank goodness it's a Chevy, but no.

7) Do you drive the car everywhere? We've gone over 150,000 miles the last three seasons. I would be dead and the car would be, too.

6) You're not as fat in real life as you are on TV—why? Because the camera adds five pounds. (Now don't say, "What, so you have five cameras then?")

5) Have you ever been to this place, it's this small place over by this one town by a bridge . . . ? My aunt's friend's sisters used to have a place . . . Okay, let's take a moment, folks. We've done 250-plus shows. Do you really think I've been everywhere? Ha ha.

4) What was the place where the guy had on the T-shirt that says "I love ribs"? No idea.

3) Do you really not like eggs? No, I don't like them just as eggs, but I'm cool with them in dishes.

2) Do you eat it all? No, but sometimes they have to pry it out of my hands because it's so good. Otherwise I'll eat so much I'll go into a food coma.

1) Here's the number one question everyone asks me—drumroll, please: What's your favorite diner, drive-in, or dive? IMPOSSIBLE. That's like asking what was your favorite day of your life! There's not just a dish, location, or person. I'm happy I'm not able to define one of them as my favorite; that would make it hard to continue on with the show. Instead, I have a ton that go into my top 100 places.

DO YOU EVER BURN YOUR MOUTH SO BADLY YOU CAN'T TASTE ANYTHING? I haven't burned it that bad, but I've burned the top and bottom back of my throat and the side of my mouth, and I had hot cheese smeared under my goatee and burned my chin. Hot grease from a Philly cheesesteak ran down my arm and burned my armpit. I've burned my feet because I wear flip-flops like a genius in the kitchen. You see, when I prepare for a show I don't eat before filming because I want my palate to be fresh. Maybe I'll have a cup of coffee and a banana. But if I've sat back and watched this guy make a chili cheesesteak, by the time he's done I want to eat it—and it's the hot center that nails me.

WHAT ARE YOUR FAVORITE TYPES OF RESTAURANTS TO SHOOT? The funky, more dive-style kind of place is my favorite, not because they don't all have great merit but because they're probably the most surprising. You walk in and they're completely jacked up—and they end up nailing you with some crazy-good food. There might be no sign out front, or it's in an industrial area of town, or it may look like a drive-up Fotomat, as Paradise Pup does. Picturesque places you just expect will be good, but expect the unexpected and you set yourself up to have your mind blown. Walk into Hob Nob Hill, an old-school San Diego restaurant, and you feel like you're going to be eating country club food. It's comfort food, but *legit* comfort food. I mean, these people are making their own corned beef. Don't judge a book by its cover. Slow down; you just have to look around.

WHAT ARE YOUR FAVORITE FOOD CITIES? Salt Lake City is definitely one of my favorite cities for food; so is Phoenix, and I love Cleveland, too. We've shot some stuff down there that I am just a fan of. One of the things I tell people is if it's a really hot or really cold climate, it's likely that people will have good food there. My theory is it's because you have to spend more time indoors. Now I'm not saying that you can't find great places elsewhere—I'm just saying the likelihood is high for great eateries in these places.

WHAT FUNKIER FOODS HAVE YOU FOUND? There's food that I probably would not go to a restaurant, look at it, and say, "I will have that, that sounds fun." Like the turducken at Alpine Steakhouse— hang on a second, you're going to stuff a chicken into a duck into a turkey and cook it how long? And I'm going to eat it? Sometimes my producers really have to challenge me to take a bite. They'll say, "It's okay if you don't," and I end up saying, "Give me the lamb's tongue." If I say I like it, I like it; if I say I love it, it's off the hook, then it's off the hook. If I don't like it, you'll *never* hear me say, "MMMM, this is delicious."

So I've had chicken gizzards; lamb, beef, and calf balls; calf brain; pig ears; pig tail. But at the bottom of my list, unquestionably, not even if hell freezes over or lottery money is offered: I WILL NOT EAT LIVER. You could hide keys to a Lamborghini sports car under a piece of liver, and even if you told me they were there, it would end up being somebody else's car, even though I really feel compelled, especially when it's a signature item for these folks, to eat it. And no, I do not like peanut butter or caviar on burgers. One thing we probably won't see on the show is a liver and egg sandwich or a lot of sweets. This is me, Guy Fieri, and hey, it's my road trip.

WHAT IT TAKES TO PULL OFF TRIPLE D

A DAY IN THE LIFE OF DAVID PAGE: NOTES FROM THE CREATOR AND EXECUTIVE PRODUCER

As a native New Yorker, I was probably born to create *Diners, Drive-Ins and Dives*. Diners have always been a part of my life. But more than just diners, I've always loved all the little places, the mom-and-pop joints, the local favorites that serve up real food made by people who care. When I went to college in Oklahoma that meant the café with the killer chicken-fried steak. When I worked at a television station in Houston it was Greek cooking at a joint on the ship channel. When I worked overseas for NBC News it was weisswurst at the outdoor stand under the elevated train in East Berlin. And the falafel joint outside Tel Aviv. As my daughter, Hannah, said to me, "Every time we talk about a place you've been to, you talk about the food there." She's right. For me at least, traveling is a chance to search out more local food. And Triple D has proven I'm not alone.

I'm also far from alone in making the show. In addition to having the most talented and remarkable host in the business, I've been lucky enough to assemble a staff that's the best of the best. No one works harder or better than they do. And much of the pleasure of doing Triple D is the constant collaboration—folks in and out of my office all day, others on the phone, reviewing our work together, changing it, improving it, everyone committed to making it the best it can be. And it's all happening at the same time. While we're shooting, writing, and editing segments and episodes for seasons three and four, we're researching segments for seasons five and six, and scouting and scheduling cities to visit for seasons seven and eight. And always double-checking everything to make sure our standards keep going up—that no one becomes complacent.

So, how's it work? Well, first we have to decide where to go. Not as easy as it sounds. We want as much geographical diversity as possible, but you can't just throw a dart at the wall map and say, okay, we're shooting there. Logistically, we ask if the place will work when we want to go. If it's upper Michigan and our shoot window is December, we have to consider if the Camaro will end up in a three-foot snowbank. Are there any conventions in town booking up the hotels? Can Guy and the crew get there on time from wherever else they are? And the biggest question of all: How's the food? There are a few cities—sorry, I'm not gonna tell you which ones—that simply have proven unbookable because there aren't enough places with food and story good enough to qualify for the show. But our research staff is the best. If it's there, they'll find it.

Once they do, the producers take over. They digest the research, call the restaurants, dig even deeper, and then talk with Guy and me about the dishes to focus on and the elements of the story that are the most interesting. Once we've got a plan, they start preparing in detail for the shoot. What foods do we need, how many steps are involved, how many times will we need to make various parts of the dish to get close-ups. They plan each shoot day down to the minute to ensure that everything runs like clockwork (well, almost everything—you just can't plan for the restaurant owner who accidentally pours scalding water down Guy's leg, causing him to jump into the prep sink to avoid a nasty burn).

On location, the shoots start early. Which means my day back at home often does, too, with phone calls from the field, usually questions or new ideas from a producer or crew, sometimes other issues—like what to do when the Camaro suddenly won't start (and, oh yeah, that happened while Guy was shooting in it, and he ended up stuck in the middle of an intersection). When he's not in the middle of that intersection, Guy and I will confer as well. He'll often call with a new item or some other change to the plan now that he's actually seen the location. And we'll go over what he's planning to say in the very beginning of the segment when he's driving up and heading into the restaurant. That's critically important—because Guy has to summarize the reason we're here and telegraph the great ride that's to come—and it can't be changed once the shoot is done and the tapes are back in the office. And the ideas for those are his—it's essential that what he's telling the viewers comes from his perspective, his experience, his real reaction to the place. Occasionally I'll correct his pronunciation of the New York Jewish dishes I grew up with. He's got Mexican and barbecue down pat.

Meanwhile, the people in the office are working on multiple shows and segments. I'm holding story meetings with writers and the senior writer to discuss how they're going to take the ten hours of tape that was shot in the field and turn it into a six-minute segment that's honest, coherent, and most of all, enjoyable. I'm reviewing scripts in progress and partially edited segments to make each piece come together just right. We usually go through multiple revisions, then further revisions based on notes from the network. Finally, after *only* twenty-seven hours of audio postproduction to make sure the viewers hear every fork clank and sauce sizzle to truly share what Guy experienced, we lock it all up, send it to the network, and get back on the treadmill to do it all again.

HOW WE FIND THE FUNKY

BY DAVID PAGE

For a show about visits to restaurants all over the country, nothing is more important than deciding which restaurants to include. That's the job of the Page Productions research department, a team of five uniquely talented individuals who could find a homemade meatloaf in the middle of the Gobi Desert.

The first step is deciding which cities to visit. We want to cover as much of the country as possible in a season. Wherever we go, the plan is to shoot seven different locations and mix them up into different episodes in coming months. So the challenge for each researcher is finding not just one suitable location—hard enough in some towns—but seven. And all of them must meet the highest culinary bar, as well as offer history, story, and characters viewers will want to spend time with.

So how do the researchers do it? Well, each works on one city at a time. Once a city has been selected and the researcher assigned, she or he digs into every available resource—reading foodie websites, blogs, and local publications, including newspapers, weeklies, and local and regional magazines. But that's just the first step. The people behind those resources—bloggers, food writers, and so on—all get called and asked for their suggestions and opinions, and the names of others we should talk to as well. They're also very useful in warning us away from popular places we'll probably hear about that folks love but where the food really doesn't hold up. The researcher also calls local businesses, museums, chambers of commerce, visitors' bureaus—and anyone we know and trust—asking for suggestions only locals would know. We routinely ask Guy for any places he knows about in a given town, and he also reaches out to his friends who may live in a specific area. And we comb through every single e-mail we've received from viewers about joints in a particular city (we've received hundreds of thousands of e-mails to date—and every single one is filed by location to be used as a future resource). In some cases, we'll select a location suggested by e-mail as a Viewer's Choice segment and ask the viewers who wrote in to visit Guy on set and be included in the segment. We also rely heavily on the recommendations of restaurant owners we've already featured on the show. When we return to a city we've previously booked, those individuals are at the top of our contact list and, considering their firsthand knowledge of our process, they're some of the most helpful, most knowledgeable sources we have.

At first the list of possible locations is enormous. But it's whittled down through an exhaustive process of contacting each restaurant and speaking with the owner and chef to determine the authenticity and originality of each location. Is the food legit (homemade, fresh, culinarily interesting—even if it's basic and simple)? How can we be sure? Is the place real? What's the history, the story? What's the passion that drives the owner and chef? We find out what they do, where they're from, and what inspires them. We learn about their menus, the stories behind their recipes, and the history of their restaurant. We learn about their customers, their traditions, and the philosophy behind the food they prepare. We work with each prospective location to collect photos of the restaurant, the food, and the "characters," and to gather sanitation reports, menus and, most important, detailed descriptions of how key menu items are prepared from start to finish—with unrelenting attention to every detailed element of the process (freshness of product, validity of cooking methods, and so on). The researchers have a keen eye for what food is legitimately homemade and which locations are organically *real*—as opposed to themed replicas of the gems we seek out on DDD. The strongest locations are closely examined by coordinating producer Kat Higgins and me, and with the selection of the most suitable locations in a region, a shoot pod is born.

THE DUDE WHO DROVE THIS TO G&A HAS BEEN IN THERE FOR TWENTY YEARS . . .

THE HOME TEAM

Meet the krew who are the wizards behind Triple D's curtain, doling out heart, courage, and brains 24/7.

DAVID PAGE

Creator and Executive Producer

KAT HIGGINS

Coordinating Producer

DREW SONDELAND

Post Production Producer

ROBERTA BRACKMAN

CEO and General Counsel

MARIA CARRERA

Senior Production Manager

WADE BARRY

Writer

MARGARET ELKINS

Senior Writer

RYAN DODGE

Assistant Production Coordinator

ERIN HALDEN

Writer

RICK BERLAND

Editor

ELIZABETH WINTER

Editor

JEFF MANDELL

Researcher

BRAD KEELY

Editor

KRIS AUSAN

Researcher

JAMIE VINCENT

Office Production Assistant

IAN LOGAN

Editor

KATHRYN BROWNING

Researcher

MEDIA KREW YEARBOOK

DAVID CANADA
Location Sound Engineer

NICKNAME: "Big Bunny"

FAVORITE PRANK: Picking just one moment would be like trying to count all the fish in the ocean—it just can't be done. But any time Guy cooks with uncommon animal parts that at one point had a job . . . Well, you'd best keep on your toes, if you know what I mean.

BEST THING YOU'VE EATEN: There's no way to choose the best thing I've ever eaten, but if you get a chance to go, the Red Iguana in Salt Lake City has the best-tasting and biggest selection of homemade mole sauces I've ever come across. I had three servings of the puntas de filete a la norteña. The Red Iguana also happens to be the one location where my mom and dad were able to come and see me work. Hi, Mom and Dad!

FAVORITE ROAD STORY: It's always the next one. . . . I'm incredibly fortunate to work with my friends, who have become part of my family over the years and thousands of miles we've all traveled together.

BIGGEST TURN-OFF: Noisy vent hoods. (I have to make sure you all hear Guy burn his mouth.)

BRYNA LEVIN

Producer

NICKNAME: "Pirate"

FAVORITE "GUY MOMENT": I don't have a favorite Guy moment (I have many), but one thing I always enjoy (sometimes a little tensely) is watching Guy walk into a place for the first time. He walks around the kitchen, lifts lids, opens doors, and asks a few questions. In just a few minutes, he's able to get a really good read on what kind of place it is and almost immediately gauge the quality of what they're doing in the kitchen. What's their proportion of dry goods to fresh refrigerated ingredients? How clean is the line? How much food are they holding hot? It's where his experience as a restaurateur really shows up. Often people we're shooting with think he's mostly a TV guy, but the reality is, he's a chef and restaurant guy first, and as soon as he starts talking to the owners, they realize he's one of them.

FAVORITE ROAD STORY: I don't have a great story, but I will say we have an amazing group on the road and I've made some true friends traveling with the crew the past two years, including Guy, who is a wonderful person to have in your corner. Guy is one of the funniest people I know; he makes us laugh so hard we have to stop shooting until we can recover. Once we were trying to shoot a simple shot of Guy walking across a parking lot. It was raining, and Guy was having trouble finding his motivation and started doing these goofy, funny walks. It was hilarious physical humor; we were all laughing so hard we were crying and all he was doing was walking. If it weren't for Guy and the crew, it would be so much harder for me to leave my family so frequently. They make being away from home a lot less difficult and a whole lot more fun.

FAVORITE OVERALL LOCATION: There is really no way to pick just one. I have so many favorite locations, some for the food, some for the people, some for the great rapport Guy has with the owner. I work so closely with the owners for a few weeks, then spend two very long shoot days with them, virtually taking over their restaurants and bossing around everyone in the place. It's a great experience (I'm bossy by nature—all producers are), and the people who can cope with that and do everything we need them to do (make the same forty-gallon batch of chili four times in forty-eight hours), maintain a good attitude about the experience, and have fun with us will always have my deep appreciation.

JEREMY GREEN
Producer

NICKNAME: "Silent Bob"

FAVORITE "GUY MOMENT": We're at Mambo's Café in Glendale, California, outside shooting Guy's stand-up with the Camaro. Across four lanes of traffic, on the opposite street corner, is a full-scale film crew shooting a scene for an episode of a TV drama. Guy begins laughing at our usual high jinks during the stand-up, and this builds in volume until he's asked—from across four lanes of traffic, mind you—if he could hold it down because they're filming.

FAVORITE OVERALL LOCATION: It would have to be Sonny's Famous Steak Hogies (*sic*) in Hollywood, Florida. Not because of the food or the restaurant in particular, but because of one moment. This was my first location to shoot for Triple D, and I'll always remember the look on the face of John, the owner, when we wrapped with Guy that day. These were good people doing honest food, and I just remember the smile on John's and the entire staff's faces after we finished shooting. This is when they began to understand just what Triple D was all about and what was in store for their little restaurant in the future. I guess this was when I began to understand it as well. Always will remember that.

BIGGEST TURN-OFF: Anything that's high maintenance.

BIGGEST TURN-ON: Aviator sunglasses.

KARI KLOSTER
Producer

NICKNAME: "KareBear"

FAVORITE "GUY MOMENT": I had so much fun watching Guy cook potato knishes with Angelo at Flakowitz in Boynton Beach, Florida. Guy showed great respect for Angelo's fifty-five-plus years of baking experience. They had so much fun together that Angelo often forgot the camera was even there.

FAVORITE ROAD STORY: One of the chefs we had a great time cooking with this year left us with some lasting memories and a few catchphrases. No matter what question we asked him he answered with "cool, cool" or "totally, totally." So now whenever anyone says either the word "cool" or "totally," everyone else chimes in with the opposite word in duplicate: "cool cool" "totally totally."

FAVORITE OVERALL LOCATION: Super Duper Weenie in Fairfield, Connecticut, will always be near and dear to my heart since it was my first location. The dogs were dynamite and the laughs between Gary and Guy were nonstop.

BIGGEST TURN-OFF: Coming back to my computer and finding that the crew had changed my screen background from Care Bears to a photo of Hannibal Lecter.

BIGGEST TURN-ON: Showing up at a restaurant that has a big cup of coffee waiting for me.

NEIL MARTIN
Production Assistant

NICKNAME: "Boy Band"

If I may . . . I'd like to first take one short moment to express my most sincere level of gratitude for the opportunity to be a part of such a unique experience. I really feel as if I'm doing charity work for great people all over the country. I'd like to thank Guy, David Page, my fabulous crew, and the person who got me into this thing, my roomie Maria, who deserves a lot of credit for taking care of all of us and our needs while we're away from home.

FAVORITE ROAD STORY: We were shooting in Sacramento at Jamie's Broadway Grill, across the street from an ABC affiliate, which invited Guy to be on a morning show while we did the setup. We turned on the TV in the bar at Jamie's and watched Guy talking. Then the camera switched to a live traffic camera positioned on top of their tower, and it was pointed straight down at Jamie's parking lot to show the Camaro. In that same shot, Fraggle (Ron Gabaldon) was outside sweeping the lot for the shoot. I immediately ran outside to let him know there was a live camera on him. I ran back inside to keep watching, and he started doing a waltz with the broom! When he did a little dip, we almost burst a gut laughing. They went back to a shot of Guy talking, and then back to Fraggle, who had put down the broom and started doing snow angels on the blacktop. The shot stayed on him for a good seven seconds before the host checked her monitor to see what was going on.

BEST THING YOU'VE EATEN: Also a very hard question to answer. But I do have an answer. I love French toast, it's something I had all the time when I was a kid growing up, and when I got to taste the Cap'n Crunch french toast at the Blue Moon Café in Baltimore, I made sure I made it the moment I got home!

BIGGEST TURN-OFF: When Matt or Anthony tells me that I suck at forking. At the shoots, the close-ups of all the dishes being forked usually show me. My advice for them is to shoot it right the first time . . .

BIGGEST TURN-ON: My biggest turn-on is easy: shooting beauties!

JEFF ASSELL
Audio Engineer

NICKNAME: "Butterbean"

FAVORITE "GUY MOMENT": When we show up at a location there's a great deal of fun to be had, but a good amount of seriousness as well. The chefs sometimes feel the pressure of having a camera on them as they present their wares not only to Guy, but to the millions of DDD fans. We were in the Midwest, and one such owner was shaking like a leaf before the camera started to roll. We did our best to assure him that he'd do fine, but he was so tense! Guy walked in and saw how nervous he was and engaged him in a very eloquent conversation about why they'd each decided to spend their lives cooking and giving the best experiences they could to their customers. He made him realize that they shared common ground—that Guy wasn't just the "rock 'n' roller," but also a thinking man and a very serious chef. Instead of shooting a twitchy chef and a larger-than-life TV personality, we watched two chefs just hang out and have fun. They went over recipes and had a ton of laughs. By the time we were done we had a seriously great segment, the food was spectacular, and you'd never be able to tell that our chef was nervous at all. They had a ball, and so did we!

BEST ROAD STORY: We often work long hours in challenging locations, so after shooting we occasionally have a few drinks and just decompress. One such night was at the Havana Hideout in Lake Worth, Florida. We were sampling some of Chrissy's sangrias (along with her awesome Cuban sandwich) and enjoying the night air after the sun went down and the gear was put away. It was my first shoot, and I was enjoying hanging out on the patio when open-mike night began. With a bit of prodding, Meltdown borrowed a guitar and went to the stage. The twist was that to participate people had to sing original songs that they'd written. Meltdown, being quite a talented musician, began crooning out songs that were either very touching or downright hilarious. He rocked that guitar and had everyone's attention. By the end I had a damp napkin from mopping up tears from laughter. I walked away that night knowing I'd found a special enclave of personalities, and I knew there'd always be another surprise around the corner. Thanks again, Meltdown.

BIGGEST TURN-OFF: The sound of metal on metal drives me nuts. Let's say there's an aluminum spoon. And this spoon is going to be used to scrape the stubborn remnants of an ingredient from a stainless-steel bowl. And my mike is three inches away from the offending contact. Need I say more?

BIGGEST TURN-ON: I love to laugh, and the DDD crew has many different kinds of senses of humor. We have PG jokes, and we have the Unrated. But one thing's for sure: if you're going to spend long hours for days on end with the same people in tight and often sweltering places where knives are readily available, you better be able to tell a joke, and laugh at one.

RON GABALDON
Trailer/Camaro Driver, Production Assistant

NICKNAME: "Fraggle"

FAVORITE "GUY MOMENT": I don't have one particular favorite, but I enjoy watching him give advice and guidance to the restaurant owners he likes. Having DDD come to a place has grand effects on the business operations, and Guy has a lot of experience and business sense to pass on to restaurant owners who want to expand.

FAVORITE PRANK: Guy seems to have a penchant for throwing food with uncanny accuracy. I'm not sure where this stems from, but I suspect he didn't have enough sports toys growing up. I guess there was no league for Roast Beef Football, so he went into the culinary arts instead. At any rate, his aim is so keen that if there had been a Pastrami Sandwich World Series he would be the Mr. October of the National Deli League.

FAVORITE ROAD STORY: We have a lot of fun in our travels, but one of the craziest things to happen was at Harry's Roadhouse in Santa Fe, New Mexico, when out of the blue Gene Hackman stops in for lunch. I think Guy and he are working on a movie version of DDD tentatively titled *The French Bread and Pulled Pork Connection*.

BIGGEST TURN-ON: What doesn't turn me on? The travel, the people I meet—and most of all I get to eat the best food across the nation. And, I suppose, sunsets, walks on the beach, and ponies.

MATT GIOVINETTI

Camera

NICKNAME: "Beaver"

FAVORITE "GUY MOMENT": The crew loves it when Guy eats interesting things like rabbit, octopus, chicken gizzards, cow tongue, lamb tongue, pig ear, pig snout, and turtle because inevitably Guy's on-camera antics and hilarity ensue. At Cattlemen Steakhouse in Oklahoma City, Chef David Egan cooked Guy one of the house specialties—brains and eggs. According to the patrons at Cattlemen and Chef Egan, brains are an acquired taste, and complicating matters, Guy really doesn't like eggs. So after much torment and teasing, Guy finally put a forkful in his mouth, chewed maybe once, then frantically looked around for something, anything, to dull the taste of brains and eggs in his mouth. At arm's reach on the serving line was a plate of tasty-looking fried nuggets. Thinking they were perhaps hush puppies or fritters, Guy grabbed one and took a bite, only to find that he just bit into another house specialty—lamb fries.

FAVORITE OVERALL LOCATION: It's so hard to pick just one, but my top three are:

- Dixie Quicks in Omaha because we were welcomed like family and Chef René is one of the kindest people I've ever met, cooking some of the finest food I've ever eaten.

- Panini Pete's in Fairhope, Alabama, because Pete and his team were fantastically friendly and completely accommodating. Plus, you just gotta love paninis and beignets.

- Vito and Nick's in Chicago because Rose has the biggest heart and the thinnest crust pizza this side of anywhere. Rose loves to cook and made us a special meal off the menu after we wrapped. She even baked us a cake. It was just like going to Grandma's house.

BIGGEST TURN-OFF: For me, beautiful lighting in every scene is the name of the game. My biggest turn-off is walking into a kitchen and seeing a mixed bag of fluorescent lights in the ceiling and no lights under the grill hood. Meltdown and Boy Band spend lots of time on ladders replacing lights so that the pictures you see on screen sizzle in HD.

BIGGEST TURN-ON: Making food look as great as it tastes is all about the backlight, highlights, and the proper mix of soft and hard light. I love lighting and shooting the magazine-style beauty shots of the tasty entrées we feature. It's when I feel most like an artist.

WHAT YOU DON'T SEE IS THE COP CAR BEHIND ME, PULLING ME OVER FOR EATING AND DRIVING. (OF COURSE THE CREW SHOOTS IT.)

MARK FARRELL
Production Assistant

NICKNAME: "Meltdown"

FAVORITE "GUY MOMENT": The crew was on Bourbon Street in New Orleans one evening. We came across a teenager playing acoustic guitar on a corner, trying to play loud enough to be heard over the rock and jazz coming out of the local bars and pubs. We listened to the kid for a bit and then Guy put some money in his open guitar case. The kid looks up and recognizes Guy and asks for a picture with him, which Guy gladly does. We stay and listen a bit more and as we do, people start coming up and asking Guy for autographs and pictures. To help the kid out, Guy will take pictures and give autographs if they tip the kid. Then people want Guy *and* the guitar player in the pictures with them. The kid made good money and became a mini-celebrity in his own right that night.

BIGGEST TURN-OFF: All my clothes, and thus my hotel room, smelling like grease and barbecue smoke for days.

BIGGEST TURN-ON: A cute chick in glasses.

MIKE MORRIS

Producer

NICKNAME: "Father Time"

FAVORITE "GUY MOMENT": It's a series of them, and Guy gets me every time. During the shoot, I'll be watching the monitor with headphones on, and Guy will get everyone on the crew in on it. If we're working with ground meat, he'll lob over a ball of it. One time he slapped my notes with a huge slab of beef fat!

FAVORITE LOCATION: We enjoyed Voula's in Seattle because the people who run it are some of the nicest people you'd ever want to meet. But they are spontaneous, and their sense of humor exactly fits Guy's. We've become good friends with them all, and just being there was watching magic happen in front of a TV camera.

FAVORITE ROAD STORY: When we were at Harry's Roadhouse in Sante Fe, New Mexico, we were just getting ready to send Guy over to the other crew when one of our crew came up behind me and said, "Gene Hackman is here having lunch." I went over and introduced myself, and asked if we could have Guy interview him. He agreed, and he couldn't have been nicer. Guy did a great interview with him, and he added so much to the story.

BIGGEST TURN-ON: The biggest pleasure I get is working with the crew on the road and then seeing the finished piece on TV. We've become good friends, and working with them is seamless. The Page staff in Minnesota works miracles. And I've made so many friends among the people who own the great restaurants we've featured on the show.

(LEFT TO RIGHT) DA KREW AT MOOCHIE'S MEATBALLS AND MORE: FATHER TIME, MELTDOWN, BEAVER, OWEN, AND ARNIE (ALL ALIASES, TO PROTECT THE INNOCENT).

ANTHONY RODRIGUEZ
Director of Photography

NICKNAME: "Chico"

FAVORITE "GUY MOMENT": There are two . . . and they both involve something Guy doesn't like. We've seen him eat a lot of odd foods. We get to laugh while Guy snacks on things like calf fries, tongue, menudo, and pig ear . . . but the first was at a diner in Kansas, where Guy had to eat the one thing he hates more than anything else: liver. He couldn't even be near the grill while it cooked, the smell made him so sick. We had to go wait in a hall laughing and shooting most of that segment from the back door. The second was the Duane Purvis Peanut Butter Burger at the Triple XXX in West Lafayette, Indiana. Guy took a bite, couldn't even swallow it, stood there, food in mouth, and asked for his mommy . . . a classic, classic moment.

FAVORITE OVERALL LOCATION: A tough one—there are many, for many different reasons: Matt's Big Breakfast in Phoenix, now some of my good friends and the best breakfast anywhere; Franks Diner in Kenosha, Wisconsin, an awesome joint; Victor's 1959 Café in Minneapolis, my home-town local joint. But if I had to pick one, it'd have to be the Bayway Diner in Linden, New Jersey. Not only is the food ridiculous and the owner, Mikey Giunta, an awesome dude, but it was the first place we ever shot. It was the place where Guy got out of the car and Page, Big Bunny, and I looked at each other and went, "Oh no," and then minutes later, we were like old friends. It just clicked—it all clicked—and we knew we had something special.

FAVORITE ROAD STORY: All of us on the crew spend upward of two hundred days a year on the road together, so I have whole books' worth of stories from the show: driving through the Rocky Mountains in a snowstorm, baseball games any time we can catch them around the country, dinners with the whole gang, concerts, the times we stop shooting 'cause we just can't stop laughing, and simply hanging around with the crew. We spend so much time on the road, away from our friends and family, but the fact that we're all a family out here *on* the road is the real story. We all love what we do, and we get to do it with friends; can't beat that.

BIGGEST TURN-OFF: A midsummer kitchen, somewhere in the middle of the country where there's not a lot of wind, in an old building with no ventilation, no air conditioner in the kitchen, and temps hitting up to 130-plus degrees . . . add in the DDD crew and all our gear, and I guess that's the sauna in Flavortown.

BIGGEST TURN-ON: Thin-crust pizza, a good bark on a brisket, baseball, being on the road shooting DDD, then going home to my girls when it's all over.

KATE GIBSON
Producer/Director

NICKNAME: "Ask Kate"

FAVORITE "GUY MOMENT": Guy is an amazing talent and a perfect match for DDD. He's not only a good interviewer, but he's also a good listener. It was always a joy for me to hear him coax people's personal stories out of them. He's very good at it, so that was always a high point in my day.

However, if I had to pick just one moment, it would probably be when Guy coerced our PA Mark into sticking his whole head into a batch of blue corn pancake batter. I can't recall, however, if any money changed hands. I think he just wanted to see if Mark would do it. Mark was bald at the time, which added nicely to the effect (it was just a blue gooey sphere emerging from the bowl), as did the makeshift garbage bag jacket he wore when he was dunking.

FAVORITE LOCATION: I really have two . . .

The first is Hillbilly Hot Dogs, the almost hidden West Virginia joint that consisted of two school buses (for customer seating) backed up to a hot dog stand. Sonny and Cherie, the owners, were wonderfully warm hosts. Their sense of humor was everywhere in this place and it made it fun to shoot. They let people write on the walls of their school buses, they had a huge hot dog called a home wrecker, and they made a hamburger the size of a hubcap. Their hot dog stand even had its own original theme song. It was a great shoot, and they couldn't have been more fun to work with. Kitschy, fun people + great location = fabulous TV.

The second location I loved was Mike's Chili—but only because it was my first real shoot. From the second I came to DDD, I fell in love with the hardworking crew (you can't make these guys take a break, seriously!). I fell in love with our executive producer, David Page, who was exacting, but only because he wants the best show possible (and it shows). I fell in love with Guy, who has the gift of connecting with almost everyone. That shoot has real meaning for me, as it launched so much in my career and in my life.

FAVORITE FOOD: We shot a place in Arizona called Joe's Farm Grill, and most of their ingredients—from herbs to fruit—were grown on the premises. The sandwiches and burgers all had a fresh crunch; their fries were terrific—it was always a pleasure to eat there. Although it was often tough to decide what you wanted to eat. My favorite item on their menu was baked potato fries. Anyone who knows me will tell you that I'm a terrible eater—fat, fried, and bacon laden, that's how I like my food. So when you come up with a dish that covers fries in cheese, bacon, chives, *and* sour cream, you're talking about my heaven.

FAVORITE ROAD STORY: On DDD I met my boyfriend, David, or as they call him, Big Bunny. And thank God, my life has never been the same. So at the risk of sounding schmaltzy, my love story will always be my favorite DDD story.

CRAIG ALRECK
Sound Tech

NICKNAME: "Arnie" (The Terminator! *Ya*)

FAVORITE "GUY MOMENT": Watching Guy repeatedly take time out of a hectic day to sit down and interact with people and kids on a real level. Guy is never so full of himself that he won't enjoy "regular people time."

FAVORITE OVERALL LOCATION: Matt's Big Breakfast—loved the people (Matt, Ernie, Christopher, and staff) almost as much as the pesto pork chops! Crazy-good food! *Das good, ya.*

BEST THING YOU'VE EATEN: Smoque Barbecue—hands down, one of the best I've had anywhere. . . . Please ship to Arnie, *ya.*

FAVORITE ROAD STORY: Chillin' with Guy and crew at the Hank Williams Jr. concert in Pittsburgh, then after the concert wrestling a Pittsburgh Steeler (big lad). Held my own, *ya,* thank you very much.

BIGGEST TURN-OFF: Overhead music, kitchen fans, honking horns during stand-ups, camera mikes, loud refrigerators, other miscellaneous noises.

BIGGEST TURN-ON: Kickin' it with Guy makes every day a great day to be at work. Not every job gets to be that much fun. (Well, maybe NFL and MLB stories . . .)

SIDE NOTE: After working with countless talents for what feels like *forever,* I can tell you that Guy Fieri is the real deal. He's one of the most genuine hosts. He's as real off camera as he is on.

DD&D PRANKS: HALL OF FAME

We spend a lot of time together. These crews are on the road six to ten days at a time. It's a twenty-hour day, and we work hard and need to unwind. Boy, do we laugh. These are my brothers and sisters, and I couldn't do it without them. Being away from my wife and kids is hard, but these guys are my friends, and let's just say we get creative when we blow off steam.

GUY'S TOP FIVE

1. Feeding the Bunny This is the longest ongoing prank we've pulled. Here's how you know the prank's coming: I'm interviewing the owner, and I say, "Blah, blah, blah—by the way, do you have any pets?" The Bunny will start to back up, 'cause he knows maybe we've got a two-foot-long chili dog coming at him from Hillbilly Hot Dogs in Lesage, West Virginia, or a huge piece of apple pie with whipped cream. We ask the owner if he'd like to feed the Bunny, and while he's doing that we sneak up alongside and squirt vinegar or hot sauce into his mouth.

I'M A FRIEND TO ALL ANIMALS. HERE I AM GENTLY FEEDING "DA BUNNY."

2. Scaring the Pirate Whenever the Pirate is putting on my makeup, she'll be looking at me intently, and at least once an episode I'll startle her while she's making me up. So we run the camera and she'll jump and look at me, always like, "I knew you were going to do that"—but she still jumps.

3. Hide 'n' Seek with Foreign Meat Everybody loves to get in on this one—hiding a meat item in somebody's stuff. We were shooting somewhere, maybe Jamaica Kitchen in Miami, hiding the pig tails in each other's gear, bags, cameras, and mixing equipment. I said, "Listen, don't you go and hide it in my luggage." So Kleetus, one of my best friends, is keeping an eye on it, but it turned out later that they'd stuffed one in the pocket of his bag—it smelled to high heaven.

4. Stealth Food Fights If anybody's not paying attention to what's going on, we take a piece of fat or a pickle and whack them with it. I'm not kidding you, it's the funniest thing in the world.

5. The Terminations At the end of every one of their shoots for a year and a half, Arnie (a strong guy), Meltdown, and Chico would take a series of photos of Meltdown being terminated by Arnie . . .

- Meltdown doing something jovial, with a clowny face.
- Arnie standing behind him, arms crossed, hat and sunglasses on.
- Arnie grabbing Meltdown from behind.

TERMINATIONS BY CHICO

Every location had a unique something—smoked meat or whatever—so every ending would have Meltdown being put into the barbecue, or what have you. We would sit on the edge of our seats, and if we shot late and they didn't do the Termination, everybody, even in the home office, would be upset—where is it!?

MORE FOND PRANK MEMORIES
FROM THE ROAD KREW

THE PIRATE: Since I don't pull pranks, I'll have to tell tales on myself. I'm in New Hampshire, in the lobby of our hotel, waiting to meet Guy and go to our location, a great diner called the Red Arrow. He's late, so I call him and he says, "Where are you? I'm waiting for you in the lobby." My stomach drops, and I run over to the front desk to see if there's more than one lobby. There isn't. This is back when we used to drive not only from town to town, but from state to state every day. Guy eventually says, "You're in New Hampshire? I'm still in Maine; I thought we were driving down this morning." I completely panic and of course think it's my fault (I'm the producer, so anything that goes wrong is my fault; that's the nature of the job). I don't know what to do, but I go to the location and hope that Guy's going to make the four-hour trip in two hours—not inconceivable. As I'm pulling into the parking lot, there's Guy doing a live television interview with local TV. Of course I open the window and start yelling at him, I make an obscene gesture, and he's laughing so hard he's doubled over—both of us oblivious to the fact that the local crew is still rolling. I'm gullible. But I had it easy the rest of the day: Guy was so pleased to have completely fooled me that he would have overlooked anything I might have actually messed up that day.

SILENT BOB: We're at Sonny's Famous Steak Hogies (*sic*) in Florida and it's my first shoot for Triple D. During a shoot, I have my notebook with me at all times, so I can take copious notes on the details of the shoot. Well, it seems that every time I set my notebook down, Anthony would add little notes of his own to my long list of things. Notes like, "Tell the owner he's sexy . . . very sexy," and things of that nature. Well, I set my notebook down to go wrestle with a Hobart mixer, and when I turn around I see John Nigro, the owner of Sonny's, peering over my notebook. My mind raced to think of what page I left it open to, but all I could think about was the gentle John Nigro reading Anthony's scribbled sabotage and then misinterpreting everything I said or did from that point on as some sort of sexual advance. I jumped from the mixer, in what felt like slow motion, and yelled, "Noooooooooo!" before slapping my hand down, safely slamming the notebook closed. This was greeted with cackles from the crew.

CHICO: The classic and consistently funny prank—well, funny to everybody but Bryna—is when Guy refuses to shoot something unless she speaks or does something in "pirate." But my favorite prank (it's hard to pick just one) was at a barbecue place. KareBear came out to tell Guy we were ready to start shooting in the kitchen. He said to her, "Are you sure?" She said, "Yes, we're all set." And Guy responded, "If I make it into the kitchen and you're not there and ready to shoot, you have to chug barbecue sauce." KareBear took the challenge: "You're on." Guy stood up, stretched, KareBear looked away for a split second . . . and Guy took off, running like Carl Lewis for the kitchen, hurdling over the counter. Kari came running up the other side as fast as she could. It was a close race, but Guy got there first, so he grabbed a bottle of BBQ sauce and filled her mouth with it. The moral of the story: don't bet against Guy.

SILENT BOB, CHICO, BUNNY, AND BOY BAND: Here's the story of one of the few times that Guy got got. On one of our DDD adventures, Guido threw out the line, "Ya know, I always seem to be pullin' the pranks, but they don't get thrown on me very often." That happens to be true, but shortly after he mentioned this we had the chance to turn the tables on him. You see, Prankology 101 teaches you two things: Never, ever call yourself out, and always expect that what comes around goes around.

We're shooting at a great Italian joint in New York, and the owner/chef, Joe, says to us in a perfect New York accent, "Eh, does Guy got a good sense of hum-ah?" We said, "Well, what do you have in mind?" Joe goes on, "Well, we do dis ting to our purveyors—we get one of our line cooks, da little guy, Mario, to go sit in dat fridge ovah dere, and den we have da purveyor open it up, and den Mario goes and yells, 'Surprise!' Usually gets 'em good, real good." All of us on the crew look at each other, and we collectively say, "Done!"

So as Guy is getting ready to shoot, we send Mario into the fridge. We're not talking about a walk-in, just a regular-size restaurant fridge. We started shooting, and Joe was showing Guy how he makes his fresh mozzarella, working the cheese with his hands, and he said, "Eh, Guy, couldya go in dat fridge and grab da heavy cream in dere?" (It had been twenty minutes, and Mario was in shorts.) Guy walked over and opened the door, and it was quiet just long enough to make us think it didn't work . . . then he let out a loud "Whoaaaaa!" leaping right out of his flip-flops, about as high as Jordan's dunk in the '88 All-Star Game. He just started laughing. What really got him was when Mario handed him the cream from inside the fridge and said, "Here ya go, Guy." Guido then looked at me, Boy Band, Bunny, and Silent Bob and pointed at each of us (while still laughing hysterically) and said, "You're dead, you're dead, you're dead, and you're dead." And that's okay, 'cause as you learn in Prankology 101, that's the name of the game . . . and game on.

WHERE'S MY NOSE AND MOUTH? DO I HAVE TO PAY EXTRA?

"THE HUNCH" IN FOUR EASY STEPS

Honestly, the Hunch came to be out of sheer necessity. The first time I assumed the position I was in Philly eating cheesesteaks, and I noticed the guys were positioning themselves like prisoners guarding their food. You see, otherwise grease could go down your hand onto your shirt—so you've gotta keep your arms up. It's all about natural gravity flow. Which takes me to my wardrobe on set: I wear these bowling shirts, and I've just got one per show lined up. If I trash one, we've got to shoot the whole thing over. When I started to show restaurant owners my technique, they'd say, "No, you're not doing it right; let me show you." So "the form" has been refined by experts all across the country; I can't, in good conscience, take all the credit.

Bottom line, the Hunch plays Triple Duty: 1) protects the shirt; 2) positions the food nicely, showing it off for the camera; and 3) prevents me from needing to shower six times a day.

PROFESSIONAL HUNCHING WILL BECOME A SPORT—JUST YOU WAIT AND SEE!

FOOD RIFFS

PIZZA GOTTA HAVE HEART One thing I do love is pizza. I mean, I love cheese steaks, tacos, and fried chicken, but to me pizza has life to it, and when people make pizza that way, it's the mom-and-pop difference. Even if they're just using so-so pepperoni and cheese, if it's made with **HEART** it's gonna taste good. Like Vito and Nick's in Chicago—my God, that's one of the best—or Pizza Palace in Tennessee, or Pizzeria Luigi in San Diego, which is like being in Napoli; these people really believe in their pizza.

My ideal pizza: thin crust, light on the cheese, heavy on the zesty sauce, real quality ingredients (I don't care if it's salami or pepperoni, but not with so much processed fat that it melts all over in a greasy mess), maybe some artichokes or olives—but always cooked crispy at a high, high heat.

BARBECUE ALL ABOUT SOUL Full disclosure: I own two barbecue restaurants, Tex Wasabi's Rock-n-Roll Sushi-Que, and I'm on a professional barbecue team called the Motley Q with my brothers in 'cue, Mike Zemenick ("Mikey Z"), Ron Walker ("UnYawn"), Robert Riley ("Pit Boss"), and Matt Sprouls ("Mustard"), and we compete in a bunch of contests, especially the American Royal in Kansas City. I've been barbecuing and smoking stuff intensely for the last ten years, six of them with this team. So when I go to a barbecue restaurant, I walk in there with a little bit of an opinion. The rule is—with all food, granted, but with barbecue joints in particular—someone there has got to be in love with the barbecue. I dig all of it: Carolina barbecue, with that vinegar that bites the back of your jowls; Kansas City; or Texan—I'd eat all three every time, pork or beef. But barbecue has got to have **SOUL**, the same way pizza has got to have heart. The key question is: How much of this is your job, and how much of this is your hobby?

So check out Wilson's Barbeque in Connecticut, BBQ Shack in Kansas, or Smoque in Chicago, where they're knocking out the whole hog on a smoker outside, or Barbecue King Drive-in in North Carolina, where they serve it drive-in style. These guys have got the right 'tude with the 'cue.

DINERS A FAMILY AFFAIR To fit the category, a diner does not have to be in a stainless-steel car. Diners have to be a home away from home, a place where people feel really comfortable, where the food is memorable. This is why we go, to feel part of the **FAMILY**.

BURGERS QUALITY COUNTS

Quintessential **QUALITY** makes all the difference in a burger. I don't care if you grill it on a flattop, sauté it in a pan, or grill it over wood or charcoal; no matter how you cook it, and no matter how you stuff it or top it, quality is the key, and less is more. With good meat that's seasoned well and served hot and juicy, and a quality bun, you've got it made. White Manna in New Jersey makes a simple pressed burger with onions; at Hodad's in San Diego the burgers are so legit, especially the bacon patty. Cooked correctly and garnished correctly, that is it.

BREAKFAST CHEAP AND EASY

This is going to sound wrong, but very simply, breakfast needs to be **CHEAP** and **EASY**. I want to apologize to everybody out there. You've anointed me the Culinary Captain of the USS *Flavortown,* and I have got to explain to you that the ship does not visit many breakfast ports because the Captain doesn't dig eggs. Don't like them scrambled, poached, over easy, over hard, in a fox, on a boat, on a moat, in a car, with a candy bar—I don't care. I don't care if it was laid by a golden goose, I am not eating it. So I'm sorry, I really am. When I had calves' brains and eggs recently, I could eat the brain part . . . Now, we would never not feature a place on the show because I don't like eggs, but if they have something like blue corn waffles on the menu, all the better.

LATINO FOOD ALIVE WITH FLAVOR

Latino food is fresh. You may deep-fry it, braise it, barbecue it, or skewer it a million different ways, but its flavor is **ALIVE**. Now, I'm not talking about heat; Latino food can be misinterpreted. I mean that you want to get up and have a fiesta when you eat it. Allow it to be itself. Don't mess with it; don't try to take it to other realms.

I mean, the picadillo at Victor's Café 1959 in Minneapolis—though cooked down, it's still **ALIVE** with flavor. Pupas are fantastic; the carne adovada tacos at Lone Star in Salt Lake City—oh my God!—talk about fresh Mexican food heating all your senses, tasting all the ingredients individually. It creates this Mariachi band of flavor in your mouth.

SEAFOOD FRESH

Less is more, **FRESH** is best, and don't rob nature of its beautiful flavor; leave it alone. Serve an oyster simply done—that's treating it with respect, as at Casamento's in New Orleans. Or at Kelly's Diner in Massachusetts, the one-claw lobster served on the most nondescript lobster roll and mixed with celery salt, just a touch of mayo, and a sprinkle of lemon—that's seafood done right.

SUPER DUPER WEENIE

EST. 1992 ★ FOR THE LOVE OF RIGHTEOUS RELISH AND SNAPPY DOGS

Now, I'd heard a lot about a place called Super Duper Weenie in Connecticut. My friends Alex and Steve live there, and they invited me over to their house for dinner. What comes rolling down the driveway for dinner but this Super Duper Weenie wagon. I'm telling you I did some great field testing, which brought us here to Fairfield and the Super Duper Weenie world headquarters.

★ TRACK IT DOWN ★

**306 Black Rock Turnpike
P.O. Box 320487
Fairfield, Connecticut 06825
203-334-3647
www.superduperweenie.com**

Gary Zemola is the big weenie wizard who is serious about his dogs. He's a culinary school grad who fell in love with an old hot dog truck that he saw a painting of in a 1977 edition of a book by John Baeder titled *Diners*. He found the truck in 1991, gutted it, redid it (restoring the look by referencing the painting), and started doing hot dogs his way. He slices the dogs lengthwise, grills them till browned and crispy, and scratch-makes all the toppings, from sweet relish to hot relish to chili for all kinds of combos. The Dixie dog has the chili and coleslaw, the Chicago has dill pickle and hot relish. Folks just couldn't get enough of them; the truck got to be overwhelming, says Gary, and he couldn't keep up. So with his neighbors John and Lorin Pellegrino and the help of their parents, he opened the world headquarters, where they're now turning out two thousand dogs a week.

The number-one top-selling dog is the New Englander, with sauerkraut, bacon, spicy brown mustard, chopped onion, and sweet cucumber relish (see recipe on page 34). That's bananas, that's relish. The hidden surprise is the bacon, and the sweetness of the relish is the amalgamator. Where has that been all my life? He's also got a hot relish he uses on three of the dogs. He starts with red and green bell peppers that have been salted and drained, then adds chopped onion, water, red wine vinegar, garlic cloves, fennel seed, and sugar. He covers the pot and gives it a quick simmer, then shuts it off so it doesn't become mush and lets it steep. Then he adds pickled cherry peppers and red pepper flakes. He blends it and puts the finished hot relish on the New Yorker hot dog, which also has kraut (fortified with chopped bacon and caraway), red onion sauce, and mustard. Makes a nice balance of salt to sweet to heat—and has great crunchy crust from the split dog.

They do everything well here, from fresh-cut fries to soup to chicken fingers, and don't forget you can rent the old truck for church socials or birthday parties. Go ahead and build your own: I did a dog with red sauce onions, bacon, and fistfuls of two types of cheese (taking a page from our boys at the Squeeze Inn in Sacramento); melted it under a pan; then topped it with chili, slaw, onions, and both sweet and hot relish. I called it Frankenstein. It was dy-no-mite.

[GUY ASIDE]

Some good friends of mine, Alex and Steve, live in Greenwich, Connecticut. We had gone on a tour together to see some of my favorite diners for one of their birthdays—Penguin, Mike's City Diner, Chaps Pit Beef, Kelly's Diner. So I was in town shooting *Guy's Big Bite* and went to visit them in Greenwich, and they in turn had a party and said, "You're going to love the food—we're bringing in this ice cream–looking truck called the Super Duper Weenie." They were bringing in a hot dog cart, what? But it blew my mind. It's the quality of the hot dog, the way you cook it, and the condiments. These guys have *righteous* relish. I must have had half of everything. I called our executive producer, David Page, and for some reason the restaurant was on file but hadn't gotten past research; so I pulled it out of the fire and we shot them. These guys are passionate. Sure, you can't eat hot dogs every day of your life, but when you do, keep it about quality, not quantity. Go for the knockouts.

THE WIZARD OF WEENIES—THE KING OF CONDIMENTS—HAS NOTHING ON UNDER THE APRON.

Sweet Relish

ADAPTED FROM A RECIPE COURTESY OF GARY ZEMOLA OF SUPER DUPER WEENIE

This relish would be good on a flip-flop.

MAKES 2 QUARTS

6 cucumbers, peeled and sliced ½ inch thick

2 Spanish onions, roughly chopped

1 green bell pepper, roughly chopped

1 red bell pepper, roughly chopped

¼ cup kosher salt

1 cup cider vinegar

¾ cup sugar

1 tablespoon celery seeds

1 tablespoon yellow mustard seeds

1. Toss the cucumbers, onions, and peppers with the salt. Put the mixture in a colander over a bowl and refrigerate overnight.

2. The next day, rinse the vegetables under cold water and place them in a pot. Add the vinegar, sugar, celery seeds, and mustard seeds. Bring the mixture to a boil over medium heat. Remove from the heat, cover, and let sit for 20 minutes.

3. Transfer the mixture to a food processor, in batches if necessary, and pulse to desired consistency.

ANUDDA TAG BY GUIDO AND KREW.

I ALWAYS WONDERED WHERE THE DOUBLEMINT TWINS ENDED UP.

ONE WEENIE HITS DA FLOOR, AND EVERYONE SCATTERS.

THE GHOSTBUSTERS RIG DOESN'T HOLD A CANDLE TO THE SUPER DUPER WEENIE WAGON.

WHAT'S A GIRL LIKE YOU DOIN' IN A WEENIE JOINT LIKE THIS?

OWNER'S NOTE: The number one question asked by visitors about the show? "Is Guy really like that?" The answer is yes, he's as fun and entertaining when he's not on camera—the kind of guy you want to hang out with, smoking cigars, playing pool, and having a good time. When we were taping the show, he was pretending to cut my hair with an immersion blender.

Recently I was at a taping of *Guy's Big Bite* for an episode called "Gridiron Grub." I made a green tomato and apple relish, and Guy made these incredible brined roasted turkey legs—they practically tasted like ham—and cheddar-stuffed pretzels. Great time. —Gary Zemola

VALENCIA LUNCHERIA

EST. 2003 ★ COME AND GET YOUR . . . VENEZUELAN BEACH FOOD?!

You know what kinda joints we look for on Triple D, right? Crazy places, like this one here in Connecticut, a Venezuelan restaurant. Now, here's the kicker: when one of the dudes who owns it wanted to learn more about Venezuelan cooking, he bounced out of the United States, cruised down to Venezuela, started as a dishwasher in a restaurant, learned a bunch of stuff, came back to the States, and opened Valencia Luncheria with his partner, Luís Chavez.

★ TRACK IT DOWN ★

**172 Main Street
Norwalk, Connecticut 06851**
203-846-8009
www.valencialuncheria.com

Chef Michael Young, a graduate of the Culinary Institute of America, had his first arepa in Manhattan and was like, wait, there's gotta be more of this, I've gotta have it. An arepa is a kind of Venezuelan sandwich made with a corn cake and filled with just about anything: coconut and shrimp, Brie and mango, fresh mozzarella and chorizo. The taste is out of this world. Michael learned from the source in Venezuela and introduced something new to Norwalk.

For his arepa stuffed with pernil—that's pork butt—the pork's almost pickled, it's brined so long in water, vinegar, sugar, salt, bay leaves, rosemary (that's not Venezuelan, that's Michael's influence), and chipotle sauce; the pork soaks up that brine for seventy-two hours. Then it's generously sprinkled with cumin, onion, garlic powder, adobo, black pepper, white pepper, and a pureed cold vegetable sauce. A little water in the pan and he cooks it for three hours covered, three hours not, so it gets a nice crust. It's pulled and stuffed into a fresh arepa. Where has this been all my life? So tender and moist—the arepa has such great texture, that's capital-T tasty right there.

Michael and Luis do roast chicken with garlic and jalapeño, and empanadas with a choice of fourteen different fillings, including spinach and cheese, black beans and cheese, Nutella and cream cheese, and chicken machada (shredded chicken). There's no fooling around with this flaky, crusty empanada and tender chicken: ting, tang, waddabaddabingbang, it's awesome.

They do mussels in a chorizo cream sauce, banana leaf–wrapped mahimahi with a pineapple sauce, and their own take on a South American seafood classic, ceviche. For the house ceviche they blanch the shrimp and bay scallops for ten seconds, then quickly cool them down in ice water. They use a trinity of juices—from three oranges, three limes, and three lemons—then they add a little olive oil for richness, followed by a little chipotle sauce, chopped fresh tomatoes and cilantro, sliced red and green bell peppers and red onion, and a dab of that international elixir, ketchup. They serve it with freshly made tostones (double-fried flattened plantains), and a garnish of avocado. Fresh and handmade, it's an orchestra of flavor, and nobody's taking a solo right now—excellent.

You get a little music going in the background, some birds singing and waves crashing, and I've got my feet in the sand already.

"YEAH, WE BAD!"

[GUY ASIDE]

When somebody wants to do something and immerses him- or herself into the culture, I'm a fan. Michael went above and beyond the call of duty to make this restaurant happen. When we say funky we don't mean tchotchkes on the wall; we mean out of the ordinary. Venezuelan beach food? Why not just do Puerto Rican or Mexican? If you're going to put yourself out like that you want to back it up, and this cat backs it up. I just want to go back, can't get enough of it. Right on. It's a cultural experience that's about more than just eating—food made right in front of you, loud, every bit like a luncheria, making the dough from scratch. A CIA grad busting out and doing this—it's just what you love to hear.

Chicken Tamarillo Arepa

ADAPTED FROM A RECIPE COURTESY OF CHEF MICHAEL YOUNG OF VALENCIA LUNCHERIA

You cannot say that any state is like any other in the United States; there are food and cultural differences. Well, the same thing is true in Latin America: the cultures are so varied. People think a torta and an arepa are the same, but it's just not true. Check these out. Michael says in Venezuela they always griddle the arepas, but at Valencia Luncheria, he's all about the deep-fryer. And this filling is also rockin' in the empanada (see page 40).

MAKES 5 TO 6 AREPAS

Filling

1 (4-pound) chicken

¼ cup olive oil

1 large Spanish onion, halved and thinly sliced

1 red bell pepper, stemmed, seeded, and thinly sliced

1 green bell pepper, stemmed, seeded, and thinly sliced

5 garlic cloves, chopped

1 (28-ounce can) San Marzano whole tomatoes

¼ cup Worcestershire sauce

2 tablespoons pureed canned chipotle

2 tablespoons adobo seasoning

1½ tablespoons dried oregano

Kosher salt

Freshly ground black pepper

1 bunch of fresh cilantro, chopped

Arepa Dough

2½ cups warm water

1 teaspoon kosher salt

2 cups masarepa (see Note)

Canola oil (for the griddle, or deep-frying)

1. **FOR THE FILLING**: Put the chicken in a deep pot and add water to cover. Bring the water to a boil over medium-high heat, reduce the heat, and simmer until the chicken is fully cooked, about 1 hour. Remove the chicken from the stock and cool. Strain and reserve the stock. When the chicken is cool enough to handle, remove the skin and shred the meat with your hands.

2. Heat the oil in a large skillet over medium heat. Sauté the onion for 10 minutes, then add the bell peppers and garlic and sauté for another 5 minutes. Crush the tomatoes with your hands and add them to the skillet along with their juices and about ½ cup of the reserved chicken stock; simmer for 5 minutes.

3. Add the shredded chicken, the Worcestershire sauce, chipotle puree, adobo, oregano, and salt and pepper and simmer for another 10 minutes. Add more stock if the mixture seems too dry; the filling should be moist but not soupy. Fold in the cilantro just before serving.

4. **FOR THE DOUGH**: Pour the water into a large bowl and stir in the salt. Slowly pour in the masarepa, stirring constantly. Turn the dough onto a board and knead until smooth and firm. Let the dough rest for 10 minutes covered with plastic wrap. Form the dough into 5 or 6 disks ½ inch thick and 5 inches across.

5. Heat a griddle over medium-high heat. Brush it with a little oil. Toast the arepas until golden, about 5 minutes per side. After you turn them, put a light weight on top, such as a baking pan. You can also deep-fry the arepas: heat the oil in a deep pot to 350°F, and fry until golden brown, about 3 minutes. Drain on paper towels.

6. Cut the arepas open, leaving one side attached. Stuff the chicken mixture inside and serve.

NOTE: Masarepa is a type of cornmeal that can be purchased in Latin markets, or find the Goya brand on www.latinmerchant.com.

Beef Picadillo Empanadas

ADAPTED FROM A RECIPE COURTESY OF CHEF MICHAEL YOUNG OF VALENCIA LUNCHERIA

Dig into one of Michael's bad-boy empanadas.

MAKES 8 TO 10 LARGE OR 14 TO 16 SMALL EMPANADAS

Empanada Dough

2 ¼ cups all-purpose flour

1 ½ teaspoons kosher salt

4 ounces (1 stick) cold unsalted butter, cut into ½-inch cubes

1 egg

⅓ cup ice water

1 tablespoon distilled white vinegar

Beef Picadillo

2 tablespoons olive oil

1 small white onion, diced

2 garlic cloves, minced

1 pound ground beef

1 tablespoon tomato paste

2 to 4 tablespoons pureed canned chipotle

1 teaspoon adobo seasoning

Kosher salt

Freshly ground black pepper

Vegetable oil, for deep-frying (optional)

All-purpose flour, for assembly

1 to 2 large egg whites, beaten, for assembly

THIRTY-SEVEN TRIES, STILL COULDN'T GET EVERYONE TO LOOK THE SAME WAY . . .

1. FOR THE EMPANADA DOUGH: Sift the flour and salt into a large bowl. Cut in the butter using a pastry blender or your fingers until it resembles coarse meal with some pea-size pieces.

2. Mix the egg, water, and vinegar in small bowl. Use a fork to stir the wet ingredients into the dry, until just incorporated and shaggy. Turn the mixture onto a lightly floured surface, gather it together, and then knead just until the dough comes together. Form into a flat disk, wrap in plastic wrap, and chill for at least 1 hour.

3. FOR THE PICADILLO: Heat the olive oil in a large skillet over medium heat. Sauté the onion and garlic until browned, about 7 minutes. Turn the heat to medium-high, add the beef, and cook thoroughly, breaking it up with a wooden spoon, about 10 minutes. Stir in the tomato paste, chipotle puree, adobo, and salt and pepper to taste. Cool before assembling the empanadas.

4. Preheat the oven to 375°F, or heat oil in a heavy pot to 350°F. Lightly flour a cutting board and roll the cold dough into a circle about ⅛ inch thick. Cut the dough into 7- to 8-inch disks. Paint half of 1 disk with some egg white. Place a scant ¼ cup picadillo in the center and fold the dough over to form a half-circle. Crimp the edges closed with a fork. Repeat with the remaining dough and filling. Paint the tops of the empanadas with egg white. (Or make mini empanadas with 4- to 4½-inch circles and ⅛ cup of the filling. Adjust the cooking time accordingly.) Bake the empanadas on rimmed baking sheets until golden brown, about 45 minutes, or deep-fry for 3 minutes. Serve hot.

WILSON'S BARBEQUE

EST. 2005 ★ HOLY SMOKES, THIS IS GOOD

The thing about people and barbecue is, if they love it they really love it. It's kind of like a club or a special organization, and it's always great to run into other members and hear what they're doing with their barbecue, like up here in Fairfield, Connecticut, at Wilson's. I'd heard it's on point.

Who would think, good barbecue in Connecticut? Ed Wilson, that's who—a former backyard barbecuer who decided to get serious about doing it right. He's been all over the country figuring out what kind of barbecue he likes best. He says Wilson's is a celebration of regional barbecue styles, with Texas-style brisket, Memphis baby back ribs, St. Louis ribs, and all kinds of sauce, from holy chipotle to sweet tang tomato-based to Eastern North Carolina–style—atop pulled pork, of course. He does a Memphis dry rub with a cumin kicker—this is not his first rodeo—and pops the pork into a just-over-185°F

★ TRACK IT DOWN ★

**1851 Post Road
Fairfield, Connecticut 06824
203-319-7427
www.wilsons-bbq.com**

[GUY ASIDE]

So I was trucking right along, wandering around Wilson's dining room, and I look over and there's a picture of Ed and one of my best buddies, Mikey Z from the Motley Que BBQ team. I was like, get out of town! Turns out it was taken at the barbecue camp we were all at in Houston, Texas, seven years ago! Ed's the nicest dude in the world, with his pork-chop sideburns and cowboy hat. Wilson's is one of those places you long to go back to.

smoker for sixteen to eighteen hours so that it just falls apart. He took it out of his big-boy barbecue, and I said, "Stand back, because I'm a bark shark." (Bark is the brown crust on the outside. . . . Sooo good.) It was talking to me—phenomenal. When pulled together in the sandwich, it's huge: the sauce is not too vinegary or too hot, there's a crunch of slaw and a little bark. I wouldn't do a thing different.

The Eastern Carolina sauce uses cider vinegar, salt, black pepper, sugar, and a little red chile flake with ketchup (see page 44 for the recipe). It's ridiculous—if they made that sauceboat human-size I'd get in it. They do a dozen homemade sides, like mashed sweet potatoes, black-eyed pea salad, and collard greens, to go along with what Ed calls "competition-quality barbecue." And he has some interesting twists, like his chicken. He makes a brining liquid with 2 gallons of water, kosher salt, sugar, onion, garlic, black pepper, pickling spice, and Old Bay seasoning. He simmers that a bit, hits it with some ice to cool and dilute it, adds the chicken for an overnight bath, then dry rubs them for smoking. They go for six hours and they're ready. There's no joking, that bird's smoking. The rub's not overpowering, and the meat is monster tender. This guy has his Ph.D. in delicious.

As Ed says, "Remember, barbecuing is a year-round sport."

THIS BBQ WILD MAN SURPRISED ME AT MY BIRTHDAY IN CALIFORNIA THIS YEAR.

Wilson's Barbeque Award-Winning Eastern Carolina Vinegar Sauce

ADAPTED FROM A RECIPE COURTESY OF ED WILSON OF WILSON'S BARBEQUE

Like I said, ridiculously good; I'd dive right into it if I could.

MAKES 3 CUPS

2 cups cider vinegar

½ cup water

1 tablespoon red chile flakes

2 tablespoons sugar

1½ teaspoons Worcestershire sauce

1½ teaspoons kosher salt

1½ teaspoons freshly ground black pepper

1 cup ketchup

Whisk the vinegar, water, chile flakes, sugar, Worcestershire sauce, salt, pepper, and ketchup in a medium saucepan over low heat. Simmer the sauce for 30 minutes.

ED JUST WOULDN'T LET THE CREW AND ME TAKE A PICTURE . . . "PEEK-A-BOO!"

Black-Eyed Pea Salad

ADAPTED FROM A RECIPE COURTESY OF ED WILSON OF WILSON'S BARBEQUE

As with all their sides, this is homemade and tailor-made for barbecue.

MAKES 8 TO 10 SERVINGS

Vinaigrette

⅓ **cup red wine vinegar**

1 tablespoon whole-grain mustard

1 tablespoon brown mustard

¼ **cup olive oil**

¼ **cup canola oil**

Kosher salt

Freshly ground black pepper

Salad

1 (#10) or 6 (15.5-ounce) cans black-eyed peas, rinsed and drained

1 small red onion, chopped

1 red or green bell pepper, or half of each, stemmed, seeded, and finely diced

1 small jalapeño chile, stemmed, seeded, and minced

1 garlic clove, minced

¾ **cup chopped fresh flat-leaf parsley leaves**

Kosher salt and freshly ground black pepper

1. **FOR THE VINAIGRETTE:** Whisk the vinegar with the mustards. Gradually whisk in the oils until emulsified. Season with salt and pepper.

2. **FOR THE SALAD:** Toss the black-eyed peas with the onion, bell pepper, jalapeño, garlic, and parsley in a large bowl. Pour the dressing over the peas and toss to combine. Taste, season with salt and pepper, and serve.

DI PASQUALE'S

EST. 1914 ★ NOW THAT'S OLD-SCHOOL ITALIAN

With a name like Guy Fieri, it's obvious that I'm going to love Italian food. If you find yourself in Baltimore and you're looking for some good Italian, check out this place. They're cranking their own pasta, making their own mozzarella, casing their own sausage, and doing it old-school in the back of a market.

> **★ TRACK IT DOWN ★**
>
> **3700 Gough Street**
> **Baltimore, Maryland 21224**
> **410-276-6787**
> **www.dipasquales.com**

It all started by making a sandwich and adding a table in the store. Then they added another table, and another, and eventually they had a full menu of homemade Italian. It's the food that owners Louis Di Pasquale Jr., his wife, Mary, and their sons and daughters (Louis III, Anna Marie, Angela, Donna, Joe, and Robert) grew up on, and they're keeping the place faithful to tradition. It all started when Louis Jr.'s father, Luigi Di Pasquale Sr., and his wife, Giovanna, opened a grocery a block away in 1914. So this crew was born and raised in the Italian food business. They even use fresh pasta for their beef lasagna. And they make two hundred pounds of mozzarella every week, be-

OWNER'S NOTE: There have been many memorable moments over the years— memories centered around the privilege of working side by side with parents and siblings, sharing stories and banter the way only a close family can. Hard work, dedication, loyal employees, and, most important, the support of family have brought Di Pasquale's to its fourth generation. As Di Pasquale's approaches its hundredth anniversary, there is much to be thankful for, and more and more friends with whom to celebrate—Guy Fieri and DD&D included. Mark your calendars for 2014! —Donna Di Pasquale Tutrani

cause they use it on just about everything from sandwiches to lasagna. It's salty on the outside, firm on the inside, and it melts in your mouth.

The Di Pasquales pull from Sicily for their arancini, using arborio rice stuffed with ground beef and pork, peas, and mozzarella and fried with a bread crumb crust, then served with marinara. If I'd been taught how to make those at home, I never would've *left* home. The rice has a nice firm center but is creamy on the outside. Winner, winner, rice ball dinner. And the locals are loyal. Any time you see old Italian guys sitting around telling stories over espressos, it makes it that much more exciting. If I weren't going to go back to have the mozzarella and sausage and the whole thing, I'd go back just to hang out with those cats.

I ATE FROM ONE END OF THE STORE TO THE OTHER!

Arancini

ADAPTED FROM A RECIPE COURTESY OF SABRINA DI PASQUALE OF DI PASQUALE'S

MAKES 8 LARGE ARANCINI

Meat Sauce

3 tablespoons olive oil

1 small celery rib, minced

1 small carrot, minced

3 tablespoons minced onion

1 pound ground beef

Salt and freshly ground white pepper

½ cup tomato paste

¼ cup water

½ cup frozen sweet peas, thawed

Rice

46 ounces (5¾ cups) low-sodium
   chicken or beef stock

1 pound arborio rice

1 teaspoon butter

¾ teaspoon ground saffron

¾ cup grated Parmesan cheese

Freshly ground black pepper

Salt

IT'S GONNA BE A GREAT DAY WHEN THE GIFT IS BIGGER THAN YOU!

Assembly and cooking
Vegetable oil, for frying
1 cup all-purpose flour
1 ¼ cups warm water
Salt and freshly ground black pepper
2 cups fine unseasoned dried bread crumbs
About 2 ounces very fresh mozzarella cut into 1-inch cubes, at room temperature
Hot marinara sauce, for serving

1. **FOR THE MEAT SAUCE:** Heat the olive oil in a medium skillet over medium heat and sauté the celery, carrot, and onion, stirring occasionally, until the onion is translucent. Add the ground beef and stir with a wooden spoon to break down any chunks; the beef should be as fine as possible. Season with salt and pepper to taste.

2. Stir in the tomato paste and water. Once the mixture begins to simmer, turn the heat to low, cover, and cook for 30 minutes. If the mixture begins to stick, add a touch more water. Remove from the heat and add the peas. Cool to room temperature.

3. **FOR THE RICE:** Bring the stock to a boil in a medium pot over medium heat. Add the rice, butter, and saffron and simmer, uncovered, stirring occasionally, until the liquid is absorbed and the rice is tender but al dente, about 18 minutes. Stir in the cheese and pepper, taste, and add salt if necessary. Spread the rice on a rimmed baking sheet and cool to room temperature.

4. **TO ASSEMBLE AND COOK:** Heat the oil in a deep-fryer or large pot until a deep-fry thermometer reads 330°F. Whisk the flour, water, and a pinch of salt and pepper in a deep bowl to make a smooth batter. Put the bread crumbs in a shallow dish.

5. Divide the rice into 8 portions. Flatten one in your palm while forming an indent in the middle. Place about 3 tablespoons of meat sauce and a mozzarella cube in the indentation. Mold the rice up around the filling. Once all the arancini are formed, dip each into batter and then coat in bread crumbs. Fry the rice balls until golden brown, about 11 minutes.

6. To serve, ladle some hot marinara sauce on a plate, and top with an arancini.

G & A
RESTAURANT

EST. 1927 ★ HOME OF OLD-SCHOOL CONEY ISLAND HOT DOGS

In 1927 Greek immigrants by the name of Gregory and Alex Diacumacos opened a hot dog stand in Baltimore, serving Coney Island-style dogs with their own chili sauce recipe. Now, it was a hit—I mean a big hit—and eighty-two years later it still is.

> **★ TRACK IT DOWN ★**
>
> **3802 Eastern Avenue**
> **Baltimore, Maryland 21224**
> **410-276-9422**
> **www.gandarestaurant.com**

It all began when owner Andy Farantos' great-uncle Gregory partnered up with his cousin Alex and started a tradition. Andy's father, James, took it over in 1966 with his brother, and then Andy's turn came in 1988. They've kept all the old recipes and all the crowds packing in, too.

They've got the old chili sauce going on the dogs. Andy starts with fresh ground beef and water, adds paprika, celery salt, and chili powder, and mixes it all up in a big pot while standing on milk crates for leverage. He brings it to a hard boil, then simmers it for about two and a half hours. It's a nice and juicy dog with a crazy meat concoction on top. The chopped white on-

OWNER'S NOTE: Enjoy all your cooking endeavors and follow Guy around the country. When it comes to *old-school eats* . . . Guy is the goods! —Andy Farantos

ions are perfect; the bun's nice and steamed—and it costs a dollar ninety. If I were a college student I could live there.

They've got quite a verbal shorthand system going for ordering: they'll be yelling it out across the room and Andy's making it right then, no writing it down. For example, three up means three with everything (which is chili, onions, and mustard: that's standard). If you hear "two hold the chili," he's making two with onion and mustard. He lines up twelve dogs along his arm and has them dressed in ten seconds flat. They serve fresh-cut fries with homemade gravy. Nothing wrong with that at all!

He also makes sliders starting with clarified butter, hits them with cheese, and uses onion water for steam. And the Coney Island burger is like a meatloaf, with onions, eggs, garlic, Worcestershire sauce, bread crumbs, salt, and pepper; he breads the patties with cracker meal, fries them up, and lets them sit overnight to tighten up. He steams them and tops them with onion and paprika before serving. Hit those with some onion and chili sauce on a bun and it's rockin'.

MAD "DOGS UP DA ARM" SKILLS . . .

QUIZ

Andy says he's got three up, five hold the onion, two hold the chili. What does that mean? *(See answer below.)*

[Answer: 3 hot dogs with chili, mustard, and onion; 5 with mustard and chili; and 2 with onion and mustard.]

Old-School G & A Sliders

ADAPTED FROM A RECIPE COURTESY OF ANDY FARANTOS OF G & A RESTAURANT

Note from Andy: You know, this was Guy's favorite item when he gave us a visit. It seems very easy at first, and really it is. The keys are the 20 ground beef (which is 80 percent lean), the rolls, and the grill. Coming from a little village of Sparta, Greece, our main source of cooking, without a doubt, was Grandfather's brick oven. The oven was fueled by charcoal and dry wood collected in the mountains of his olive fields. Here we use a seventy-five-year-old cast-iron griddle. We clean it with butter and a grill screen. This preserves the flavor in the cast iron. The difference is in the taste . . . quite noticeable.

MAKES 8 BURGERS

1 large Spanish or white onion, grated or chopped fine in a food processor

1½ pounds 80/20 ground beef, at room temperature

¼ cup clarified or melted butter

Fine sea salt

Freshly ground black pepper

8 slices American cheese

8 mini burger rolls, buttered and lightly toasted

Ketchup, mustard, pickle slices, and any other condiments and garnishes you prefer

1. Wrap the grated onion in damp cheesecloth and wring out as much liquid as you can into a small bowl. Add about ¼ cup water and set aside. Discard the solids.

2. Preheat a griddle or cast-iron skillet over medium-high heat. Portion the ground beef into 8 balls. Do not ball up tight. Pat the balls loosely to avoid pushing the fat out of the meat. This will allow all the natural flavor to be absorbed into the meat as it cooks.

3. Pour a few tablespoons of clarified butter onto the griddle. Spread it evenly with a spatula. Lightly sprinkle the burgers with salt and pepper. Cook the burgers to order—we prefer medium. The trick here is to sear the ground beef on both sides, about 1 minute on each side, to lock in the juices. Then move the patties to indirect heat, or turn the heat down, if you want them cooked more.

4. Top the burgers with American cheese. Pour a little bit of onion juice around the burgers; the steam will melt the cheese into the meat. This truly makes the difference in the taste. Put the burgers on the buns and add your favorite condiments.

Fresh-cut Fries

ADAPTED FROM A RECIPE COURTESY OF ANDY FARANTOS OF G & A RESTAURANT

Note from Andy: My family used vegetable oil and a single-propane-tank stove with one eye to make our French fries. Although we harvested the best olive oil in the world in Greece, vegetable oil is our preference for fried potatoes. There's nothing that complements good ole diner food better than fresh-cut fries. I should know because we go through five hundred pounds a day. A great option would be to top them off with hearty beef gravy, which is also homemade.

MAKES 4 SERVINGS

5 large Idaho potatoes
Water
Kosher salt
Vegetable oil, for frying

1. Peel the potatoes, leaving on thin strips of skin. Cut the potatoes in half lengthwise, then turn them flat and slice into ½-inch-thick slices. Turn the slices to a flat side and cut into ½-inch-thick fries. Soak the fries in salty water until you are ready to fry.

2. Fill a pot one-third of the way with vegetable oil and heat to 350°F. Be careful not to add more oil or the pot will overflow and cause a kitchen disaster.

3. When you're ready to fry the potatoes, drain them in a colander and blot off excess water so the cut fries are as dry as possible. Fry the potatoes in batches; as far as doneness, this is your preference. Fry for 5 minutes for lightly fried, and up to 8 for well done. Drain the fries and sprinkle immediately with salt.

"FOLLOW ME IN HERE. YOU'LL SEE WHY I'M SMILIN'."

Rice Pudding

ADAPTED FROM A RECIPE COURTESY OF ANDY FARANTOS OF G & A RESTAURANT

Andy says, "Please remember, the constant stir is not optional. It's imperative. Just take your time and enjoy the feeling of good old-school homemade cooking. Nothing compares to that . . ."

MAKES 8 SERVINGS

1½ cups sugar

3 large egg yolks

2 teaspoons vanilla extract

1 quart (4 cups) whole milk, divided, plus a bit more as needed

½ cup medium-grain white rice

Ground cinnamon, for garnish

1. Put the sugar, egg yolks, vanilla extract, and ½ cup of the milk in a mixing bowl. Mix old-school style with a whisk—no electric mixers, please.

2. Put the rice and the remaining 3½ cups of the milk in a medium saucepan and bring to a boil over medium-high heat. Reduce the heat and simmer, stirring frequently, until the rice is almost cooked, about 10 minutes.

3. Give one more brisk beating to the milk and egg yolk mixture and then pour it slowly into the hot milk while vigorously whisking. Bring back to a simmer, whisking the whole time, until thickened, about 5 minutes. The custard will thicken as it cools; you can add a little extra milk now if you think you want it thinner. (Alternatively, Andy's method to thin it is to gradually add a few ice chips a little at a time, while vigorously stirring—do not use ice cubes or too many ice chips, as the sauce can break or become too liquid. When it looks like the consistency of a cream of broccoli soup, he says you know you're done.)

4. Grab a ladle and spoon the pudding into 8 serving dishes. Sprinkle cinnamon over the tops and serve warm or chilled.

KELLY'S DINER

EST. 1996 ★ WHERE THE OLDIES ARE NEW AND THE WAITRESSES ARE WITTY

....

It's pretty amazing, but all over the country places like this one in Somerville, Massachusetts, are booming again fifty or sixty years after serving their very first meals. The all-American classics are as popular as ever, or even more so.

> **★ TRACK IT DOWN ★**
> ....
> **674 Broadway**
> **Somerville, Massachusetts 02144**
> **617-623-8102**
> **www.kellysdiner.net**

Diners are places where you just want to hang out, soaking up that classic waitress attitude. As waitress Marion Birch says, she can say almost anything to the customers because they come in expecting that. And there's nothing better than homemade favorites that won't break the bank. For owner Jay Holmes, the diner is the perfect fulfillment of a childhood dream. As a kid he and his dad were obsessed. His dad had a Pepperidge Farm cookie route, and he'd wake Jay up early in the morning to ride with him. When it came to lunchtime they'd always find a different diner to go to. They'd talk about how it would be great to own a diner one day. So when this place became available, Jay and his dad went to take a look. By then it wasn't even a restaurant anymore—it was a tree nursery in Newcastle, Delaware. They practically couldn't see it through all the trees, but his dad had a good imagination and Jay was able to locate the walk-in, so they shipped it to Somerville and restored it, and more than thirteen years later it seems as if the corner it sits on was made for it. And the food is classic and fresh. They go through 150 dozen eggs a day, from crabmeat eggs Benny on down. Jay's corned beef hash is made the way his grandfather did it, and it's the bomb.

But Jay's not shy about inventing things with new twists, like meatloaf topped off and baked with a mushroom Alfredo sauce. That's some meatloaf with a plus. He does what the locals love, like Portuguese sausage and even a lobster sandwich. You see, he calls up his fish guy, Joe (not every diner has a fish guy Joe), and gets a deal on culls (one-claw lobsters) so he can make the sandwich at a diner-friendly price. See page 57 for the recipe—fresh as can be. Keeping prices down is part of being a real neighborhood diner, and this really is the neighborhood place. But don't try to come for dinner; they're only open for breakfast and lunch. When you're sitting in the middle of Kelly's, it's tough to remember the diner hasn't been here forever.

HA HA HA, HE'LL NEVER BE ABLE TO EAT ALL OF THIS.

ONE OF THE FOUNDING FATHER JOINTS OF TRIPLE D.

Lobster Sandwich

ADAPTED FROM A RECIPE COURTESY OF JAY HOLMES OF KELLY'S DINER

Jay buys the one-claw lobsters, known as culls, because they're cheaper than the two-fisted. If you can't find them, you'll just have extra meat for these well-stuffed rolls. (Or you can make two.) This is so simply made, but it blows your mind.

MAKES 1 SANDWICH

2 (1¼-pound) one-claw, hard-shell lobsters

1 teaspoon freshly squeezed lemon juice

Large pinch of celery salt

Large pinch of white pepper

2 tablespoons mayonnaise

Romaine lettuce leaf

1 top-split hot dog bun, lightly buttered
   and toasted on a griddle

Chopped fresh flat-leaf parsley
   leaves, for garnish

1. In a large pot, bring at least 1 gallon plus 1 quart (20 cups) water to a boil over high heat. Plunge in the lobsters, cover the pot, reduce the heat, and simmer for 6 to 7 minutes, depending on the size of the lobsters. Remove the lobsters with tongs and set them on rimmed baking sheets to cool. When they are cooled to room temperature, remove the meat from the claws and tails and rip it into large chunks (I do this with my hands; I don't chop it).

2. Sprinkle the lemon juice, celery salt, and white pepper over the lobster. Fold in just enough mayonnaise to coat the meat and hold it together—not a lot. Put the lettuce leaf in the bun and top with the lobster mixture. Sprinkle parsley on top to garnish.

[GUY ASIDE]

Back when we were filming the original show—a one-hour special—we went all around the country. I had limited time, and David Page was flying us all around to shoot different areas. Every time we'd go to shoot at a new location he'd have contacted somebody to drive a different car; as you may recall, that's when he learned that I'm a Chevy man. So this is where we got to meet the red 1967 that we currently use on the show: in Somerville, Massachusetts. Later on for my buddy Steve's birthday we flew around for a few days to different places, and this is one of the places I took him. Wow, these cats are busy. I'd like to throw a big shout-out to one of my diner favorites, a special character and one of the coolest waitresses in the world: Joanie Batzek. Whazzup, Joanie?

MIKE'S CITY DINER

EST. 1995 ★ DINER NIRVANA IN THE SOUTH END

When I think of Boston I think of the Tea Party; I think of the Sox, of course; and now I think of a place called Mike's City Diner. It's not because the owner's an immigrant living the American dream or because President Clinton has eaten here; it's because of the way they're cranking out an American favorite: turkey.

They're doing up and serving up four home-cooked turkeys a day here: the all-American meal from a guy who came to the states at age eight from Lebanon. Jay Hajj started working in the food business as a dishwasher in his teens, then worked his way up. He bought this place fourteen years ago and left the original name but got right to work on his own menu, filled with fresh, homemade local favorites. When he tried his hand at turkey it was an instant hit. He says it kinda happened by accident: that

★ TRACK IT DOWN ★

1714 Washington Street
Boston, Massachusetts 02118
617-267-9393
www.mikescitydiner.com

he had no place to put the turkeys but on top of the steamer, and because it was an open kitchen it grew and got out of control. People couldn't believe their eyes—fresh-made turkey on the bone. He's got platters, sandwiches, turkey salad, turkey meatloaf, all made fresh every day, Jay's way.

He has a special contraption that's inspired by beer-can chicken stands that holds the turkey upright, cooking from the inside and outside in the oven. He doesn't season the bird, but he makes a homemade gravy seasoned with California bay leaves and serves a stuffing with cumin, white

WALKING INTO A DEN OF HUNGRY LIONS . . . BRAVE.

pepper, seasoned salt, and veggies, and mashed potatoes, sweet and white. The turkey is super tender, and the gravy is money.

This is the kind of place people want to keep lining up for, and a big part of that is basic American home cooking, Thanksgiving any time you want it. Jay says he feels like he won the lottery—and so do we.

[GUY ASIDE]

So we go to Boston, and just like anybody else I get stereotyped into thinking about what kind of chowders and seafood sandwiches Mike's City Diner is going to make. It's a common name, and so forth. These places gotta have great food, but they've gotta have heart and soul, too, and Jay Hajj, the owner, is one of the neatest guys you'll ever meet. I recently had Jay on *Guy's Big Bite*. The dude roasts these turkeys every day—stands 'em up his way. Everything comes out great. My cousin Rooker Price still goes to this place for the Pilgrim Sandwich. I took one of my friends on a tour for his birthday—five places on the East Coast—and Mike's City Diner was one of them. Every year I get asked if I'll do it again. What a great place. Do yourself a favor: expect a line. In fact, better get in line at lunchtime if you want to get in for dinner-time. (Joke!)

Mike's City Diner's Famous Pilgrim Sandwich

ADAPTED FROM A RECIPE COURTESY OF JAY HAJJ OF MIKE'S CITY DINER

Take note, Jay puts so much turkey in his Pilgrim Sandwich he should call it the "Good Night." With the gravy and the stuffing you need to eat it with a fork and knife—unless you've mastered the big bite, of course.

MAKES 1 SANDWICH

1. First, select a braided roll (or roll of your choice) and cut it open. Spread cranberry sauce on the bottom of the roll and then spread stuffing (see recipe on page 61) over the cranberry sauce.

2. Next, place sliced turkey on top of the stuffing and follow with gravy, if you like. Top off with the other half of the roll and enjoy.

"GUY, YOU DON'T THINK I CAN DO IT . . . DO YOU?" (NICE HUNCH, JAY.)

Mike's City Diner Stuffing

RECIPE COURTESY OF JAY HAJJ OF MIKE'S CITY DINER

MAKES 6 CUPS STUFFING

5 cups chicken stock or low-sodium chicken broth

1 cup chopped celery

¾ cup chopped carrot

¾ cup diced onion

2 teaspoons poultry seasoning

1 small bay leaf

½ teaspoon dried oregano

½ teaspoon ground cumin

½ teaspoon kosher salt

Freshly ground black pepper

6 cups cubed French bread, day-old is best

1. Preheat the oven to 350°F. Put the stock, celery, carrot, onion, poultry seasoning, bay leaf, oregano, cumin, salt, and pepper to taste in a medium stockpot and boil for 15 minutes.

2. Spread the bread cubes evenly over the bottom of a roasting pan. Remove the bay leaf from the stock, then pour the stock over the bread and let it sit for 3 minutes. Stir well, then bake until golden brown, for about 30 minutes.

MUSTACHE BILL'S DINER

EST. 1959, RE-EST. 1972 ★ PANCAKE PORTRAITS: FROM CYCLOPS TO GUY'S HEAD

We started our New Jersey diner tour here at the South Jersey Shore on Long Beach Island. The locals around here know that when the rain starts coming in from the Atlantic, it's time to come into Mustache Bill's for some hot coffee and a homemade breakfast.

★ TRACK IT DOWN ★

....

8th Street and Broadway
Barnegat Light, New Jersey 08006
609-494-0155

Every basic you'd want is on the menu, as owner Bill Smith says, but every basic is done the best it can be done by Mustache Bill himself. He's been doing it all his way—including the custom paper-towel headband he wears—for the past thirty-seven years. You see, he worked in this place as a dishwasher when he was fourteen. After going off to college he came back and bought the place in 1972. It's half job, half love, and totally what a New Jersey diner should be. All-American diner food.

Bill makes chipped beef fresh every day, using high-quality chipped beef that's kinda like wet jerky, served over rye toast—it's money. And of course at a classic diner you're going to get pancakes. He's got blueberry, strawberry, banana walnut—as Bill says, he's a pancake maniac.

You can even get them done freehand. He did my portrait—in pancake—and it was scary. His pancake weirdness didn't stop with my face; the Cyclops has a fried egg in the middle of it and a few blueberries around the edge. Somehow Bill makes it work, and the yolk never gets broken on the flip. Up there with some of the best pancakes I've ever had (minus the egg part, of course).

[GUY ASIDE]

When we got to Long Beach Island there was a torrential downpour, and the town looked abandoned. Here I was in shorts, and it was cold out. It was an adventure. Little did we know that our executive producer, David Page, has a beach house there. When we went back the next year, it was like two different worlds.

Funny thing about this dude making the pancake of my head—I was like, there's no way it's going to work, but he knocked it out, and later it inspired me to make pancake art with kids. I took it to Miami and had great success with it, teaching kids about whole grains and organic food coloring. He was a real inspiration to me, which is something I love about the show.

THE MUSTACHE MAN, BUSTIN' OUT SOME PANCAKE ART.
QUESTION: IS IT THE NIÑA, THE PINTA, OR THE SANTA MARIA?

Chipped Beef

ADAPTED FROM A RECIPE COURTESY OF BILL SMITH OF MUSTACHE BILL'S DINER

Note from Bill: Some people like this served on home fries or white toast, which is the most popular choice. I personally like it on rye toast, and so does Guy! I use a quality brand of dried beef, such as Alderfer's.

Kitchen note: For the dried beef, the Alderfer chipped beef is sold only in East Coast supermarkets, under the Knauss label. Under the Alderfer brand it can also be ordered from alderfermeats.com.

MAKES 4 TO 6 SERVINGS

2 quarts (8 cups) milk

1 pound dried beef

8 ounces (2 sticks) plus 2 tablespoons unsalted butter, at cool room temperature

1 cup all-purpose flour

¼ teaspoon freshly ground white pepper

Home fries or white or rye toast, for serving

1. Get the milk going in a large saucepan over medium heat. When it's almost hot, add half of the dried beef. Don't let the milk boil; it should just start to steam by the time you finish the next step.

2. Next, heat a large frying pan over medium-high heat. Press the 8 ounces butter and the rest of the beef into the pan with a spatula. The idea is to melt the butter quickly without overcooking the beef. When the butter is bubbling, add the flour, and cook, stirring, until the flour is toasted and the roux starts to bubble a little, about 4 minutes. Stir the mixture into the steaming milk. Cook, stirring, until the mixture bubbles and thickens enough to coat the back of a spoon. If you've done it all right, the mixture will thicken quickly as you stir it.

3. Remove the chipped beef from the heat and let it rest for 5 minutes. Stir it again and add the remaining 2 tablespoons butter and the white pepper. Serve hot over home fries or toast.

RITZ DINER

EST. 1985 ★ THE SECRET HIDEOUT OF THE BAKERS' ELVES

They're baking it all here. Every day all day, bake, bake, bake. They've got cheesecake, carrot cake, cookies, lemon meringue pie, babka, chocolate, chocolate, and more chocolate. They must have twenty little elves downstairs, but they swear it's just two bakers.

★ TRACK IT DOWN ★

**72 E. Mount Pleasant Avenue
Livingston, New Jersey 07039
973-533-1213**

David Feldman and his mother, Marion, have been putting on the Ritz for twenty-three years. Their clientele wants something out of the ordinary, says David, and that means making just about everything from scratch, from breakfast to dinner and all those fresh-baked desserts.

"MOM . . . GUESS WHAT I JUST DID?"

Made fresh every day, these pies are crazy looking. They're made out of one piece of oversize dough that's rolled out and put in the pan, edges overlapping. The apple pie's got ten to fifteen apples in there and cinnamon sugar and butter sprinkled on top (no mixing concept here); then the dough is just pulled up around the top and the whole thing is packed in. (I know what this is—it's Speed Pie.) A sprinkle of confectioners' sugar outta the oven and it's good pie—a light flaky crust, my oh, my oh what a pie. The Ritz is a family joint that's keeping sweet. But this family joint is also serving up homemade savory dishes, like a tower of goods called the Pork Chops Giambotta—check it out on page 67.

FINALLY THEY'RE DISTRACTED ENOUGH THAT SHE CAN GET A BITE IN.

Pork Chops Giambotta

ADAPTED FROM A RECIPE COURTESY OF DAVID FELDMAN OF RITZ DINER

The Ritz serves these chops up with gaufrettes—that is, waffle-cut French fries.

MAKES 2 SERVINGS

4 (8-ounce) boneless pork loin chops

Kosher salt

Freshly ground black pepper

2 tablespoons olive oil

8 ounces sweet Italian link sausage, sliced ¼ inch thick

1 large Spanish onion, halved and thinly sliced

8 ounces mushrooms, such as cremini, portobello, or shiitake, or a mix, sliced

4 garlic cloves, sliced

2 red bell peppers, roasted, peeled, seeded, and thinly sliced

½ cup roughly torn fresh basil leaves

Waffle-cut French-fried potatoes, for serving

1. Heat a grill over medium-high heat. Preheat the oven to 375°F.

Season the pork chops with salt and pepper. Grill the chops to leave grill marks on each side, transfer to a baking dish, and roast in the oven until cooked through, about 12 minutes.

2. While the chops are roasting, heat a large skillet over medium-high heat; add the olive oil and heat. Add the sausage and onion and cook, stirring occasionally, until the sausage is brown and the onion starts to caramelize. Add the mushrooms and garlic and cook, tossing, until the mushrooms are cooked through. Add the roasted peppers and basil and cook 1 more minute.

3. To serve, place one pork chop on a plate, top with some of the veggies and sausage, put a second pork chop on top, and finish with more veggies to make a tower. Put the fried potatoes around the pork chops and serve.

BIG JIM'S IN THE RUN

EST. 1977 ★ ITALIAN CLASSICS IN THE RUN

....

If you're from Pittsburgh, you probably know about the neighborhood called the Run, and you gotta be from Pittsburgh if you know about this place: Big Jim's in the Run. Now, it's nothing fancy on the outside, but on the inside they're cooking up old-school Italian, and the locals say it's better than ever.

★ TRACK IT DOWN ★
....
201 Saline Street
Pittsburgh, Pennsylvania 15207
412-421-0532
www.bigjimsrestaurant.com

Here you'll find baked ziti and homemade lasagna, hand-stuffed shells, and a veal parm that's as big as your head, all made Big Jim's way. In 1977 the owner's uncle bought the building and turned it into Big Jim's. Big Jim's nephew, Vito Bochicchio, bought the place in 1992 with a couple of partners to keep the tradition alive. Most of the recipes were handed down from Vito's grandmother, who brought them with her from Italy.

Partner Gary Burdick is cranking them out, like the one-of-a-kind red sauce that has fresh green peppers, celery, carrots, and onions pureed with olive oil; he adds oregano, basil, garlic, salt, and pepper and lets it sauté about five minutes. It all cooks down with some tomato sauce for about five or six hours. Those pureed vegetables give it some good texture, and it's light, fresh, and sweet—delicious. The meatballs are made with eggs, oregano, a lot of basil, salt, pepper, pecorino romano, granulated garlic, and panko bread crumbs. Gary's tweaked the original

[GUY ASIDE]

This is a funky joint on a corner in a residential section. There's no glitz or glamour; you can just drink in the history. There's a picture of Big Jim and crazy memorabilia on the wall, it's an old building, and the regulars have been coming for years—and any time I get a veal parmigiana sandwich, I'm happy.

Funny thing—we were outside shooting the stand-up intro and an older guy starts yelling at me. He says, "Where are those girls?" The crew's trying to move him out of the way, and I'm like, "What, excuse me? What girls?" He yells, "The three hot girls on the TV show with you!" He's talking about the T.G.I. Friday's commercial! I think he thought they were on a show with me. He wanted nothing to do with me, just the girls.

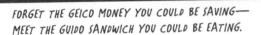

FORGET THE GEICO MONEY YOU COULD BE SAVING— MEET THE GUIDO SANDWICH YOU COULD BE EATING.

a little: he uses the panko because it doesn't have flavor to it and it lets the meat flavor come through. They roll the balls about 4 ounces each and bake them. Great texture, not overcooked, and made the right way.

And the pizza—let me tell you, the dude they have in the back is really throwing some skins (okay, tossing the dough). Felt like I was in Italy. One of the biggest hitters here, though, is the veal parm sandwich. Gary pounds *two* pieces of veal—that puts the shamalama in the ding-dong—dips them into unseasoned flour, then into an egg wash, then into panko; and then fries them up for three to four minutes. He then takes a bun that's clearly from Paul Bunyan's bakery, puts on some marinara and provolone, and melts it under the broiler. When you look in the dictionary under ridiculous, that veal parm is right there. Every part of this sandwich blows my mind, from the super-tender veal and the melted provolone to the crusty Italian bread, all cooked up in a brick joint across from a little old ballpark. Yeah, that's exactly what I expected to find.

It's hard to find good wedding soup in restaurants, but not at Big Jim's; it's one of their biggest sellers. He makes a fresh pot every day from scratch—including the chicken stock. They use escarole instead of spinach, a mound of little meatballs, and dark- and white-meat chicken. I tell ya, I took a culinary stroll with that escarole—felt like I was at the reception.

Big Jim's Meatballs

ADAPTED FROM A RECIPE COURTESY OF GARY BURDICK OF BIG JIM'S IN THE RUN

MAKES 10 LARGE MEATBALLS

Oil, for the baking dish

2 eggs

1 tablespoon granulated garlic

1 ½ teaspoons dried basil

1 teaspoon dried oregano

1 teaspoon kosher salt

1 teaspoon freshly ground black pepper

2 pounds ground beef

1 cup panko (Japanese bread crumbs)

¼ cup grated pecorino romano cheese

1. Preheat the oven to 400°F. Lightly oil a shallow baking dish.

2. Mix together the eggs, garlic, basil, oregano, salt, and pepper in a large bowl. Add the beef, panko, and cheese and use your hands to thoroughly combine. Form the mixture into 10 meatballs and put them in a baking dish, leaving about an inch between them. Cover with foil and bake for 20 minutes. Remove the foil and bake for another 10 minutes, or until lightly browned.

3. Remove the meatballs from the oven and let sit for 15 minutes to let some of the juices absorb back into the meatballs. Serve with your favorite pasta and the marinara sauce on page 71.

Marinara Sauce

ADAPTED FROM A RECIPE COURTESY OF GARY BURDICK OF BIG JIM'S IN THE RUN

This sauce is meant for Big Jim's meatballs!

MAKES ABOUT 2 QUARTS

6 celery ribs

2 carrots

1 Spanish onion

1 green bell pepper, stemmed and seeded

1 cup olive oil

3 tablespoons granulated garlic

1 tablespoon dried basil

1½ teaspoons dried oregano

1½ teaspoons kosher salt

1 teaspoon freshly ground black pepper

2 (28-ounce) cans crushed tomatoes

1. Roughly chop up the celery, carrots, onion, and bell pepper. Put them in a food processor with the olive oil and pulse until very finely chopped, but not liquefied.

2. Heat a heavy-bottomed pot over medium heat, add the vegetable mixture, and sauté for 15 minutes, stirring occasionally to keep the mixture from scorching.

3. Add the garlic, basil, oregano, salt, and pepper and sauté for 3 minutes to help release their flavors. Add the crushed tomatoes and simmer for 1½ to 2 hours, stirring occasionally to keep from scorching.

KELLY O'S DINER

EST. 2001 ★ WHERE GUY MET HALUSKI

There's almost nothing scarier than trying to open a restaurant, especially for someone who doesn't have any formal culinary training, but that didn't stop one former bartender right here in Pittsburgh. She took out a small loan, bought a little joint in a strip mall, and turned it into a neighborhood favorite.

> **★ TRACK IT DOWN ★**
>
> **Pines Plaza Shopping Center**
> **1130 Perry Highway #28**
> **Pittsburgh, Pennsylvania 15237**
> **412-364-0473**
> **www.kellyos.com**

It all tastes like Mom made it here, and Mom is Kelly O'Connor. She's been called Kelly O her whole life. She serves what she likes to eat and has her whole family pitching in—her daughter, her son, and her mom, Tootie. It's Tootie's cooking that got it all started: fresh bolognese, roast turkey, hot meatloaf sandwich, and a Pittsburgh favorite—haluski—even though they're not Polish. They've got the boiled cabbage, onions, garlic salt, bacon, and noodles. I could eat this stuff every day. I mean, there's a little bit of bitterness from the cabbage, the sweetness of the onion, the saltiness of the bacon—gave me a *haluskination*. It was one of the biggest surprise dishes I've had on Triple D. I told Kelly I'd go home and make it that weekend—and I did, and I've made it a billion times since (see page 75 for one of my versions).

IF YOU HOLD THE CARROTS REALLY STILL, THE MICROPHONE CAN PICK UP "THE CARROT WHISPERER."

Then there's the fried mush. That's polenta cooked, chilled, and sliced up for frying or grilling until crispy. They serve it with butter and syrup . . . for breakfast. I added bacon to "Guy-ify" it. They also make creamy polenta with bolognese sauce and pecorino romano cheese. It's comfort food. Another Kelly O favorite is turkey potpie soup from scratch; I threw in some dry rub and cooked it up with her. I tell ya, there isn't a person walking out of there without a smile.

. . . .

OWNER'S NOTE: Guy has totally helped a girl out. I am so thankful! I could never express my gratitude fully. Next to Christ, Guy's my hero. My business is freakin' booming. I've had thirty-two thousand hits to my website since my show aired in February, and there's six thousand more every time it airs again. People from seventeen different countries have visited my website. And I've met the most incredible people—from France, Switzerland, and every state in America. —Kelly O'Connor

Haluski

ADAPTED FROM A RECIPE COURTESY OF KELLY O'CONNOR OF KELLY O'S DINER

Kelly O's recipe here is simple and basic, but fantastic. Trust me.

MAKES 8 TO 10 SIDE-DISH SERVINGS

1 head of green cabbage, core removed and leaves separated

4 ounces (1 stick) unsalted butter

2 large Spanish onions, julienned

1 tablespoon garlic salt, divided

1 pound sliced bacon, cooked, drained, and crumbled

5 cups wide egg noodles, cooked al dente and rinsed in cold water

1 teaspoon freshly ground black pepper

½ cup grated Romano cheese

1. Bring a large pot of water to a boil. Add the cabbage leaves and cook until crisp-tender, about 5 minutes. Drain and julienne.

2. Melt the butter in a large skillet over medium heat. Add the onions, sprinkle on half of the garlic salt, and let the onions sweat for about 10 minutes, stirring often. Stir in the cabbage and cook, stirring all the while, until the onions and cabbage start to caramelize, about 10 minutes.

3. Stir in the crumbled bacon, the noodles, the remaining garlic salt, and the pepper, and let the haluski cook for 5 more minutes or so. Plate it up and top it off with Romano cheese.

Guy Fieri's Holy Haluski

RECIPE COURTESY OF GUY FIERI

One of the most amazing things about Triple D is getting inspired by people and bringing that inspiration into my own life. Kelly O introduced me to haluski (see page 74) and I will tell you this: ever since then I've made haluski gone wild, with jalapeños, shrimp, and chicken; for fine dining and for lunch.

MAKES 6 TO 8 SIDE-DISH SERVINGS

2 ounces (½ stick) unsalted butter, divided

½ pound thin-sliced pancetta, diced

2 large onions, sliced ¼ inch thick

1 medium head of green cabbage, cored and sliced ½ inch thick

1 cup carrots, cut in ¼-inch julienne (about 2 carrots)

1 tablespoon fresh thyme leaves, chopped

1 teaspoons kosher salt

2 teaspoons freshly ground black pepper, divided

8 ounces wide egg noodles

3 tablespoons minced garlic

3 tablespoons capers, rinsed and drained

1 cup green peas, preferably fresh shelled, but frozen can be substituted

¼ cup white wine

1 tablespoon freshly squeezed lemon juice

2 tablespoons chopped fresh Italian (flat-leaf) parsley leaves

1. Bring a large pot of salted water to a boil for the noodles.

2. In a large Dutch oven, melt 1 tablespoon of the butter over medium heat and add the pancetta. Cook, stirring, until crisp, 12 to 14 minutes. Remove the pancetta to a paper-towel-lined plate to drain. Reserve.

3. Strain the fat from the pancetta from the pot, wipe the pot clean, add back in 2 tablespoons of the pancetta fat, and melt the remaining butter along with it in the pot. Reserve the remaining pancetta fat for another use or discard.

4. Add the onions, cabbage, carrots, and thyme. Season with the salt and half of the pepper. Stir to coat the vegetables with the butter. Cover and cook until the cabbage is wilted and almost tender, about 10 minutes. Uncover and simmer until the cabbage is very tender, about 10 minutes more.

5. While the cabbage cooks, add the noodles to the boiling water and cook according to the package directions.

6. Increase the heat under the Dutch oven to high and cook, stirring, until the cabbage and onions are golden, about 10 to 12 minutes. Add in the minced garlic and capers. Cook for 1 minute and add the peas, then deglaze the pan with the white wine and add the lemon juice. Add three quarters of the pancetta, combine well, and remove from the heat.

7. Drain the noodles and add to the pot with the cabbage. Toss well to coat the noodles with the cabbage and onion mixture. Sprinkle with the parsley and the remaining reserved pancetta. Serve immediately.

NOT JUST "SEEN," "EXPERIENCED"—THAT'S MORE LIKE IT.

NADINE'S BAR AND RESTAURANT

EST. 2001 ★ A NEIGHBORHOOD BAR WHERE HOME COOKING IS SACRED

Here on the south side of Pittsburgh, things have been around for a while. You've got hundred-year-old houses and places like this. It'd been a neighborhood bar for decades. Now it's called Nadine's, and it's become a local favorite for something else: real home cooking.

★ TRACK IT DOWN ★

19 S. 27th Street
Pittsburgh, Pennsylvania 15203
412-481-1793
www.nadinesbar.com

Everybody was doing fast food, and Nadine Voelker wanted something different; so she bought a local place and amped it up with the food she was doing at home. And home it is: her daughter, son, and husband all work shifts. If she's really busy, the customers will come and help. Every day she serves a special, from monster meatballs and spaghetti to roast beef so good it's almost illegal. The meat's great, and I'd eat an old army boot with that gravy. Just what I expected when I drove up to this hole in the wall—didn't you?

And get this: most menu items top out at $5.95. A lot of Nadine's customers say she's their second mother, running a family dining room for the entire neighborhood. If a bigger guy pulls up, she'll give him more, plus seconds if he wants it. She has every customer's name, and when it's their birthday she puts their name up on the birthday banner.

Nadine serves a jumbo sandwich of fried bologna, jalapeños, onions, cheese, and deli mustard on toasted bread. That's caramelized goodness right there. She's also serving a hot sausage, salami, and capicola signature pasta—the meat-to-pasta ratio must be fifty-fifty. (Her sons grew up on this; they were football players.) Winner, winner, Italian dinner.

MATT WAS A Q-TIP FOR THE
ANNUAL HALLOWEEN PARTY.

[GUY ASIDE]

There are some iconic things about Pittsburgh that you think of if you don't know the city—the Steelers, coal mines, Three Rivers Stadium—but what I think makes the town special are the small nooky pubs. Here's your all-American-Joe location where everybody knows your name—a workingman's bar. Coming here was like stepping back into another dimension for me, like out of a storybook. This is one of those places I wish were in my hometown. You feel like you're at your mom's or best friend's parents' restaurant. If you want something, Nadine will cook it. Thanksgiving Day, Easter, and New Year's Eve—if you don't have any money, it doesn't matter, she'll feed you—but people don't take advantage of her generosity. I hope people know how lucky they are to have Nadine's—she's amazing.

Home-style Roast Beef Sandwich with Gravy

ADAPTED FROM A RECIPE COURTESY OF NADINE S. VOELKER OF NADINE'S BAR AND RESTAURANT

This recipe's on like Donkey Kong—jump over the barrel, get the hammer, and save the girl.

MAKES ABOUT 10 SANDWICHES

5 carrots, cut into large chunks

Ribs from 1 bunch of celery, leaves removed

1 onion, peeled, ends trimmed, halved root to stem

6 pounds beef top round, trimmed

2 garlic cloves, halved

⅔ cup olive oil

½ cup steak seasoning mix (such as McCormick's Montreal Steak Seasoning)

4 ounces (1 stick) unsalted butter

½ cup all-purpose flour

1 tablespoon veal demi-glace (found in your local grocery store)

20 slices white bread, for serving

Mashed red potatoes, for serving

1. **FOR THE ROAST:** Preheat the oven to 350°F. Place the carrots, celery, and onion in the bottom of a roasting pan. (Nadine uses the vegetables instead of a rack.) Add enough water to just cover the vegetables.

2. Cut four X's in the sides or top of the meat and push in the garlic pieces. Rub the entire roast with olive oil and then dredge it in steak seasoning.

3. Heat a large skillet over medium-high heat and sear all sides of the meat. Set the meat on top of the vegetables, cover the pan with foil, and roast until a meat thermometer inserted in the meat registers 130°F for medium-rare, about 2 hours. Transfer the roast to a cutting board and let it rest for 30 minutes.

4. **TO MAKE THE GRAVY:** Strain the roasting-pan juices; discard the vegetables. Melt the butter in a skillet over medium-high heat. Whisk in the flour. Stir in the roasting pan juices and the demi-glace, and simmer until thickened.

5. Slice the roast beef very thin. Put the slices in the gravy. (Nadine likes to smother the beef in the gravy.) Plate up the sandwiches with the meat between two slices of white bread and ladle more of the gravy on top. Serve with mashed red potatoes.

"THANKS FOR WATCHING, FOLKS. WE'LL SEE YA NEXT WEEK!"

MANCI'S ANTIQUE CLUB

EST. 1924 ★ LOCAL FLAVOR, EVERY WHICH WAY

Back in the day, a guy named Greg Manci started serving beer at his gas station. Over the years, the pumps went away but the place became a legendary local hangout. Today, people say things are better than ever; Manci's offers a unique experience that they just can't quite explain. After hearing that, I had to check it out.

> ★ TRACK IT DOWN ★
>
> **1715 Main Street**
> **Daphne, Alabama 36526**
> **251-626-9917**
> **www.manci.net**

I was actually just a little freaked out, but not by the food. The place has been fantastic for years, but especially since 1994, when Gwen Manci started serving food at her husband Alex's bar. She got back to something she's always loved. Her father had owned a few drive-ins, and she had cooked beside him from the age of thirteen. Now she's serving up Gulf oysters, piled-high burgers, a steak sandwich to the max, and their signature dish: seafood po'boys. Gwen is po'boy royalty. She mixes some eggs up with milk, a little hot sauce, and beer. Her dry mix is flour, some black pepper, and Cajun seasoning. Then she throws eight large deveined and butterflied shrimp into the wet, then the dry (eight per po'boy), then lays them down in the fryer. She butters the po'boy bun and griddles it, and spreads it with a tartar sauce made with mayonnaise, pickle relish, red onion, white onion, and a little chopped caper. As she says, it makes the shrimp taste "wooh." With some lettuce and tomatoes stacked on with the shrimp, when you look up po'boy that's what should be in the dictionary—you taste the fresh shrimp, the crunch of the lettuce, fresh veggies; and that is some really good tartar sauce. Same with their spider sandwich (soft-shell crab po'boy): it just works.

Now, back to the freaky bit, the decor: the place is full of just about every crazy thing you can possibly think of, from guns to taxidermy to old trophies, plus a Chinese rickshaw and something that looks like Abe Lincoln's top hat. The majority of it was put in there by Alex's dad, and he and Gwen go on living with it. Gives the customers plenty to talk about! From behind the bar Alex is responsible for making this joint the self-proclaimed Bloody Mary Capital of the World. To go with the drinks, they've got hand-cut steaks, fresh grilled shrimp, and something called the Jazzy Burger—topped with the local favorite sauce, Jezebel. Gwen uses fresh horseradish root for that extra kick, along with dry mustard, apple jelly, pineapple preserves, and black pepper. Wow, that's weird. It's good, don't get me wrong—I mean it's tangy, spicy, sweet, sour; one of the most interesting sauces I've ever had.

[GUY ASIDE]

My wife, Lori, gives me the hardest time because I won't throw things away. She now takes my stuff and puts it out in the garage and says my office will become a museum of the places I've been. I was at Manci's for about an hour before I could focus on the food. It has the craziest stuff on the wall you've ever seen. So I was interviewing Gwen, and I looked over and there were four crusty old bottles sitting on a board in a store room—1920s Pabst Blue Ribbon bottles. That's one of the beers I like. I came home with one of the greasy old bottles, and Lori said, "Oh my God, what's this?" And I said, "It's an antique." She cleaned it about ten times to get the grease off and stuck it in my office.

Manci's feels like a speakeasy. I was sitting there shooting the show, and a siren went off all of a sudden, like in the game Operation when you hit the sides and the nose lights up—only much louder. I'm not kidding you, I went through the roof. As I sat there and recovered, it went off again, and I was like, "This is nuts!" Well, there happens to be a painting of Adam (you know, Adam of Adam and Eve) in the women's room, and there's a painted wooden fig leaf covering Adam, and when a woman goes into the restroom, if she lifts the leaf, the siren goes off. Now, mind you, this is a one-stall restroom, so everyone in the restaurant knows what you're up to. Had me in stitches!

And they make this crazy sauce; every region has its own goofy sauce. When we go to a location the researchers and the producer will grab the menu and order what the place is known for, then they send me a folder showing how it works and we go on to making the items. But when I first get to the locations I always start digging around—I go through the coolers, and so on, trying to find out if there's something I don't know about the place. So when I found pineapple preserves, horseradish, dried prepared mustard, and apple jelly, I said, "You make what? We've got to make this." These things are the quintessential novelties of the show.

Cheddar Cheese Burgers with Jezebel Sauce

ADAPTED FROM A RECIPE COURTESY OF GWEN MANCI OF MANCI'S ANTIQUE CLUB

Get your Jazzy Burger on with some crazy good sauce.

MAKES 4 BURGERS

1 tablespoon Tony Chachere's Creole Seasoning

2 teaspoons Dale's Seasoning (can be
purchased at www.dalesseasoning.com)

1 teaspoon kosher salt

1 teaspoon freshly ground black pepper

2 pounds ground round

1 to 2 tablespoons vegetable oil

1 cup shredded Cheddar cheese

8 slices smoked bacon—cooked, of course

4 hamburger buns

Jezebel sauce, for serving (recipe follows)

Your favorite condiments and lettuce, sliced
tomato, and red onion, for serving

O TO 60 IN ONE WEEK.

1. Use your hands to work the seasoning mixes, salt, and pepper into the beef. Be careful not to overwork. Shape the meat into four ½-inch-thick patties.

2. Heat a large, heavy skillet over medium-high heat. Add the oil and heat. Cook the burgers to the desired degree of doneness. Top each burger with ¼ cup cheese and 2 slices bacon right before it is done.

3. While the burgers are cooking, warm your buns (hamburger buns, of course). Serve the burgers with Jezebel sauce, condiments, lettuce, tomato, and red onion.

Jezebel Sauce

ADAPTED FROM A RECIPE COURTESY OF GWEN MANCI OF MANCI'S ANTIQUE CLUB

MAKES 1 PINT

8 ounces apple jelly

8 ounces pineapple preserves

6 ounces prepared horseradish, drained

Scant ½ cup dry mustard

Coarse ground black pepper

Whisk together the apple jelly, pineapple preserves, horseradish, mustard, and a generous amount of black pepper in a medium bowl.

SOMEONE MUST HAVE RANSACKED THE JOINT. IT LOOKED WAY DIFFERENT WHEN I WAS THERE.

Spider Sandwich (Soft-Shell Crab Po'boy)

ADAPTED FROM A RECIPE COURTESY OF GWEN MANCI OF MANCI'S ANTIQUE CLUB

Behold the po'boy technique of po'boy royalty.

MAKES 4 SANDWICHES

Vegetable oil, for deep-frying

1 cup milk

¼ cup lager beer

1 egg

1 teaspoon hot sauce

2 cups self-rising flour

1 tablespoon Cajun seasoning

2 teaspoons kosher salt, plus more for seasoning the crab

2 teaspoons freshly ground black pepper, plus more for seasoning the crab

4 large soft-shell crabs, cleaned

4 po'boy buns, toasted

Tartar sauce, lettuce, sliced tomatoes, onions, and pickles, for garnish

1. Heat the oil in a deep-fryer or heavy pot to 375°F. Whisk the milk with the beer, egg, and hot sauce in a shallow bowl. In another bowl, whisk the flour, Cajun seasoning, and 1 teaspoon each of salt and pepper.

2. Season the crabs with the remaining salt and pepper. Dip a crab in the milk mixture, making sure you coat it well. Dredge the crab in the seasoned flour, covering the crab completely with flour. Fry in the hot oil until golden brown, about 3 minutes. Repeat with the remaining crabs. Serve the crabs on the po'boy buns with tartar sauce, lettuce, and sliced tomatoes, onions, and pickles.

ALPINE STEAKHOUSE

EST. 1932 ★ WHERE TURDUCKEN'S KNOCKIN' FOLKS OUT OF THE COOP

When you're thinking about turkey, you're probably not thinking of a joint like this. The Alpine Steakhouse is more of a sirloin and sausage kind of place, but wait until you hear what they're doing with turkey; it's going to blow you away.

Seriously, man, they take a chicken, they shove it in a duck, they put the duck inside the turkey, and then they stuff it with all sorts of things. It's called a turducken, and it's just one of the home-made specialties that transplanted New Yorker Mark Rebhan and his son Matt are cranking out at the restaurant and butcher shop first opened by Mark's dad more than thirty years ago.

See, his dad came to Florida to retire, but that didn't last too long; he got back into business, and then Mark came down in 1975. So one day Mark hears of something called a turducken. I asked Matt how he responded when his dad said, "Guess what? You're going to start boning chickens, ducks, and turkeys, making all the stuffing, throwing it all together, and then sewing it up like a football." Mark says, "Basically, he just put one on the counter and started doing one himself, and we just did it side-by-side."

Piecing this bad boy together is kind of like a culinary action movie for a guy like me. They make their own andouille sausage, and Matt does such a mac daddy job sewing up the bird that

> **★ TRACK IT DOWN ★**
>
> 4520 S. Tamiami Trail
> Sarasota, Florida 34231
> 941-922-3797
> www.alpinesteak.com

he's gotta have a spring clothing line coming out. He makes it look easy. Superbird takes twelve to thirteen hours at 200°F to cook. You should smell it— holy moly. When you start eating it, you pick up the richness of the duck, the andouille flavor; and the chicken has a lighter texture than the turkey. It's a flavorfest, all right—and that's before the gravy. It's like somebody shot off all the fireworks at the same time.

[GUY ASIDE]

They say we're going to go here. I say, eh, sounds good . . . wait, they've got what? A turducken? Then we've got to go for sure. I was so excited for weeks to actually see someone make one. And they lay it down like surgeons. If they'd been in the medical field instead, they'd own half of Florida. Dynamite. The following Thanksgiving I made it at my house—I almost had to call the 800 help line, but I ended up kicking butt with it.

While the turducken's in the oven, these guys serve oysters Rockefeller to get you started. They begin with several tablespoons of butter in a frying pan, a cup and a half of chopped celery, chopped green onions, chopped parsley, kosher salt, white pepper, cayenne, chopped garlic, fennel; do a flambé of Pernod; and then toss in spinach. Stuff the oysters, dust them with Parmesan, and broil for a bit. Now, I've had a lot of oysters Rockefeller, but the spinach and jacked-up anise flavor from the Pernod—that's money. Seems Mark and Matt just have a way with stuffing things with flavor. Starter or entrée, these guys really are talkin' turkey.

THE DUDES WILL SOON START THE STEER-GOAT-A-PIG!

The Turducken

Boneless Turkey Stuffed with a Boneless Duck and a Boneless Chicken ("One Big Bird")

ADAPTED FROM A RECIPE COURTESY OF ALPINE STEAKHOUSE

Be brave, get a buddy, and tackle the birds.

MAKES 20 TO 25 GENEROUS SERVINGS

1 (4-pound) chicken, butterflied through the back, wings and all bones removed

About 9 tablespoons olive oil

About 7 tablespoons blackening spice, divided

1 (6-pound) duck, butterflied through the back, wings and all bones removed

1 (25-pound) turkey, butterflied through the back, wings attached, boned except for drumsticks

2 tablespoons chopped garlic

Cornbread Dressing (recipe follows)

Spinach Stuffing (recipe follows)

Andouille Sausage Stuffing (recipe follows)

3 red bell peppers, roasted, peeled, seeded, and cut into strips

2 tablespoons kosher salt

Gravy, for serving

Special equipment: large 3-inch-deep roasting pan, rack, parchment paper, butcher's twine, trussing needle or large sewing needle

1. Heat a large skillet over medium-high heat until very hot. Rub the chicken all over with a tablespoon or two of olive oil and 2 tablespoons of blackening spice. Place the chicken skin side down in the hot skillet and cook until golden brown, 1 to 2 minutes, then turn over and brown again for a minute or two. Do the same thing with the duck. Refrigerate the birds until you are ready to assemble the turducken.

2. Place the turkey on a large cutting board, skin side down, with the legs toward you. Rub the meat with 3 tablespoons of olive oil. Sprinkle with 1 tablespoon of blackening spice and the garlic. Pat a ½-inch layer of cornbread dressing over the meat. Top that with a ¼-inch layer of spinach stuffing. Scatter about 2 cups andouille sausage stuffing over the spinach stuffing. Top that with 6 to 8 slices of roasted bell pepper.

3. Place the chilled duck skin side down on top of the peppers. Layer the stuffings and peppers as above, using a bit less sausage stuffing. Repeat with the chicken. Press down gently with your hands to compact all ingredients.

4. TRUSSING THE TURDUCKEN MAY TAKE ANOTHER PERSON'S HELP: Lift the sides of the turkey together. Have a helper hold the bird closed. Starting at the legs and working toward the neck, sew the turkey together with the butcher's twine and trussing needle, making the stitches about 1 inch apart. Sew up the neck opening. Cut the twine and then sew up the openings by the legs.

5. Since the turducken has no boney frame, very carefully roll it breast side up and truss the legs with twine. For extra support, tie butcher's twine around the body at 3-inch intervals.

6. Preheat the oven to 250°F. Set the turducken on the rack in the roasting pan. Add ½ cup water to the pan. Rub the breast and legs with 2 tablespoons of olive oil, then sprinkle with the remaining 2 tablespoons or so of blackening spice and the salt. Wrap the drumsticks with aluminum foil. Place parchment paper over the entire bird. Loosely tent the roasting pan with aluminum foil. Bake until a meat thermometer inserted just above the thigh into stuffing at the center reads 165°F, 12 to 13 hours. Remove all of the foil and the parchment paper and turn the oven up to 325°F. Roast until golden brown and crisp, another hour or so, basting occasionally with the drippings.

7. Remove the turducken from the oven and let it rest in the roasting pan for at least 1 hour. Transfer to a carving platter and remove all of the twine, including the stitching along the spine. To serve, cut the turducken in half lengthwise, then crosswise into 1-inch slices. Serve warm, with your favorite gravy.

Andouille Sausage Stuffing

ADAPTED FROM A RECIPE COURTESY OF ALPINE STEAKHOUSE

MAKES 4 SERVINGS (IF SERVED APART FROM THE TURDUCKEN)

1 ½ pounds coarsely ground pork

1 ¼ teaspoons liquid smoke

1 teaspoon chopped garlic

½ teaspoon kosher salt

¼ teaspoon paprika

¼ teaspoon dried thyme

¼ teaspoon freshly ground black pepper

Pinch of cayenne pepper

Pinch of red pepper flakes

Pinch of ground mace

Pinch of ground allspice

Pinch of ground bay leaf

Pinch of ground sage

1 tablespoon bacon fat

1. Mix the pork, liquid smoke, garlic, and seasonings and spices in a large bowl.

2. Heat a large skillet or griddle over medium-high heat, add the bacon fat, and then brown off the sausage mixture. Once the sausage mixture is cooked through, about 7 to 8 minutes, remove from the heat. Chill until ready to use.

Spinach Stuffing

ADAPTED FROM A RECIPE COURTESY OF ALPINE STEAKHOUSE

MAKES 4 SERVINGS (IF SERVED APART FROM THE TURDUCKEN)

4 ounces (1 stick) unsalted butter

1 large Spanish onion, chopped

2 pounds frozen chopped spinach, thawed and excess liquid removed,
    or 1 ½ pounds fresh spinach, chopped

½ teaspoon ground fennel

½ teaspoon kosher salt

¼ teaspoon ground white pepper

Melt the butter in a large skillet over medium-high heat. Add the onion and cook until tender. Stir in the remaining ingredients and cook, stirring occasionally, for 5 minutes. Cool to room temperature before using.

LIKE GORILLA BBQ, THEY'LL SPELL IT OUT FOR YA!

Cornbread Dressing

ADAPTED FROM A RECIPE COURTESY OF ALPINE STEAKHOUSE

To make poultry stock, Alpine Steakhouse simmers the turkey, duck, and chicken carcasses in one gallon of water with some celery tops and onion skins for two hours.

MAKES 12 SERVINGS (IF SERVED APART FROM THE TURDUCKEN)

2 pounds fresh cornbread, cut into ½-inch cubes and
dried overnight, or dried cornbread stuffing

8 ounces (2 sticks) unsalted butter

1½ cups chopped celery

1½ cups chopped Spanish onions

6 cups poultry stock

1½ pounds ground pork

¾ cup cold water

2 tablespoons fresh chopped sage

1½ teaspoons kosher salt

½ teaspoon cracked black pepper

1½ cups chopped fresh flat-leaf parsley leaves

1. Put the cornbread into a large mixing bowl. Melt the butter in a large skillet over medium heat. Add the celery and onions and cook, stirring, to soften the vegetables and release their flavors. Add the poultry stock and let the mixture simmer while you continue.

2. Fold together the pork, water, sage, salt, and pepper in a large bowl. Heat a medium skillet over medium-high heat, add the pork mixture, and brown until fully cooked. Add the pork, along with the warm stock and vegetables and the parsley, to the cornbread. With a spoon or spatula, fold everything together so that the mixture is saturated with stock. Season to taste. Chill before using.

MATTHEWS CAFETERIA

EST. 1995 ★ SOUTHERN COMFORT ON MAIN STREET

. . . .

It's only ten miles from Atlanta, but when you cruise down Main Street in Tucker, Georgia, it looks like it did fifty years ago. Especially this local landmark, a third-generation joint where folks say the food is better than ever.

> ★ TRACK IT DOWN ★
> . . . .
> **2229 Main Street**
> **Tucker, Georgia 30084**
> **770-939-2357**
> **www.matthewscafeteria.com**

Matthews is the kind of small-town cafeteria the South used to be full of. Good home cooking done the right way every single day. That's the way Michael Greene grew up working beside his father, Charles, and his mom, Alice. Alice's father started this place, and Mike's running it today. So it's his responsibility to make sure that everyone's getting exactly what they expect. The biscuits are made fresh every morning. They start with 3½ pounds of flour, 17½ pounds of shortening, and nonfat buttermilk, and he hand-makes (literally) some winner flaky biscuits even before the peppery sausage gravy—which would be good out of a shoe. We've done biscuits and gravy all over the country, and these were hands down some of the best.

. . . .

OWNER'S NOTE: It's been out of control—the numbers are staggering since the day after the show aired; it's been phenomenal. We've got people from all over the country coming in just because they saw us on the show. You all did a wonderful job, and it's been a godsend. We're just tickled. —Mike Greene

They're also stuffing these biscuits with sausage, ham and cheese, or bacon and using the same dough to make another local favorite: chicken and dumplings. Wow, if those aren't some of the most tender dumplings I've ever had. This place is about the country food. There are sweet potatoes, fried chicken, and Brunswick stew. They smoke the chicken out back for that stew—unexpected for sure. They start with a good chicken stock and then go wild with dry mustard, creamed corn, Worcestershire, vinegar . . . it goes on and on. First I get barbecue, then smokiness, then I get soup, the spiciness of chili, the Buffalo wing sauce; it's like Metallica playing with the Philharmonic.

Matthews is a great place. As Mike says, they change by staying the same here; let everybody else change.

[GUY ASIDE]

This is one of those places that's a staple of a community. It's Southern scratch cooking; they're making it all. Kind of like Sweetie Pie's in Missouri: they serve so many people so fast, and it's a buffet of fresh-made food.

And Mike is hysterical! I've cooked with quite a few characters in my life, you name it, but the dude was a riot. I like being quick, but this dude was tit for tat all day long. I watched the show recently and I was like, man, it was a culinary Smothers Brothers. And the Brunswick stew was a trip, nuts. I'd never seen stew like this; talk about some crazy stuff: creamed corn, tomatoes, ketchup, a ton of Worcestershire sauce. So since then I've learned Brunswick Stew is like clam chowder: everybody has their own style. The spectrum is wide, and this was a wild one. They tried to get me to do chicken livers, but after recently having had (at Joe's Gizzard City) my fill of gizzards, I wasn't sure I could take on livers that day.

The great thing about working with Mike is he doesn't have any measuring techniques. I kept calling him on it; one day I'll send him a measuring cup, not that he needs it.

Brunswick Stew

ADAPTED FROM A RECIPE COURTESY OF MIKE GREENE OF MATTHEWS CAFETERIA

Matthews Cafeteria smokes chicken parts in an outdoor smoker for ninety minutes at 350°F. You can also use boiled chicken, but in that case don't use the bones; just bring the water to a simmer, and then add the skin with the other ingredients.

MAKES 16 SERVINGS

5 pounds smoked chicken, whole or parts

1 gallon (16 cups) water

2 (14.5-ounce) cans diced tomatoes, with juice

1 large onion, chopped

¼ cup dry mustard

¼ cup white vinegar

2 tablespoons Worcestershire sauce

2 tablespoons freshly ground black pepper

2 (14.5-ounce) cans creamed corn

¼ cup ketchup

¼ cup of your favorite barbecue sauce

Hot sauce, to taste

Kosher salt, to taste

1. Remove and reserve the chicken skin and pull the meat off the bones. Chop the skin and meat very fine. Put the bones and the water in a large pot and simmer for 30 minutes. Remove and discard the bones, then add the skin, tomatoes, onion, mustard, vinegar, Worcestershire sauce, and black pepper and simmer for 30 minutes.

2. Stir in the chicken, corn, ketchup, barbecue sauce, and the hot sauce to taste, and bring just back to a simmer. Simmer for another 30 minutes, stirring often so that the stew doesn't stick to the bottom of the pot. Taste and season with salt. Refrigerate the stew overnight, reheat, and enjoy.

THe HIGHLANDER

EST. 1992 ★ SERVIN' UP SCRATCH BAR FOOD

You know, finding great bar food is way more than just a menu, it's a whole experience. Like here in Atlanta at this joint called the Highlander. It's a dive bar in a strip mall, where they're heavy on tattoos and serious about scratch cooking.

★ TRACK IT DOWN ★

**931 Monroe Drive NE
Atlanta, Georgia 30308
404-872-0060
www.thehighlanderatlanta.com**

The food here is so much better than it needs to be. It's a neighborhood place where Jeff Merback and his partners decided to take a chance and open in a strip mall. They set out to be the place that was still open at the end of the night. That meant their clientele was going to be bartenders and waiters and chefs, so they couldn't just throw out your typical grub. The dude running the kitchen's got it down. Ice Jahumpa is from West Africa, and he's loading the specials board with some head-turners like oxtail soup and curried goat. And their chili is done with a twist—a jerk twist. It starts with ground beef and spicy sausage, red onion, colorful bell peppers, red and black beans, and peeled tomato, and that pot is mixed with a puree that's got a veggie and chicken stock base with roasted garlic, habañero, Ice's own jerk seasoning, spiced rum, and tomato paste. Then he throws in some brown sugar, black pepper, thyme, onion powder, dried mustard, bay leaves, Maggi sauce, cilantro, chile flakes, celery seed, allspice, white pepper, cumin, and chili powder and rounds it out with cayenne. It simmers for a couple hours, and it's got chunks of meat, great spice and color. It is legit chili.

Their corn fritters are golf ball–size and are served up with their roasted red pepper rémoulade. He does fish-night specials, caprese salad, sliders, Jamaican jerk chicken wings, marinated lime chicken, and potato skins. He even does the bar staple, mozzarella sticks. Here, however, they're wrapped in pasta. First comes the all-egg-yolk egg wash, and he makes bread crumbs with Italian seasoning. After rolling the mozzarella in a pasta sheet, sealed on the edge with the yolk, he trims it, pinches the ends, rolls it again in the egg wash, then the bread crumbs, and fries it. These are served with marinara sauce that's made with roasted garlic, onions, peppers, red wine, herbs, and spices. The pasta sheet around the cheese holds it together and gives it a great texture. Whatever the hour, you've got comfort food. Come and get it.

From mohawks to yuppies, this place is the place to hang out.

[GUY ASIDE]

Here are some dudes who wanted a place that's open when they get off work in the restaurant biz, so they got together to create the Highlander, and it works. There's some crazy ink and artwork on the ceilings, and it kinda feels like home. The stereotype is that a wild bar won't have good food or the food will have been frozen. But I met Ice, the chef, and he made some bomb fried mozzarella for me. Ninety percent of the places you go in the country, fried cheese is a preprocessed, frozen, fried, funky little log. But I'm telling you, these guys make it themselves— and their mozz is money!

GUIDO AND THE HIGHLANDERS WILL BE ON TOUR THIS SUMMER.

Pasta-Rella Highlander Style

ADAPTED FROM A RECIPE COURTESY OF BRANNON AMTOWER OF THE HIGHLANDER

You'll never go back to the frozen, funky little mozzarella sticks.

MAKES 18 CHEESE STICKS

1 egg yolk

⅓ cup cold water

2 cups plain dried bread crumbs

2 teaspoons Italian seasoning

Fresh 10 by 15-inch egg pasta sheets, for wrapping

1 pound block part-skim mozzarella, cut into ½ by ½ by 4-inch sticks

Vegetable oil, for frying

Grated Parmesan cheese, for garnish

Marinara sauce, hot, for dipping

1. Whisk the yolk and water in a small bowl. Mix the bread crumbs and seasoning in a shallow dish. Slice the pasta sheets in half lengthwise. (Keep the pasta sheets covered with plastic wrap or a towel so they don't dry out.) Place a cheese stick on a short edge of one sheet of pasta, roll to enclose the cheese with a slight overlap, and cut. Fold the ends of the pasta as you would wrap a present. Dip the entire stick in the egg wash and roll in the bread crumbs. Repeat with the remaining cheese sticks and pasta.

2. Heat oil in a deep-fryer or heat a few inches of oil in a heavy-bottomed pan until a deep-fry thermometer reads 350°F. Add the sticks a few at a time and fry for approximately 1½ minutes or until deep golden brown. Don't move them around too much and don't overcook or the cheese will spill out. Drain on a rack. Repeat with all of the cheese sticks.

3. Sprinkle Parmesan cheese over the hot marinara sauce and sticks and serve.

CASAMENTO'S RESTAURANT

EST. 1919 ★ HOME OF THE OYSTER LOAF AND CHAMPION SHUCKERS

Here in New Orleans, everybody knows Magazine Street. It's full of history and restaurants. You'll find the best of both at this place, where they've been doing it old-school for close to ninety years.

★ TRACK IT DOWN ★

4330 Magazine Street
New Orleans, Louisiana 70115
504-895-9761
www.casamentosrestaurant.com

This place has been busting at the seams since 1919, when Joe Casamento shucked his first oyster. And third-generation owner C.J. Gerdes is still shucking 'em like Grandpa did. Mike Rogers is his five-time-champion number one shucker. (He showed me how to do it so that mine didn't look like a frog in a blender; you've got to get your thumb working for you.) They give you all the condiments on the table and you mix your sauce yourself—horseradish, hot sauce, lemon, ketchup—and down it goes, fresh, vibrant, nice and smooth. On the average Friday they go through twenty-five sacks—that's 120 oysters per sack. A lot of the regulars can't wait to come back, which makes it pretty tough in the summertime, when they close up shop for three months.

They also serve an oyster loaf, which is a mess of fresh fried oysters on two slabs of fresh-baked white bread toasted with butter and dressed with lettuce, tomato, and mayo—and a lot of people hit it with a little Tabasco. C.J. drops the oysters straight into corn flour and fries them in hot boiling lard in pots on the stove. I felt the Philly Hunch coming on. It doesn't get any fresher tasting. And I'll send anybody who says they don't like oyster sandwiches over for a chat with C.J. I like the way they loaf.

They'll "loaf" fried trout and serve some of the best fried shrimp in the city, and fried crabs that are dunked in egg wash, then salted corn flour, and fried up. (Be sure to cover the top with a screen when you fry these, as the moisture in them makes them splatter.) That's some great crab flavor, and it's been one of the staples since C.J.'s grandpa's time.

Mike expertly tossed me some oysters from across the room, straight into my mouth. Yep, I'll be performing here again.

[GUY ASIDE]

Casamento's is lined with wall-to-wall white tile, and as soon as you make it in the door you find a dude who's a champion in oyster shucking.

I found myself on a ladder in this place rummaging around in the attic and looking at the old equipment their grandfather used. It felt like stepping back in time.

HE DID ALL THESE IN LIKE . . . TWO SECONDS AND HAD TIME TO TWITTER A FRIEND.

Oyster Stew Casamento's

ADAPTED FROM A RECIPE COURTESY OF C.J. GERDES OF CASAMENTO'S RESTAURANT

Check out this delicately seasoned stew that's yet another of their fine fresh oyster conduits.

MAKES ABOUT 3 QUARTS, 8 TO 12 SERVINGS

5 ounces (10 tablespoons) unsalted butter

1 medium onion, finely chopped

½ cup chopped fresh flat-leaf parsley leaves

1 tablespoon kosher salt

4 to 6 dozen shucked raw oysters, with their liquor, about 2 quarts

5 cups milk

HANDS DOWN, AN OYSTER INSTITUTION.

1. Put the butter and onion in a large pot over medium heat and cook, stirring occasionally, until the butter starts to simmer and the onion softens a bit. Add the parsley and salt and simmer for another minute or so. Stir in the oysters and their liquor and bring to a simmer for a minute or two.

2. Add the milk and cook until it starts to rise in the pot. Do not let it come to a full boil and overflow. Serve immediately.

PARASOL'S

EST. 1952 ★ HOME OF BEEF PO'BOYS AND HOT MUFFULETTA

On Triple D, we love to go to the places our fans send us, and this time it's New Orleans, where e-mailer Ross Liner goes nuts for the po'boys.

★ TRACK IT DOWN ★

**2533 Constance Street
New Orleans, Louisiana 70130
504-897-5413**

The roast beef po'boy is the one that made Parasol's the local legend it is. It's served with lots of TLC by Jeff Carreras, who bought this place more than ten years ago and kept it the way it's always been. The recipe was handed down. He trims the meat and boils it for about an hour and a half, unseasoned, but don't worry; he'll get your taste buds dancing in a little bit. He uses the water from the beef to make the gravy, which is made with flour, oil, black pepper, garlic powder, salt, and Kitchen Bouquet for color. He makes that gravy every day. Wow, I wouldn't kick that out of a sandwich. He slices the beef thin once it's cold (suspiciously like jerky at this point, but hold on), pours the gravy on top, and bakes it, covered, for about an hour. He spreads the bread with mayo, lettuce, tomatoes, sliced pickles, beef, and gravy, then toasts the whole thing for a couple of minutes. Yes, with the lettuce and all. And that roast beef is capital-T tender, juicy, nice and sloppy.

[GUY ASIDE]

Parasol's is known for doing one of the biggest Saint Patrick's Day parties in New Orleans, four blocks wide, and this is the center of it, in a great old building from the 1800s—an awesome joint that's famous locally.

So we were in the middle of the shoot here in this hot kitchen, making the beef po'boy, and all of a sudden this girl comes in and interrupts the shoot. She's nice enough, big fan of the show, okay. I assume she knows the owner, and the owner thinks she knows me, and he's thinking he's doing the right thing by letting her interrupt us. It takes us fifteen minutes to figure out neither of us knows her. Why is she here? So funny, and totally perplexing.

Tradition matters here. I could get busy on their gumbo and their boudin balls, which is a pork, rice, and herb sausage rolled up in a ball and fried. Another New Orleans classic is the muffuletta, done their way. He grills the prosciutto (I think that's illegal in Italy), the ham, the salami. He butters the bun, layers up the meat, then tops it with the olive salad (carrot, cauliflower, green and black olives, and red pepper in a vinaigrette) and cheese and toasts the whole sandwich for a couple of minutes. First warm muffuletta I've ever had, and it is ridiculously good. Jeff is a designated flavor hitter.

GO, GO, GO!

BEFORE THERE WAS "WHERE'S WALDO," THERE WAS "WHERE'S GUIDO" (COME ON, PLAY ALONG. . .)

Chicken and Andouille Gumbo

RECIPE COURTESY OF JEFFREY CARERRAS, CHEF AND OWNER OF PARASOL'S

Dive into a pot of this New Orleans classic.

MAKES 6 TO 8 SERVINGS

½ cup vegetable oil

1 (3½ to 4 pound) chicken, cut into 10 pieces

Kosher salt and freshly ground black pepper

1 cup all-purpose flour

3 garlic cloves, finely chopped

2 celery ribs, coarsely chopped

1 medium Vidalia or yellow onion, coarsely chopped

1 green bell pepper, stemmed, seeded, and coarsely chopped

8 bay leaves

1 pound sliced andouille sausage or pepperoni

1 quart (4 cups) chicken stock or low-sodium chicken broth

½ cup chopped green onions

¼ cup finely chopped fresh flat-leaf parsley leaves

1. Heat a 6-quart pot over medium-high heat. Add the oil. Season the chicken with salt and pepper and fry until golden brown on both sides and cooked through, 20 to 25 minutes. Remove and set aside, leaving the oil in the pot.

2. To make the roux, reduce the heat to medium and stir the flour into the hot oil, making a thick paste. Cook, stirring, until the roux is the color of dark peanut butter, about 20 minutes. Watch closely and stir constantly because roux are easily burned.

3. Stir in the garlic, celery, onion, bell pepper, and bay leaves and let them sweat until the vegetables are soft. Add the andouille, chicken stock, and salt and pepper to taste and bring to a boil. Reduce the heat to low and simmer for 1½ hours, stirring occasionally to keep the roux from sticking to the bottom of the pot and burning.

4. While the gumbo simmers, pull the meat from the chicken. Stir it into the gumbo the last 30 minutes or so of cooking.

5. Remove the gumbo from the heat, discard the bay leaves, and stir in the green onions and parsley. Serve over rice.

RANDOM THOUGHTS FROM THE '67: "I'D DRIVE RIGHT IN IF I COULD!"

DARWELL'S CAFE

EST. 2005 ★ **THE TASTE OF THE SOUTH, COMPLETE WITH A FLOOR SHOW**

One of my favorite places to live was Long Beach, California, so you've gotta know I was stoked when I found out there was a Long Beach, Mississippi. Now, if you find yourself here you have to check out this crazy shack. People around here say they're turning out some top-notch food.

★ TRACK IT DOWN ★

127 E. First Street
Long Beach, Mississippi 39560
228-868-8946
www.darwellscafe.com

From barbecue to Cajun and Creole, Darwell Yeager III—the locals call him "D"— has been serving it up just right since he opened the joint a few years back. And he's got a little front-of-the-house help from his dad, who's hard to miss, goggles, paint-splattered overalls, and all. Darwell started in the food business when he was fifteen, then did some moonlighting as a professional wrestler in his twenties. But his dad told him to get out of the ring and back into the kitchen to do what he does best. He was trained by some of the top chefs in the area on how to put it out and make it taste good.

Like his classic shrimp Creole: he takes chopped celery and sautés it in a quarter pound of butter with blanched, chopped green bell pepper, blanched sautéed onion (the blanching just makes it cook faster, says Darwell), Creole seasoning, Old Bay Seasoning, minced garlic, bay leaves, and sliced smoked sausages. He makes the roux in the pot with flour, adds some homemade shrimp stock and tomato sauce, and cooks it for forty-five minutes to an hour. Then he heats the shrimp to order, to keep them perfect and tender, and serves it all up with long-grain basmati rice, 'cause it's a flavorful rice that holds the sauces and makes for a nice presentation. He makes blackened shrimp with his own blackening seasoning: paprika (the dominant spice—three parts paprika to one part of everything else), cayenne, oregano, garlic powder, and black pepper. It's not so hot that you can't enjoy the flavor of the shrimp. And he serves grits with spicy tasso that's been sautéed in butter with chopped green onion, and tops it all with sharp Cheddar cheese. Wow, that's on point; I could put that whole pot away.

And that's not all. Darwell has a full selection of sandwiches, from pulled pork and burgers to prime rib. Prime rib? Not bad for a little joint! He says, "Daddy taught me, if you can't go top of the line, don't go at all." He drenches the ribs with soy sauce, then rubs 'em down with minced garlic; sprinkles on Tony Chachere's Creole Seasoning, black pepper, and chopped onion; and pops 'em in the oven at 350°F for two and a half hours. After they rest and cool, he slices them super thin, then sautés the rib meat and serves it on a roll with sautéed onions, mushrooms, and its juice for dipping. I'd like to have a big sixteen-layer birthday cake made out of that. Messy and good.

THE CABOOSE ON THE TRAIN TO FLAVORTOWN—ALL ABOARD!

Crawfish Étouffée

ADAPTED FROM A RECIPE COURTESY OF DARWELL YEAGER III, OWNER OF DARWELL'S CAFE

Kitchen note: Darwell does this using his own homemade crawfish stock made from the crawfish shells. We substituted shrimp stock and, in case all you can find are frozen crawfish that have already been peeled, you can too. Feel free to adjust the amount of the Creole seasoning to your taste.

MAKES 6 SERVINGS

4 ounces (1 stick) unsalted butter

1 bunch of celery, medium diced (about 3 cups)

2 red or green bell peppers, stemmed, seeded, and medium diced

1 small onion, medium diced

1 tablespoon minced garlic

1 tablespoon Old Bay Seasoning

1 tablespoon Creole seasoning, preferably Tony Chachere brand

½ cup all-purpose flour

1 quart (4 cups) shrimp stock

1 cup heavy cream

2 pounds freshly picked, steamed crawfish tail meat

Steamed basmati rice and/or French bread, for serving

2 tablespoons freshly chopped flat-leaf parsley leaves, for serving

1. Melt the butter in a 14-inch skillet over medium heat. Add the celery and sauté until tender. Add the bell peppers, onion, garlic, and Old Bay and Creole seasoning and cook, stirring, for another 5 minutes.

2. Turn the heat up to medium-high and blend in the flour to form a roux around the vegetables. Cook thoroughly, stirring, until the roux starts to brown slightly. Stir in the shrimp stock and the heavy cream a little at a time. Bring just to a boil, reduce the heat to low, and simmer until thickened, about 15 minutes.

3. Finish by adding the crawfish tail meat and simmer to heat through. Serve over rice or French bread, and garnish with the chopped parsley.

BAR-B-Q KING

EST. 1959 ★ A LANDMARK DRIVE-IN SERVIN' SAUCY FRIED CHICKEN

I used to visit North Carolina a lot when I was a kid. You see, that's where my grandma Mamie used to live, and that's where I got my love of grits. But had I known about the Bar-B-Q King, I think I would've visited even more often.

★ TRACK IT DOWN ★

**2900 Wilkinson Boulevard
Charlotte, North Carolina 28208
704-399-8344
www.barbqking.com**

When you pull in here you're headed for some killer Carolina-style vinegar-based barbecue. They've been dishing up pulled pork, sliced pork, fried chicken drenched in their secret recipe barbecue sauce, even homemade hush puppies for years at this Charlotte landmark. And it's brought right to your car.

It's a family joint, run by the same family since the start. They've had the same ordering gizmos and the same carhop service since the very beginning, along with one other thing: the same food made from scratch.

Pete Gianakis started running this place and smoking the signature pork shoulders in 1959. He retired in 2003, but no one's really sure what that means; he still shows up almost every day. Gus Karapanos, his brother George, and their uncle Steve bought the place from Uncle Pete, and Steve's wife, Maria, and Gus's niece, Amanda, also work there. Gus is in charge of putting on the pork shoulder—a hundred pounds every day. It's cooked so tender it falls right off the bone, and it's used for chopped pork, sliced pork, sandwiches, and platters. The hickory-smoked meat is served with barbecue sauce that's tangy and wow: vinegar, brown sugar, tomato, and a little somethin' that tastes like Tabasco, Worcestershire, and liquid smoke—a secret spice mixture that's cooked with lemons for three hours.

They bread the chicken before frying all day long, then submerge it in that barbecue sauce. It's like a cross between fried chicken, barbecue chicken, and buffalo wings. Oh man, I don't get surprised very often, but that is outta bounds right there. They don't need to have anything else on the menu, but they do.

I tried doing the carhop delivery, but I made it through only five orders; man, they've got some hard workers. But I think they'll do okay without me, 'cause in Charlotte this place is king, chopped and sliced, fried and dipped.

[GUY ASIDE]

A few years ago when I was doing competition barbecue at the Kansas City Royal, a couple guys came up to me saying they wanted to do a "barbecue king" show set up like a competition on Food Network, so I had the name in the back of my mind. Then right after I won Food Network Star I was in Charlotte judging a Pro Start culinary competition, and all of a sudden we go by this Bar-B-Q King on the way to the airport, and I thought it was such a great name. Then four years later we were shooting there! It was too coincidental! So we went there and I thought it was just a drive-in—it was a little hit or miss at the beginning of the show. So I thought, okay, it'll be so-so food, a novelty drive-in and so forth. But this place really blew my mind. They don't even season the big old pork shoulders, and they make some wicked barbecue sauce, but the thing that blew me away the most was when they fried the chicken and dipped it in the 'cue sauce.

They've got a real-deal carhop service. I spoke to some people the other day who went there and they complained, "We had to eat in our car," and I said, "What's wrong with that?" and they said, "Our AC was broken!" There were five of them in ninety-degree heat. I said, I would've gone out and eaten it on the hood. They said they did. So I said, "Well, how was the barbecue?" Their answer: "Totally worth it."

COMMAND CENTER O' BBQ KING.

Bar-B-Q King Fried Chicken

ADAPTED FROM A RECIPE COURTESY OF BAR-B-Q KING

Give this method a go—just make sure you're using vinegar-based, tangy Carolina-style sauce.

MAKES 4 SERVINGS

Vegetable shortening or oil, for deep-frying

2 cups water

1 cup milk

2 cups self-rising flour

2 cups finely ground cracker meal

1 (2½- to 3-pound) chicken, cut into 10 pieces

Carolina-style barbecue sauce of your choice (optional)

1. Heat the shortening or oil in a deep-fryer or deep pot to 300°F. Combine the water and milk in a large bowl. Whisk the flour and cracker meal in a shallow dish.

2. Dip the chicken pieces in the milk mixture, then roll them in the flour mixture. Dip again in the milk and roll in the flour. Fry the pieces until golden brown and cooked through, about 15 minutes. If desired, dip the hot pieces in barbecue sauce as they come out of the fryer.

OWNER'S NOTE: At the Bar-B-Q King, the food is made today the same way it was in 1959. The food is all prepared in-house. The homemade barbecue pork, barbecue chicken, barbecue sauce, and seafood would actually be enough to keep Bar-B-Q King busy, but we also have homemade items such as slaw, potato salad, hush puppies, tartar sauce, and our one-of-a-kind onion rings. Most of the people who visit Bar-B-Q King have been customers for many, many years, but thanks to *Diners, Drive-ins and Dives,* our new clientele has increased dramatically. We have people drive hundreds of miles just to come to Bar-B-Q King and try the barbecue fried chicken. All of them say they'll keep coming back! Many customers ask us every week for the recipe for the barbecue chicken and the barbecue sauce. It's dipped into our secret barbecue sauce—the ingredients have been kept a secret for almost fifty years. Only the owners know the ingredients, and Guy's not getting this one! Thank you to *Diners, Drive-ins and Dives*! And a very special thanks to Guy, his crew, and the producer, David Page. —Steve, George, and Gus

BEACON DRIVE-IN

EST. 1946 ★ WHERE GOOD FOOD, GOOD TIMES, AND GOOD PEOPLE COME "A-PLENTY"

For more than sixty years, folks around Spartanburg have been in love with this landmark called the Beacon Drive-In, and for good reason. I've never seen anything like it.

★ TRACK IT DOWN ★

**255 John B. White Sr. Boulevard
Spartanburg, South Carolina 29306
864-585-9387
www.beacondrivein.com**

This place is loud, packed, and busy, with good food at a reasonable price. And it may look like pandemonium, but let me tell you, these guys have a playbook—a system for cranking it out. In a week's time they see fifteen to twenty thousand customers. But now, wait a second . . . there are only about forty-five thousand people living in Spartanburg.

Most meals come with a mountain of French fries and homemade onion rings—a combination they call "a-plenty." The best seller is a cheeseburger topped with homemade chili underneath a-plenty; yes, the burger is under there, although it's tough to see under all the fried goodness. They've got ham and cheese a-plenty, bacon cheeseburgers a-plenty—everything's a-plenty. Owner Kenny Church showed me how to make the signature rings. They sell more than two tons of onions a week—that they slice, ring, and batter. For one day they do a thousand pounds. Shaking the rings out after battering was like mining for gold—and Kenny says, that *is* gold.

Right after the Depression the original owner, John White, started serving these mounds of good, cheap food. Kenny, Mark McManus, Steve McManus, Sam Maw, and Steve Duncan won the bid to buy it in 1998 because they were dedicated to keeping it just the way it's always been. They do all kinds of down-home cooking. The hash is not the typical corned-beef hash; it's made with beef shoulder and pulled pork and served with barbecue sauce on a bun. The pimento cheese is homemade and served in a sandwich that's pressed—like a South Carolina–style panini. The chicken stew is creamy and thick, with loads of chicken and chives, and a real-deal homemade breakfast is served; you can have a platter with grits, great bacon, scrambled eggs, and peaches. Peaches? Steve says that's just the way Mr. White did it since 1946, and if it ain't broke, don't fix it. And that means making traditional Southern iced tea filled with sugar and lemons. They say they make more than any place else in the country, thousands of gallons. But maybe the biggest tradition of the Beacon isn't the food, it's how you order it.

J.C. Strobble is a Spartanburg institution and the heart of this place. He's been calling orders here for half a century. He says, "I tell you one thing, we do not have strangers at the Beacon," and he's one amazing person. He's lost his eyesight but not his enthusiasm or his energy. In his spare time he goes to church and goes home to get some rest. He says let's rock, and man, does he. I tried calling orders. "There ya go!" he encouraged me, but I did five and lost my voice. And try being the guy who's filling J.C.'s orders; they keep coming in, and it's restaurant shorthand like you've never heard.

You're not going to find anything like the Beacon anywhere else. Great food, a one-of-a-kind experience, and some really special people you ought to meet.

THERE ARE "A-PLENTY" OF FOLKS WAITIN' FOR A-PLENTY!

Beacon Lightly Breaded Onion Rings

ADAPTED FROM A RECIPE COURTESY OF KENNY CHURCH OF BEACON DRIVE-IN

These are fantastic; try them "a-plenty" atop your next burger.

MAKES 4 SERVINGS

Vegetable oil for deep-frying, plus 1 tablespoon

3 Vidalia onions

1 quart (4 cups) buttermilk

1 egg

4 cups all-purpose flour

1 teaspoon kosher salt, plus more for sprinkling on hot rings

¼ teaspoon freshly ground black pepper

1. Heat the frying oil in a large heavy pot over medium-high heat until a deep-fry thermometer reads 325°F. Peel and slice the onions into rings about 1 inch thick (just rings, not hearts).

2. Whisk the buttermilk, egg, and 1 tablespoon vegetable oil in a large bowl. In another bowl, whisk the flour, 1 teaspoon salt, and the pepper.

3. Drop the onion rings first into the buttermilk mixture and then into the flour, making sure they are well coated with each dip. Shake the excess flour off the rings and fry in batches until golden brown, about 3 minutes. Remove from the oil, sprinkle with salt, and serve hot.

Beacon Drive-In Pimento Cheese

ADAPTED FROM A RECIPE COURTESY OF KENNY CHURCH OF BEACON DRIVE-IN

The cheese is great spread on toast and broiled until the cheese melts, or on burgers.

MAKES 1 QUART

1-pound block American cheese, coarsely chopped
1 (4-ounce) jar pimentos, drained
2 tablespoons mayonnaise

Grind up the cheese and pimentos in a food processor until almost smooth, but with some small pieces of pimento visible. Scrape into a bowl and stir in the mayonnaise.

IF YOU'RE STANDING THIS CLOSE TO DA SIGN, YOU BETTER BE READY.

UNCLE LOU'S FRIED CHICKEN

EST. 2001 ★ DIPPIN' IT ALL IN SWEET SPICY LOVE

....

You know how I like to find the funkiest joints in town—well, I found one here in Memphis, Tennessee, in a strip mall by the airport. It's Uncle Lou's, and he's doing chicken one of my favorite ways, fried and dipped.

★ TRACK IT DOWN ★

....

**3633 Millbranch Road
Memphis, Tennessee 38116
901-332-2367
www.unclelousfriedchicken.com**

This is Uncle Lou's home cooking. A few years ago Louis Martin opened his own joint, doing chicken the way his great-grandmother did, and folks just went nuts. The chicken and the sauce are bananas, and bananas is good (you know that, though, don't you?). He's even frying it whole and the crowd keeps packing in, for something fresh, hot, tasty, and cooked to order.

His seasoned flour has loads of black pepper, as well as salt, onion, garlic, and cinnamon. He dredges the pieces with a light coating, then puts them into the fryer, thigh first, then drum, then wing, then breast. Twelve minutes and it's golden brown. There's good crunch, and I can hear the sauce calling my name. It's Lou's creation and it's like a buffalo wing sauce, sort of, with red wine vinegar, honey, Cajun Chef Louisiana Hot Sauce, and a mixture he calls Corruption, with garlic, chili powder, salt, paprika, onion, sugar, lemon pepper, and hickory smoke. (He sells this and his seasoned flour online.) He called it Honey Dip Sauce when I went in there, but I said you've got to call it Sweet Spicy Love, and he changed the name on the spot. He dips that chicken in and you get the taste of vinegar backed up with the sweetness and a little heat—or more heat if you roll that way; he does that too. There's Spicy and More Spicy. As he says, it's hot enough to make your hair stand on end, like mine.

But Uncle Lou is not a one-hit wonder. Folks are loving whatever he's doing, like honey-dipped fried bologna or a dipped smoked sausage sandwich or a monster burger. His signature item, though, is his whole fried chicken, injected with Creole butter, fried, and dunked in Sweet Spicy Love, and sprinkled with Corruption. So tender and juicy, and you can really taste the garlic butter. It's off the chain, crazy good. If you live within three hundred miles of this joint you should be getting yourself over there, right quick now.

. . . .

OWNER'S NOTE: Uncle Lou's Fried Chicken was established April 4, 2001. That September, Uncle Lou's "Honey-Dipped" Chicken (now known as Sweet Spicy Love) won the best new food item at the Mid-South Fair in Memphis.

After it was featured on Triple D, things went bananas (bananas means VERY good). We put up a map of the United States the day before the show aired—August 3, 2008—and from then until May 18, 2009, we've had more than 450 out-of-state visitors. I had no idea Guy has such a loyal following. The first thing people say when they come in is, "You really did change the name to Sweet Spicy Love"—that was one of the best decisions I ever made. We now bottle and sell the Sweet Spicy Love and the Uncle Lou's Corruption; we have a display in-store, and we also have an online store at www.unclelousfriedchicken.com. It's become a chore to just keep enough Sweet Spicy Love and Uncle Lou's Corruption bottled to serve our customers. Thanks, Guy—we went from averaging six to eight gallons a week to making eighteen to twenty gallons a week. —Uncle Lou

UNCLE LOU . . . HOLDIN' POULTRY COURT.

Uncle Lou's Fried Chicken

ADAPTED FROM A RECIPE COURTESY OF LOUIS MARTIN OF UNCLE LOU'S FRIED CHICKEN

MAKES 4 SERVINGS

Vegetable oil, for deep-frying

1 whole fryer chicken, cut into 8 pieces

3 cups Uncle Lou's Fried Chicken Seasoning (available online)

Uncle Lou's Sweet Spicy Love dipping sauce (recipe follows; also available online)

1. Heat oil in a deep-fryer or heat 3 inches of oil in a heavy pot until a deep-fry thermometer reads 375°F. Line a baking sheet with paper towels.

WHO STOLE DA FRIES?

2. Rinse the chicken and thoroughly pat dry with more paper towels. Put the seasoning mix in a plastic zip-top bag. Add the chicken 2 to 3 pieces at a time, close the bag, and shake until all of the pieces are well coated.

3. Remove the chicken from the bag and shake off excess seasoning mix. Slip the chicken into the hot oil and fry until the juices run clear, about 12 to 15 minutes. Remove from the oil and drain on the lined baking sheet to remove excess oil. Serve as is, or dipped in the Sweet Spicy Love sauce.

Uncle Lou's Sweet Spicy Love

Note from Uncle Lou: A little history about Uncle Lou's Corruption. I started making it about fifteen years ago, as an all-purpose seasoning, and without Uncle Lou's Corruption there would be no Sweet Spicy Love. Uncle Lou's Corruption is the "Love" in Sweet Spicy Love. It is also great for grilling, baking, broiling, and boiling; it's great on popcorn, vegetables, salads, and dips—the sky is the limit.

We also like to serve Sweet Spicy Love on what we call Tennessee round steak—but you probably know it as bologna: Just slice bologna about ¾ thick and cook it on a grill or flattop griddle, deep-fry it, char grill it, or microwave it. Dip the meat in Sweet Spicy Love. Make a sandwich with your favorite bread, bun, or Texas toast and add your favorite toppings. You can also do this with beef, chicken, or turkey!

MAKES 6 CUPS

2 cups red wine vinegar

⅓ cup Uncle Lou's Corruption seasoning mix (available online)

2 cups hot sauce

1⅔ cups honey

Bring the vinegar to a boil in a medium saucepan. As soon as the vinegar starts to boil, add the Uncle Lou's Corruption and stir to dissolve completely. Remove from the heat and stir in the hot sauce and honey. Put into sealable containers and remember to shake well before using. Store for up to one month.

CEMITAS PUEBLA

EST. 2002 ★ DISCOVER A RARE MEXICAN SPECIALTY . . . IN CHICAGO

So check it out: here I am in Chicago, and I know you're expecting that I'm going to be eating one of those killer Chicago dogs or some pizza or Italian beef, but nope, this was all about cemitas. Just when you think you know your Mexican food, Triple D rolls into town and finds this joint.

Cemitas are a kind of sandwich made with an avocado, chipotle pepper, Mexican cheese, and a kind of bitter herb called papalo, served with various types of meat—from carne asada to al pastor to a spiced pork called carne enchilada. Cemitas are unique; you can't find them outside of Puebla, Mexico, where Tony Anteliz's mom and dad grew up. Eighty percent of the menu at Cemitas comes from Puebla. For their cemita with breaded pork, Tony follows Mama's rules for the recipe or he gets in trouble. He makes the breading mixture in a blender with chopped onion, cloves, black and white pepper, oregano, three peeled garlic cloves, ground garlic, a little bit of bread crumbs, milk, and some salt. The pork loin pieces soak in this mixture and then he breads them, lets them sit in the fridge for about an hour, and fries them up. Even the buns are a family recipe; Tony has a guy who bakes them just for him. He assembles the sandwich with the avocado spread on the bun, the chipotle, a whole lotta queso Oaxaca, and some papalo that his mother grows for

"WELL, GUY, I'LL TELL YA, YOU JUST ATE ABOUT TEN JALAPEÑOS—YOU'RE GONNA FEEL THAT!"

him in the summertime. That stuff is pungent; it makes arugula taste like iceberg. Just a dash of olive oil on the top of the bun, and that's all she wrote.

They're bringing Mexico to Chicago, literally. Every month or six weeks Tony's father heads down there to pick up their cinnamon, queso, oregano, and dried chipotles. He's using his grandmother's recipe for chipotles in adobo sauce, and he says that's what gives his cemitas most of their flavor. He uses small dried chipotles, raw sugarcane, dried thyme, dried oregano, bay leaves, dried cloves, five or six garlic heads, three thingies (big pinches) of salt, giant Mexican cinnamon sticks, and a whole lot of onions (this is cooking with Tony). About a gallon and a half of plain white vinegar and a sweet and sour pineapple brine. Top the pot off with water and let it boil for seven or eight hours. It's a classic flavor on every classic cemita.

The cemitas are just the start. He makes something that's like the Mexican cousin of the shawarma: Taco Arabe. It's the classic Middle Eastern meat on a spit. They blend serrano peppers, cloves, white pepper, parsley, salt, and white vinegar and marinate sliced pork shoulder for two or three hours. Then they stack the pork shoulder, alternating with onion, on a rotisserie. It's a beautiful big spit of meat. He slices it up and down to start with, and the juices fall like tears from the flavor angel. Then he lets the slices cook on the flattop for a little bit to get charred on the outside, and he uses a type of flat pita to wrap the meat up with pureed chipotle and adobo sauce. Mmmmm. This is good stuff.

Tony's been taught right.

Cemitas Puebla Steak Tacos with Salsa Verde

ADAPTED FROM A RECIPE COURTESY OF TONY ANTELIZ OF CEMITAS PUEBLA

Note from Tony: If the steak is really thick, ask the butcher to butterfly it and remove some of the fat—but not all, because it adds flavor. The steak should be medium thick, not too thick or too thin—about ¾ to 1 inch thick.

FINGER GUN FIGHTS, BIG COMPETITION AT CEMITAS PUEBLA.

MAKES 4 TO 8 SERVINGS

For the salsa verde

6 tomatillos, husks removed

4 garlic cloves, peeled

2 jalapeño chiles

1 ripe avocado, pitted, peeled, and coarsely chopped

½ cup water

1 tablespoon kosher salt

½ large bunch of cilantro, stems and leaves coarsely chopped

For the steak

1 teaspoon paprika

1 teaspoon freshly ground black pepper

½ teaspoon kosher salt

½ teaspoon garlic powder

¼ teaspoon ground cloves

Pinch of ground cinnamon

8 limes, halved

2 pounds skirt steak, ¾ to 1 inch thick

For the tacos
16 corn tortillas, heated in the skillet or microwave
Diced white onion
Chopped fresh cilantro leaves

1. **FOR THE SALSA VERDE:** Heat a griddle, grill, or skillet over high heat and add the tomatillos, garlic, and jalapeños all at once. Eyeball them, but do about a minute or two on each side, turning with tongs, until everything is close to getting black but not black.

2. Put the charred vegetables in the blender with the avocado, water, and salt and blend until smooth. Add the cilantro and blend again.

3. **FOR THE STEAK:** Combine the seasonings in a small bowl. Squeeze the limes over the meat evenly, using all their juices. Then rub the lime halves over the meat to get the pulp over it. Sprinkle the seasoning mix over both sides.

4. Heat a grill to medium-high. Grill the steak to your liking; we like it medium-well. Remove, let rest 5 minutes, and then slice it across the grain in angled strips. Using 2 tortillas per taco, pile in some meat, onion, and cilantro and top with salsa verde.

[GUY ASIDE]

I've been going to Mexico for years and I pride myself on my awareness of Mexican food, so for me doing DD&D, this is a culinary theme park, and today I'm going to "It's a Cemitas World"—Cemitas Puebla is why I love doing the show. I was so pleasantly surprised at how great it was, and it had a really good following.

I dig this story because it reminds me a lot of my dad and myself. Antonio and Tony are a really interesting father and son, and the father really helps support the son in going after this restaurant. Tony got the shot to do the place, didn't know how to cook, learned from his dad, and gets there every day—an enthusiastic, hard-working guy. His dad's got a connection with a radio show, and it was the first time I've ever been on Mexican radio; he just put me on the phone on-air. You think Mexican TV is crazy, you should hear Mexican radio. I speak enough kitchen Spanish to get me in trouble: takes me twenty words to get out a three-word sentence.

PARADISE PUP

EST. 1983 ★ CHICAGO CLASSICS, FRESH AND FAST

On the family-owned tour, I was right out of Chicago and found this first-generation place that was only 800 square feet. But don't let the size fool you, because for the last twenty-five years they've been jamming out tons of off-the-hook Chicago favorites.

> **★ TRACK IT DOWN ★**
>
> **1724 S. River Road**
> **Des Plaines, Illinois 60018**
> **847-699-8590**

Knowing the menu by heart isn't unusual at Paradise Pup, where brothers George and Tony Manos want you to feel like you're at a backyard barbecue. These guys started the joint over twenty-five years ago after jumping into the food biz as teens. Their father was driving by one day and saw a small for-sale sign, and went home and said, "I got a great spot for you."

OWNERS' NOTE: When we first opened Paradise Pup in 1983, Tony was eighteen and George was nineteen. The building was a wreck when we bought it and it took a lot of hard work and several coats of paint to get it ready for opening day! We spent our last fifty dollars on paint—it was our tip money we saved from waiting tables. On September 17, 1983, at eleven A.M., Tony, George, and Fannie (Mom) took the order of the first customer. He was rung up and paid with a twenty-dollar bill. No money in the drawer! Mom ran in the back room and pulled a few fives, singles, and some coins from her purse and gave the man his change. Our mom has always been good luck, and since that day we've never had to ask Mom for money again!

Being on Food Network was such an honor and a great boost for our business. It's been well over a year and we're still generating new business. People are still coming in and saying they came from fifty miles away or more because they saw us on Guy's show. One day a charter bus pulled in from Michigan—a group of Food Network junkies traveling to places Guy has been! We're close to O'Hare, and so many people every day still come in from all over the country and mention our segment on *Diners*. It truly put us on the map!

Thank you, Food Network and Guy. We love ya. —George and Tony Manos

They still don't want anyone else working the grill. What they're doing here in an 800-square-foot joint is traditional Chicago fast food, the way it oughtta be. They've got Polish sausage, Chicago dogs, and homemade Italian beef—and their burgers slathered with Merkts Cheddar require about twenty napkins. It's a third-of-a-pound patty, fresh, never frozen. The stovetop is about 750 degrees to give it a great char. They grill the buns, spread softened Wisconsin Cheddar, and put on molten hot onions, tomato, lettuce, and pickle. Oooooh, man, that's juicy. I needed a bib—or a shower. Tony said they'd hose me down in the back. The Polish sausage is topped with grilled onions; the real Chicago dog is served with mustard, relish, fresh chopped onion, tomatoes, fresh sliced cucumber, a pickle. I felt like I'd been to a salad bar; that is something good.

And the Italian beef is entirely made from scratch. They start with a top butt, douse it with lots of salt and pepper, oregano, and garlic juice, and slow-cook it for about four hours. They slice it so thin you can see right through it, then serve it in a bun dipped in the meat juices from the roasting pan. They dress it with peppers and pickled vegetables, and wow, that is so good. All those herbs and spices, and it's the thin slicing, too, that really makes the difference.

You'd think there were no other restaurants in this town the way they line up and out the door. These brothers are committed to doing it right. As George says, it's all in the quality of their food.

[GUY ASIDE]

These are the nicest guys, with a family kind of place you want to go back to. I come here every time I'm on the way to the airport in Chicago, and every time there are more people. I show up and they want me to cut the line, but I don't do that. When we were there filming, we arrived forty minutes before they opened, and there were people sleeping in their cars to be first in line. Things taste different when they come from a place like this, with cars flying by and a nearby auto body shop. I was like, "This place looks like a Fotomat drive-up, where you'd drop off your film in the old days—you could turn it into a museum and move the restaurant to the shop next door!"

Paradise Pup Merkts Cheddar Burger

ADAPTED FROM A RECIPE COURTESY OF TONY AND GEORGE MANOS OF PARADISE PUP

MAKES 6 BURGERS

A block of Merkts Cheddar cheese or any cold-pack cheese food found in a grocery store

2 pounds ground chuck (80 percent lean)

2 teaspoons kosher salt

1 teaspoon freshly ground black pepper

6 challah egg twist buns or soft bakery buns, toasted

Hellmann's Real Mayonnaise, Hunt's ketchup, crinkle-cut sliced pickles, sliced red onion (grilled, if you like), sliced tomatoes, and lettuce leaves, for serving

1. Let the cheese sit out for about 2 hours to get soft enough to spread easily.

2. Preheat a grill or griddle to VERY HOT to get the right char.

3. Season the meat with salt and pepper. Mix and form 6 balls, then flatten each to a patty.

4. Grill the burgers for about 3 minutes each side. Do not press down on the patties while cooking or all the juices will squirt out and dry out the patties! Toast the buns on the grill. Spread the cheese on top of the patties; then place the top half of the bun on top to adhere with the cheese. Remove from the grill.

5. Garnish the bottom half of the bun with mayo, ketchup, pickle, red onion, tomato, and lettuce.

6. Have plenty of napkins on hand. Enjoy!

THE ORIGINAL VITO & NICK'S PIZZERIA

EST. 1932 ★ WORLD-CLASS THIN-CRUST IN A DEEP-DISH TOWN

When you think Chicago, you probably think of that thick-crust deep-dish pizza. So you've got to stop and take a look when you find a pizza joint in Chicago that's doing the exact opposite. At Vito and Nick's, people have been piling in for their thin-crust pizza for more than sixty years.

> **★ TRACK IT DOWN ★**
>
> **8433 S. Pulaski Road**
> **Chicago, Illinois 60652**
> **773-735-2050**
> **www.vitoandnick.com**

"If I want to eat bread, I eat bread," says owner Rosemary George; and if you want to eat pizza it's going to be the way her family's been serving it since 1949—thin! The dough is made from scratch using flour, water, milk, yeast, and salt; mix it and let it sit overnight. And when the dough starts to rise, it's punched down every twenty minutes or so. After the dough is rolled out thin, Rosemary goes all the way to the edge with her sauce, 'cause she says the edges will burn otherwise. She throws on a little bit of cheese (mozzarella that's been through the grinder, not shredded) and then just about anything—sausage, onion, green pepper, and, get this one, Italian beef.

They're putting a Chicago specialty on the pizza, and the beef's homemade Rose's way. Not wasting a thing, she trims the beef, then grinds the fat, flattens it out on a roasting sheet, and seasons it with salt, black pepper, and granulated garlic. That's her base, and she puts the meat on top. It's covered with more salt, black pepper, some granulated onion, and then generously with granulated garlic, then basil, oregano, and olive oil. It's an adventure. Rose tucks the trimmings in underneath and slow-roasts the beef for eight hours. You can't get a better medium rare. She then slices it thin and tops the pizza, with a little extra cheese on top to hold it together—and I tell ya, that thing comes out of the oven looking like a manhole cover in Flavortown. And it's killer. Anyone who would come to Chicago and not come here and try this should be arrested, I'm moving in.

This joint's making a lot of people very happy, with more than sixty pies every hour. The pizza dough gets sauced, trimmed, and sent for toppings in under a minute—an assembly line like none other. Get this: to keep up the pace, these guys *throw* the pizza peels (boards) at each other across the kitchen. The explanation? When you're working a ten-hour shift, you try to walk as little as you can. It's the way they've always done it. Rose even has a technique for making breakfast pizza. She'll show you how to crack the eggs just so, placing them raw on top of the cheese pizza, with a little oregano and a sprinkle of water, and then topping with fried pepperoni before putting it in the oven. If you're gonna eat eggs, this is the way to do it—on a thin crust covered in fried pepperoni. This isn't just coming and getting a pie, this is a come-to family joint. This is an event.

[GUY ASIDE]

Here's the thing—I pulled up on a humungous street on some side of Chicago, I was sick—had a sinus cold or something—and there were trucks hauling by. And I am not really a deep-dish pizza fan, so I was thinking, I don't know if this is gonna work. But these people are making some of the thinnest, crunchiest crust in the world. They're putting Italian beef, onions, eggs, olives, and everything on top of pizza, and it's to die for. You've gotta watch these dudes throw the pizza peels—the wooden ones. They snap when they throw it, and at the last nano-second the other guy grabs it. Incredible. A year and a half later Rosemary came to one of my shoots while I was in Chi-town and asked if I wanted a pizza, cuz I couldn't make it over there before I had to leave. They took the pizza that was coming out of the oven for one of their customers (and gave him four free pizzas in exchange) so they could drive it over to me at the final location and I could have it before I left for home! So *kewl!*

Italian Roast Beef Pizza

ADAPTED FROM A RECIPE COURTESY OF ROSEMARY GEORGE, OWNER OF THE ORIGINAL VITO & NICK'S PIZZERIA

Rosemary uses her beef sliced thin in Italian beef sandwiches or cut thicker with heavy gravy for dinner as well as offering it on a pizza.

MAKES 1 SERVING

Fresh pizza dough

1 cup of your favorite pizza sauce (Rose uses a can of Stanislaus with a bit of water)

2¼ cups shredded mozzarella (Rose actually grinds hers)

4 ounces very thinly sliced rare Italian Roast Beef (recipe on page 130)

1. Preheat the oven to 475°F, with a pizza stone, if you have one, on the bottom rack. You want the stone to be very hot, so leave it in there about 45 minutes or the middle of the pizza will be mushy, says Rose. If you don't have a stone, Rose recommends using two layers of heavy-duty aluminum foil. ("You don't even need a freaking pan!")

2. Stretch a premade pizza dough to make a 12-inch round. Spread a thin layer of pizza sauce on top. Scatter just a handful of mozzarella over the sauce and top that with the roast beef. Top with the remaining mozzarella and bake on a baking sheet or directly on the baking stone until the crust is crisp and the cheese bubbly, about 15 to 18 minutes.

Italian Roast Beef

ADAPTED FROM A RECIPE COURTESY OF ROSEMARY GEORGE, OWNER OF THE ORIGINAL VITO & NICK'S PIZZERIA

MAKES 8 TO 12 SERVINGS

½ cup kosher salt

½ cup dried basil

½ cup dried oregano

½ cup granulated garlic

¼ cup granulated onion

¼ teaspoon freshly ground black pepper

1 (5- to 7-pound) roast beef round, fat cap on

½ cup extra-virgin olive oil

1. Preheat the oven to 300°F. Combine the salt, basil, oregano, granulated garlic and onion, and the black pepper in a mixing bowl.

2. Trim all the fat from the beef round. Rosemary grinds the trimmings, but you can cut them up into bite-size pieces. Put the trimmings on the bottom of a roasting pan and sprinkle with some of the seasoning mix. Put the roast beef on top and coat the beef well with more of the seasoning mix. Drizzle the olive oil over the top of the roast and pat it into the seasonings.

3. Roast for about 1½ to 2 hours until the internal temperature registers 130°F (medium-rare) on an instant-read thermometer. Remove from the oven and let stand for about 20 minutes before carving.

BBQ SHACK

EST. 1997 ★ GO WHOLE HOG, WHERE HEAT MEETS HEAT. SO GOOD THAT IF YOU PUT SOME ON TOP OF YOUR FOREHEAD YOU CAN WATCH YOUR TONGUE BEAT YOUR BRAINS OUT TRYING TO GET TO IT.

Here I was on the last leg of my real-deal barbecue-athon, in Paola, Kansas, about forty miles south of Kansas City. Now, a lot of folks think of this as cattle country, but you might change your mind after you taste some of the tasty pork at the BBQ Shack. From whole hogs to racks of ribs, it's go big or go home at this joint.

> **★ TRACK IT DOWN ★**
>
> **1613 E. Peoria Street**
> **Paola, Kansas 66071**
> **913-294-5908**
> **www.thebbqshack.com**

BBQ Shack was a big gamble that paid off big for Rick Schoenberger. He left his corporate job to turn his hobby into his business. Now he's firing up the monster smoker, cranking out the classics and some surprises—like chicken wings and homegrown jalapeño poppers. One customer says, "I send my heavyweight wrestlers down here to gain weight."

And if you order ahead, he really will do an entire hog. It starts with his homemade rub of salt and sugar, ground celery, chili powder, black pepper, granulated garlic, seasoned salt, granulated onion, paprika, mustard flour, allspice, and a little ground clove. He sprinkles it on the inside of the split hog, rubs some

OWNER'S NOTE: We actually had to move! We're in a new building now primarily due to *Diners, Drive-Ins and Dives*—we just outgrew the other place. We've just seen a second surge, because they ran the show again a week ago. A lot of the new customers would have loved to see the old place, but we've done a good job keeping the ambience. It's the same good barbecue. —Rick Schoenberger

"DADDY, I THOUGHT ONLY ONE LITTLE PIGGY WENT TO MARKET?"

olive oil on the skin, and closes it up with chicken wire before hauling it into the smoker. (I thought I'd pulled a hammy!) It goes low and slow all day. It renders down practically all the fat and cooks in its own skin, so there's just flavor galore in there. As one customer said, "It'd make a rabbit hug a hound." Good eats.

While the whole hog is a special order, Rick's everyday menu is keeping the place packed. Here in barbecue country, people won't stop raving about his brisket and his ribs, real good and real tender. He's serving burnt ends and homemade sausage, and he's even loading up the smoker with chicken wings. Most people just take 'em, fry 'em, and sauce 'em. But he seasons 'em, smokes 'em, and deep-fries 'em to order.

Along with his rub he sprinkles on dried chipotle for a kick and he smokes them for a couple hours. Amazingly, all that seasoning stays on them when they hit the deep-fryer. It's a lot of work for a chicken wing, man, but it sure is good.

Rick grows jalapeño peppers in his garden, and he makes poppers out of them the way they did before the chain restaurants got ahold of them. They're cored, then stuffed with cream cheese and with a water chestnut that's been marinated in brown sugar and soy sauce. He then wraps them with bacon, skewers them with a toothpick, and sprinkles a little dry rub on top before smoking. I've had smoked Brie, smoked mozzarella—but smoked cream cheese? That's wicked, great flavor. (And there goes the theory that cooking the jalapeños cools them down—wow! That's hot.)

Rick really is a BBQ bad boy. The rub, the smoke, all done low and slow.

BBQ Shack Chicken Wings

ADAPTED FROM A RECIPE COURTESY OF RICK SCHOENBERGER OF BBQ SHACK

Note from Rick: At the BBQ Shack, we cook up to forty pounds of wings at a time. We just dump the wings in a big plastic tub, dump some of our All-Purpose BBQ Rub on them, and mix them up. I am sure most any barbecue rub will work.

We actually bag the wings in freezer bags, one dozen per bag, and freeze them. When we get an order for wings, we grab a bag out of the freezer and fry them about two to three minutes, then serve. For hot wings, you can either mix some ground hot peppers in with your rub or after the wings have fried, put them in a container with a lid, pour a couple of ounces of your favorite hot sauce into the container, shake the wings up, then serve.

MAKES 24 WINGS

12 chicken wings, tips removed, split at the joints

About ¼ cup All-Purpose BBQ Rub (recipe follows), or your favorite rub

Vegetable oil, for deep-frying

1. Sprinkle just enough rub on the wings so you can still see the skin. You don't want the rub too thick. Then smoke the wings for approximately 2 hours at 250°F.

2. Serve the wings right out of the smoker, or cook them in a 350°F deep-fat fryer for approximately 1 minute to crisp up the skin. If the wings have cooled down, let them fry until they are warm throughout.

[GUY ASIDE]

I liked this place the minute I walked in. I mean, Rick had a signed Don Knotts photo on the wall—and I was a big fan of Barney Fife. It was a small little kitchen, but busier than all get-out. He had a big smoker on wheels out in the back, a rolling smoke machine. So, I remember we were doing the whole hog back there, but the chicken wire that we had to contain the pig wasn't long enough. I took a look around and said, get me some wire snips and a pair of gloves. After snipping some more wire off a nearby fence, I grafted the chicken-wire blanket to wrap around the pig to put on the smoker. Everyone was going, "Where did you learn to do that?" It's one of the things my dad taught me. (When I was a kid he'd make me straighten out the nail if I bent one instead of getting new one.) I asked Rick what he did when I wasn't around, and he said he has a lot of people who'll work for beer.

All-Purpose BBQ Rub

ADAPTED FROM A RECIPE COURTESY OF RICK SCHOENBERGER OF BBQ SHACK

MAKES JUST OVER 4 CUPS

1 ½ cups kosher salt (can be celery salt, garlic salt, seasoned salt, onion salt, or a combination)

1 cup sugar

¾ cup Spanish paprika

Scant ½ cup chili powder

Scant ½ cup finely ground black pepper

3 more spices of your choice, to taste

Combine all the ingredients in a bowl and you're good to go!

MY FAVORITE GAME, "WHERE'S GUIDO?" (CAN YA FIND ME?)

Jalapeño Poppers

ADAPTED FROM A RECIPE COURTESY OF RICK SCHOENBERGER OF BBQ SHACK

Most barbecue/fireplace stores sell chile-twisters for coring the jalapeños and racks that will hold one, two, or three dozen poppers upright on the grill. Start this recipe a day ahead because the water chestnuts need to marinate.

MAKES 4 SERVINGS

1 (8-ounce) can whole water chestnuts

1 cup soy sauce

½ to 1 pound light brown sugar

12 jalapeño chiles, the larger the better

8 ounces cream cheese, at room temperature

6 slices thin-sliced bacon, halved crosswise

All-Purpose BBQ Rub (see page 134)

Special equipment: jalapeño grilling rack

1. Put the water chestnuts and soy sauce in a nonreactive bowl. Add enough brown sugar to cover the chestnuts completely. It will dissolve as you put it in, so it may take a fair amount of brown sugar. Cover and refrigerate overnight.

2. In the morning, stir the mixture up. Slice the stem ends off the jalapeños and core them. Put the cream cheese into a quart freezer bag. (At the restaurant they put the cream cheese into the bag and warm it in a pan of water that is on their steam table.) Cut a little bit of the corner off the bag and use it as a pastry bag. Pipe some of the cream cheese into the tip of the pepper. Now stuff one or two chestnuts in. (You may need to cut the chestnuts in half.) Leave a little space at the top of the pepper. Wrap each pepper with a half slice of bacon and use toothpicks to keep the bacon in place. Repeat with the remaining chiles. Stand the chiles in the rack. Sprinkle a little bit of the BBQ rub over the tops for some color.

3. Heat a grill to medium-high heat. Grill the poppers with the lid closed until the bacon is done, about 15 to 20 minutes. Watch them closely; if bacon grease pools, it will catch fire. An offset fire (indirect heat) works best.

BOBO DRIVE-IN

EST. 1953 ★ STRAIGHT FROM THE FIFTIES AND STRAIGHT TO YOUR CAR

One of the things I love about Triple D is finding the kind of places that belong to the whole town. The kind of joints that feel like they've been there forever. In Topeka, that means Bobo Drive-In.

★ TRACK IT DOWN ★

**2300 S.W. 10th Avenue
Topeka, Kansas 66604
785-234-4511**

From double cheeseburgers to Coney dogs to fresh-cut onion rings made every day, they're keeping with tradition here. They've got the sweet stuff, too, like chocolate malts and their famous hot apple pie with ice cream, which Bob Bobo started serving back in 1953. It was Bob's aunt's and mom's original recipe, and it's the same today.

Richard Marsh and his wife, Tricia, bought the place a couple years ago—despite a total lack of experience in the restaurant business—after a friend in real estate called and said he'd found the perfect thing for them. It was a dream come true. They've got the original Bobo's recipes and the staff that's been the heart of this place for years. Betty Ramsey, for one, who moved here from England, has been making these all-American burgers since 1975. She presses down on the meat with equal pressure so it goes down flat, nice and thin. A little salt and pepper, cheese in the middle, and it's got a great crust on it. And they do seventy-five pounds of onions a day for the rings. They sift them in flour, shake off the excess, then dip them in the pool of milk and into cracker meal. Then dust them with salt when they come out of the fryer.

The chili comes from the original owner's recipe, and so does the Spanish sauce on the Spanish burger. It starts with ketchup, minced onion, sugar, paprika, cayenne, some more secret seasonings, and a scoop of lard, then cloves and star anise go into a spice ball and it all cooks together for forty-five minutes. Reminded me of a sloppy Joe that hasn't been ground up: good eats.

Then there's that apple pie. It's just not something you see much of at drive-ins, and nobody's making it like Jo Mendoza. They have an apple peeler that looks like Johnny Appleseed could've used it, and she makes fifty pies a day—been doing it for more than fifteen years. That's over 195,000 pies! Tricia took on a pie-eating contest against customer Lisa Bassett, no hands allowed. Lisa was laughing, but Tricia was all business and won. It was vicious. But everybody's a winner at Bobo's.

[GUY ASIDE]

Everybody loves Bobo Drive-In—a great little place. They make the apple pies down in the basement, and the coring machine is crazy—I was afraid I'd get my shirt caught or get lobotomized, one of the two. Then upstairs you get the nostalgia of a genuine drive-in—they either have it or they don't, and the ones that have it are the ones that survive.

THAT DUDE IN DA CORNER PASSED OUT FROM TOO MANY BURGERS.

Apple Pie

ADAPTED FROM A RECIPE COURTESY OF TRICIA AND RICHARD MARSH OF BOBO DRIVE-IN

Bake up a few and have your own Bobo pie-eating contest, no hands allowed.

MAKES 1 (9-INCH) PIE

Dough

2 cups all-purpose flour

1 teaspoon fine salt

1 cup solid vegetable shortening

6 tablespoons cold water

Filling

1 cup sugar

3 tablespoons all-purpose flour

¾ teaspoon ground cinnamon

⅛ teaspoon freshly grated nutmeg

**6 apples, peeled, cored, and sliced about ¼ inch thick
    (a mix of different types all year round; we use what's available)**

1. Preheat the oven to 400°F.

2. FOR THE DOUGH: Mix the flour and salt in a large bowl. Using a pastry blender or two table knives, cut the shortening into the flour to make a coarse meal. Sprinkle the cold water over and toss with a fork until it comes together. Divide the dough in half and roll out two 10-inch crust rounds on a lightly floured board.

3. FOR THE FILLING: Combine the sugar, flour, cinnamon, and nutmeg. Line a 9-inch pie pan with one crust. Mound the apples on the crust. Sprinkle the sugar mixture over the apples. Place the second crust on top and press the edges with a fork all around to seal. Bake until the crust is golden brown, about 50 to 60 minutes.

CAFE ON THE ROUTE

EST. 1998 ★ A SMALL TOWN WITH BIG FOOD ON ROUTE 66

On the final leg of my Route 66 road trip from Cali to Kansas, I find myself in Baxter, Kansas, at a joint that used to be a bank that was actually held up by Jesse James in 1876. It's called Cafe on the Route, and they've got some road food you may not expect.

You've got your apple-and-bacon-stuffed salmon, your nut-crusted catfish, pineapple garlic chicken, rib-eye in a tomato and white wine sauce—and get a load of the twice-baked potatoes and deep-fried cheesecake! Chef Richard Sanell's done everything from fine dining to amusement parks, filet mignon to corn dogs. But nine years ago he and his wife, Amy, decided to make a change. Their place was an old diner from the 1940s, back in the day when Route 66 was in its heyday. It was hopping then, and it's hopping again. They're doing total scratch cooking, like their Aztec chicken, which is battered in egg, and served with shrimp, chiles, avocado, bacon, and a rum glaze. That is outstanding—in it to win it, and why not? Richard's out to prove that you don't need to be in a big city to find people who appreciate fine cooking. And they do dig his salmon stuffed with apples, bacon, honey, and chives. He smokes it on the stovetop with hickory, oak, and a little cherrywood dust on a screen for five to six minutes, then finishes it in the oven. He does a pan sauce for it with mandarin oranges and rum that he flames, with butter stirred in—that'd be good on my hand. Talk about an orchestra of flavors—this dude's like a chef version of Lawrence Welk!

Even the basics here aren't so basic, like turkey, ham and cheese on a pita, chicken salad with walnuts and grapes, and he ain't makin' Grandma's old potato salad either. His has a nice crunch 'cause he's deep-frying the potatoes. The sauce is two parts mayo to one part mustard and a little seasoning. That's yippeeyiyay yummy. Now the Beaunilla Cheese-cake . . . that's something to check out. Made with tortillas, it's kinda like a Mexican cannoli, stuffed and fried to a golden brown. A light and flaky crust, cream cheese, cinnamon in there, and he's knocking the ball out of the park.

Still standing after more than 130 years, this place isn't the old bank or the old diner; it's Richard and Amy's place, and once you're here, you're part of the family.

[GUY ASIDE]

When we went to this place on Route 66, it was still back in the day when we would drive the car from location to location. We used to have just one crew; it was crazy what we would go through. Big props to our viewers—the show is so popular now, and we're shooting on multiple days with two crews and two locations a day. It's a big operation, and we have a full-time transportation guy who gets the '67 from location to location.

So they say this place was held up by Jesse James in 1876, then I held it up in 2007—ha ha ha.

"WHADDAYA THINK, JESSE JAMES, CAN WE HOLD 'EM UP FER DINNER FER TWO?"

Beaunilla Cheesecake

ADAPTED FROM A RECIPE COURTESY OF RICHARD SANELL OF CAFE ON THE ROUTE

This dessert looks like it'll feed eight when you get it on your plate, but not for long; just taste it.

MAKES 6 SERVINGS

1 egg

½ cup heavy cream

2 tablespoons granulated sugar

2 teaspoons ground cinnamon

1 pound cream cheese, at room temperature

1 pound (two 8-ounce packages) confectioners' sugar

6 (10-inch) flour tortillas

Vegetable oil, for deep-frying

Whipped cream, for serving

Strawberry, caramel, or chocolate sauce, for serving

1. In a small bowl, beat the egg and cream with a fork to make an egg wash. In another bowl, combine the granulated sugar and cinnamon.

2. Whip the cream cheese and confectioners' sugar with an electric mixer fitted with a whisk attachment until smooth and light. Pipe or spoon about ⅔ cup of the mixture across the center of each tortilla, leaving a bit of a border at each end. Use a pastry brush to paint egg wash around the edges of the tortillas. Fold the edges in over the ends of the filling, then roll up, applying more egg wash to the lip of the tortilla to seal, if necessary. Refrigerate for 2 hours.

3. Heat the oil in a deep-fryer or heavy pot to about 325°F. Fry one cheesecake at a time until one side is golden brown, and then flip over to brown the other side. Browning can take between 1½ and 3 minutes, so keep an eye on the cheesecakes as you put in one after the other. Remove from the oil, sprinkle with cinnamon sugar, and serve hot with whipped cream and sauce.

Fried Potato Salad

ADAPTED FROM A RECIPE COURTESY OF RICHARD SANELL OF CAFE ON THE ROUTE

I liked this potato salad so much it has inspired me. I'm working on a recipe called a baked potato salad: cube up all the potatoes and use fried potato chunks with all the baked potato trimmings.

MAKES 4 SERVINGS

2 large baking potatoes
¾ cup mayonnaise
⅓ cup yellow mustard
Kosher salt
Freshly ground black pepper
Canola oil, for frying

1. Preheat the oven to 300°F. Bake the potatoes until tender, about 1 hour. Cool and cut them into ¾-inch squares. Mix the mayonnaise, mustard, and salt and pepper to taste in a medium bowl.

2. Heat about 1 inch of oil in a deep skillet or small pot until a deep-fry thermometer reads 325°F. Fry the potatoes until golden brown and crisp, about 3 to 5 minutes. Drain on paper towels.

3. Combine the potatoes with the mayonnaise mixture, taste, and season. Serve warm.

NOTE: Serve immediately; the salad does not hold well for long periods.

NOT ME . . . AH . . . SOME DISTANT COUSIN.

DARI-ETTE DRIVE-IN

EST. 1951 ★ AMERICAN GRAFFITI GOES ITALIAN

After fifty-five years, the Dari-ette Drive-In is about as classic as they come. They've still got carhops, speaker boxes, and meals on a tray. But get a load of what's on that tray: made-from-scratch Italian food that'll spin your head around.

★ TRACK IT DOWN ★

**1440 Minnehaha Avenue East
St. Paul, Minnesota 55106
651-776-3470**

One Dari-ette regular claims, "Most of the Italian food up here in Minnesota, I don't know—it must be made by Swedes or something. So this place is just a treasure."

They've got homemade sausages and meatballs, in sandwiches or over pasta, drenched in homemade sauce and delivered straight to your car. Owner Angela Fida has been going to the Dari-ette all her life. It was opened more than fifty-five years ago by her grandparents. When they retired, her mom and dad took it over, and a few years ago they passed it on to her. And she says she loves it; it's what she was born to do. Born to crank out forty gallons of homemade tomato sauce at a time, and the recipe's a family secret. She lets the staff stir once in a while, but that's it. And she lets them roll three hundred meatballs at a time, also a family recipe. But get this—you know what they do to them? They deep-fry them. And they deep-fry their own homemade sausage, too. Now, top that sausage with mozzarella on fresh Italian bread, cover with homemade sauce, and steam until the cheese is running, and you've got the Italiano, their best seller. They do a mac-daddy meatball sandwich, Italian cold cuts, all kinds of pasta, and great old American cooking, too, from burgers and onion rings to something that looks like a pterodactyl breast, it's so big—fried chicken dipped in batter, then each piece fried to order. Nothing under a heat lamp here. It's all done the way Angela's grandparents did it. If it ain't broke, don't fix it.

ARE THEY RIOTING? . . . OH, YEAH, DANCING . . . COULDA BEEN RIOTING!

. . . .

OWNER'S NOTE: A little more history of the "ette" from Angela Fida.

My father's parents, Sarafina and Michael Angelo Fida, opened the restaurant in July of 1951. Sarafina (Mama) hired my mother, Lois, as a carhop. Mom met Dad and fell in love, and they worked side by side for forty-eight years, minus the time Dad spent in the navy during the Korean War. They raised four girls. All of us worked at the "ette" through high school. I started when I was twelve years old, when minimum wage was $1.64 an hour. I've been here thirty-six years.

The "ette" was supposed to be a large full-service Italian restaurant, but because the government was rationing supplies for the war, they built smaller, with the hope of adding on later. Minnehaha Avenue was the main road to Wisconsin before I-94 was constructed and was called Yellowstone Trail. Now we sit in the middle of a residential area.

The "ette" started with a small menu of ice cream and American foods. In the 1960s Dad added his Italian dishes—spaghetti, meatball sandwiches, Italian hamburgers, and the famous trademarked Italiano sandwich. Other trademarked foods: the Burger-ette, the Gondola, and Chick-ettes. We still serve original cherry and vanilla colas. We also make a mean Fresh Banana Malt and have a reputation for our hand-dipped deep-fried chicken. Everything on the menu is cooked to order.

I cook forty gallons of red sauce three times a week. I make six batches of meatballs and seventy-five pounds of sausage a week. Everything but the bread is made on the premises. The ice cream machine is from 1977. One fryer is from 1967, and the fountain sink is from the forties (it was in one of my grandfather's bars). All of them are in great working order, and the stainless shines like new. And I have a lot of customers who either worked here or their parents or grandparents worked here. Sometimes both.

Dari-ette Meataballas

ADAPTED FROM A RECIPE COURTESY OF ANGELA FIDA OF DARI-ETTE DRIVE-IN

Note from Angela: To make our bread crumbs, we use the heels of the Italian bread we serve; we set the leftover bread aside on a rack overnight. Then we run the hard, dried bread right through the grinder to create the bread crumbs; you could use a food processor. Note that the Italian bread we use is baked on cornmeal. We think that little bit of cornmeal adds significantly to the final meatballs, so look for that if you can.

Start these a day ahead, because the meat mixture needs to chill overnight.

MAKES 40 MEATBALLS

3 large eggs

½ cup milk

2¼ cups dried bread crumbs, preferably homemade from day-old bread

½ cup chopped fresh flat-leaf parsley leaves

1½ tablespoons kosher salt

2 teaspoons garlic salt

1½ teaspoons finely ground black pepper

3 pounds ground beef

Vegetable oil, for deep-frying

1. Whisk the eggs and milk in a large bowl. Stir in the bread crumbs, parsley, salt, garlic salt, and pepper. Chill for 1 hour.

2. Work the ground beef into the crumb mixture; be careful not to overwork or the meatballs will be tough. Chill overnight.

3. Heat the oil in a heavy pot over medium-high heat until a deep-fry thermometer reads 345°F. Using your hands, shape the meat into 2½-inch balls (about 2 ounces each). Fry the meatballs until they are just cooked through, about 7 minutes.

[GUY ASIDE]

Wow, what a crazy place. We went there back in the beginning of DD&D for the special: seven locations in one hour. We were in Minneapolis, and this was the last shoot. Picture the quintessential drive-in—you pull up on a summer day in a convertible, right out of *American Graffiti*, but it's not French fries and hamburgers but bomb Italian food you're getting. If it were in my town I'd eat there twice a week: old-school American Italian, spaghetti and meatballs, but they also do fried chicken. They deep-fry the meatballs; I remember thinking you've got to be kidding me. I played around, messing with the car-hop thing—they made me tuck in my shirt!

DONATELLI'S

EST. 1976 ★ YOUR NEIGHBORHOOD, SCRATCH-MADE ITALIAN

....

We hit all kinds of joints, but one of my favorites is Italian. Now, there's Italian, and then there's Italian. You know, the places making their own meatballs, the dough for their fresh pastas, their sauce. The folks north of the Twin Cities—well, they're on point, because they get to experience that every day here at this place.

★ TRACK IT DOWN ★
....

**2692 East County Road East
White Bear Lake, Minnesota 55110
651-777-9199
www.donatellis.com**

Donatelli's has served classic Italian American recipes from a Minnesota strip mall for more than thirty years. Chef and owner Steven Donatelle (yes, that's how he spells it) grew up next door to his father's sister, and he says his aunt was the best cook you'd ever want to meet. He learned from her how good food was supposed to taste and how it's supposed to be made, from scratch—even the pasta. Head cook Aaron Liedl is scratch-making eight different kinds in a contraption that's like the Medusa of pasta machines. This is when you know it's legit. And they're topping the homemade pasta with all kinds of homemade sauce, from creamy Alfredo to classic red sauce, made fresh every morning. They serve up a meat sauce over fresh-made mostaccioli, topped with shredded mozzarella and Cheddar that's melted, then sprinkled with Parmesan—that's money mostaccioli.

Then they're making something called spaghetti pie, super creamy, super cheesy and rich. They've got meatball sandwiches, too. The meatballs are a mixture of hamburger and ground pork, with eggs, water, house-made bread crumbs, parsley, basil, black pepper, garlic salt, onion salt, salt, and Parmesan cheese. Aaron rolls the meatballs, places them in a pan, and covers them with water, so they don't burn, and in they go to the convection oven—nice flavor, not too dense or loose. They lay the meatballs on Italian bread, sauce it with red sauce, put the shredded mozzarella on there, and melt it. They never skimp on the cheese. Great, huge sandwich.

Then there are the pizzas. They serve hundreds of those a day. Jessica Kissel's been making the dough for ten years. They have about three big bins of dough on hand at any time, and they're topping the 'za with everything from deep-dish veggie to a monster called the Heart Stopper Pizza. She tops it with sauce, then represents all the great meat groups: first sausage, then hamburger, then pepperoni, then six ham slices, then fourteen pieces of bacon . . . all atop that super-thin crust. A thick layer of mozzarella and it's into the 550°F oven. Then she takes a knife that looks like it came from *Pirates of the Caribbean* and slices the pie into squares. It's got a nice crunch to it, it's enough cheese to sink the *Black Pearl,* and it's delicious.

YEAH! DATZ RIGHT! KILLER PIZZA PIE.

Baked Mostaccioli

ADAPTED FROM A RECIPE COURTESY OF TRISH APPLEBY OF DONATELLI'S

Do it like Donatelli's, and don't skimp on the cheese.

MAKES 3 QUARTS SAUCE AND 4 SERVINGS

For the sauce

¼ cup vegetable oil, divided

2 pounds lean ground beef

1 tablespoon minced garlic

Kosher salt

1 teaspoon freshly ground black pepper

1 small onion, diced

2 (12-ounce) cans tomato paste

1 (29-ounce) can tomato puree

1 (15-ounce) can crushed tomatoes, with juice

1 tablespoon beef base, such as Better Than Bouillon

1 tablespoon chicken base, such as Better Than Bouillon

½ cup grated Parmesan cheese

2 teaspoons steak seasoning, such as McCormick's Montreal Steak Seasoning

1 teaspoon garlic salt

1 teaspoon dried basil

1 teaspoon dried parsley

For the baked pasta

Vegetable oil, for the baking dish

1 pound dried mostaccioli, cooked al dente

3½ to 4 cups meat sauce, warm or at room temperature

2½ cups shredded whole-milk mozzarella cheese

2½ cups shredded sharp Cheddar cheese

Shredded or grated Parmesan cheese, for garnish

1. **TO MAKE THE SAUCE:** Heat 2 tablespoons of the vegetable oil in a large skillet over medium-high heat. Add the beef, garlic, salt to taste, and the pepper and cook, breaking up the meat with a wooden spoon, until the beef is browned. Set aside.

2. Heat the rest of the oil in a large saucepan over medium-high heat. Add the onion and cook, stirring a bit, until soft. Stir in all of the tomato products. Fill the tomato puree can with hot water, and stir in the beef and chicken base to dissolve. Add the mixture to the saucepan along with the Parmesan, steak seasoning, garlic salt, basil, and parsley, and bring to a simmer.

3. Add the beef to the sauce, reduce the heat to low, and simmer, uncovered, for 1 hour, stirring occasionally. Taste and add salt, if necessary.

4. **TO MAKE THE BAKED PASTA:** Preheat the oven to 350°F. Lightly oil a 10-inch deep-dish pie plate.

5. Toss the cooked pasta with 2 cups of the meat sauce and 1½ cups each of the mozzarella and Cheddar cheeses. Mound the mixture in the pie dish and top with the rest of the meat sauce and the mozzarella and Cheddar. Place the pie dish on a baking sheet, and bake until bubbling and golden brown, 25 to 30 minutes. Top with the Parmesan cheese and serve.

"BOY, WHAT IN THE HECK HAPPENED TO YOUR HAIR?" . . . "I DON'T REALLY KNOW!"

VICTOR'S 1959 CAFÉ

EST. 1999 ★ A LITTLE MINNEAPOLIS JOINT DOING BIG CUBAN FOOD

I'm always looking for those small joints that make you stop and say, what in the heck? Like this little tropical-looking dive in South Minneapolis. It's a small joint, but people say Victor's 1959 Café is packed with big flavor.

This may not be Miami, but it would be hard to convince you otherwise. They've got lime- and garlic-marinated pork, steak with fried green plantains called tostones, classic Cuban sandwiches, and more—all cooked by a woman whose background is Greek. As she says, you don't have to be Cuban to cook Cuban food, but it's really great if you can learn from a Cuban. So that's what Niki Stavrou did when she opened this place with her then-husband. He's from Cuba, and the recipes that she learned from him are authentic Cuban recipes—and she's kept it that way.

The Cuban sandwich starts with a whole pork loin. Niki marinates it with lime juice, oregano, garlic, salt and pepper, and a little vinegar, places it in a roasting pan, and cooks it in the oven, covered for three and a half hours, then uncovered for thirty minutes. The pork gets shredded, the pan juices are added back in, then she layers the sandwich roll with mustard, Swiss cheese, sliced pickles, a thick slice of ham, and the pulled pork, then presses it on the hottest part of the grill on both sides. It's about as legit as they come, super juicy, the pickle fits in there great, and that great big slice of ham . . . Out of the fifty Cuban sandwiches I've had, this is in the top 5 percent.

For her ropa vieja she puts flank steak in a pot with some water, salt, cumin, and bay leaves. It simmers for about an hour and a half; then she shreds it. Next she heats a little oil and places a layer of sliced red, yellow, and green bell peppers and sliced onions on the bottom. The meat goes on top, then Creole sauce, garlic, sherry, and green peas. It's served with rice and sweet plantains: take a bit of all three at once, it's my rule. You get the deep rich tomato flavor, onions and peppers, and sweet crunchy plantain in the back. If you live within five hundred miles of this joint, make a vacation out of it.

RICKY AND LUCY GIVE IT A DOUBLE BABALOO!

[GUY ASIDE]

I love Cuban food! I love it all. Ropa vieja, picadillo, cubano sandwiches, the history, lore, cigars. I've done a bunch on *Big Bite*, cooking with sofrito and mojo, so when we go to a Cuban joint I know I have a little bit of a position—not an attitude, just a position. When I went in here to see what was going on, I was very happy. Niki's knocking it out. Cuban food is not really well known, it's tough to find. But based on my knowledge this place is pretty authentic. Everybody thinks that because Cuba's close to Mexico the food must be spicy, and people are greatly surprised to find out it isn't.

Here's my challenge: I want everybody who reads this book to go into Victor's 1959 and find out where I signed *Diners, Drive-ins and Dives*—because everybody writes on the walls.

. . . .

OWNER'S NOTE: To Anthony "Chico" Rodriguez, director of photography.

I thought you'd like to know that my dinner business has doubled since the show aired! My October, usually a slow month, was as good as my August, which is always the best month of the year; it's blowing me away. And November is looking just as good! We're meeting new DD&D fans every day at breakfast, lunch, *and* dinner. We actually have a full reservation book every Friday and Saturday night, and on weeknights we're doing what we *used* to do on weekend nights. Our new mantra is Viva Food Network!

I've designated a new spot for writing on the wall, dedicated especially for DD&D fans who have come from out of state. We've had people signing from all over the country. I feel so grateful to have had the opportunity for this wonderful exposure. Especially with the state of the economy these days, I am humbled and thankful to be able to say that business is thriving. Please share this news with your colleagues; you guys did an awesome job on the show, and I appreciate it so much. —Niki Stavrou

Picadillo

ADAPTED FROM A RECIPE COURTESY OF NIKI STAVROU OF VICTOR'S 1959 CAFÉ

Ohhh, this is good. A little bit of saltiness from the capers is right there, plus the sweetness of the raisins. I could eat this every day.

MAKES 6 SERVINGS

2 tablespoons olive oil

1 pound ground beef

1 teaspoon kosher salt

1 teaspoon ground cumin

3 cups Creole Sauce (recipe follows)

4 small red potatoes, cut into thin wedges

4 garlic cloves, chopped

¾ cup Spanish olives

¾ cup raisins

2 tablespoons capers (include a little bit of the juice)

2 bay leaves

1. Heat the oil in a large pan over medium-high heat. Brown the beef; spoon off any excess fat. Stir in the salt and cumin and cook for 1 minute.

2. Add the Creole Sauce and bring to a simmer. Add the potatoes, garlic, olives, raisins, capers, and bay leaves and simmer, stirring regularly, for 30 minutes. Discard the bay leaves and serve the picadillo with black beans and rice.

Creole Sauce

ADAPTED FROM A RECIPE COURTESY OF NIKI STAVROU OF VICTOR'S 1959 CAFÉ

MAKES 5 TO 6 QUARTS

¼ cup olive oil

1 red bell pepper, stemmed, seeded, and chopped

1 green bell pepper, stemmed, seeded, and chopped

1 yellow onion, chopped

Kosher salt and freshly ground black pepper

5 garlic cloves, chopped

¼ cup chopped fresh oregano

1 teaspoon ground cumin

1 (#10) can tomato sauce (96 ounces, or 3 quarts)

Water

4 bay leaves

1. Heat the olive oil in a large saucepan over medium-high heat. Add the bell peppers, onion, and salt and pepper to taste and cook, stirring occasionally, until the vegetables are softened. Stir in the garlic, oregano, and cumin and cook for about a minute.

2. Add the tomato sauce, fill the #10 can with water and pour that in, and bring to a boil. Reduce the heat and simmer for about 30 minutes, until all the flavors have blended. You'll have extra sauce to use for other recipes!

TWO CUPS OF THIS COFFEE AND YOU'LL NEED A SNOW SHOVEL TO GET YOU OFF DA CEILING.

AMATO'S CAFE

EST. 1968 ★ FROM FAIRGROUND TO NEIGHBORHOOD LEGEND

You know a lot of restaurants boast about home cooking, and on DD&D we look for those places that have real family recipes. Like here in Omaha where a guy named Sam Amato started serving sausage and pepper sandwiches at an eight-by-eight-foot wooden stand at the county fair and ended up here serving his family's Italian favorites.

They make sausage fresh every day, because that's the way Sam was taught when he was just a boy, cooking next to his mom and grandma. In his neighborhood everybody got a nickname, and his was Sammy Tomato-head. At his restaurant he works the room, serving up what the locals say is the best sausage in town.

He starts with boneless pork butt that he cuts into pieces, and puts in some sea salt, coarse ground black pepper, fennel seed, and the "oompah": crushed red pepper. He adds just a little water ('cause water kills sausage), squeezes it through with his fingers, and puts it through the meat grinder into natural casings. It shows up in omelets, monster chili Alfredo, and the one the started it all, the sausage sandwich. He uses a mezzaluna to chop up the roasted red pepper, puts in some marinara and olive oil, and mixes it up. He cooks the sausage on the flattop for about twenty minutes, both sides. The bread is slathered with their homemade garlic butter and griddled, the sweet pepper sauce is cooked up, and it's all put on the sandwich with the Italian sausage. The big chunks of meat in the sausage give it great texture. Get away from me, I'm eating!

Sammy's got a Sicilian take on chicken-fried steak. He uses Italian bread crumbs, Romano cheese, black pepper, and rough-chopped parsley. Take a nice beef steak, grab a bottle, and tenderize (hit the heck out of it). He does a double dip of egg wash and the bread crumbs, and it's onto the

THEY'RE SQUARING OFF, SAUSAGE MAN VERSUS PRETZEL BOY—CULINARY BATTLE ROYAL.

flattop. He heats up some of the roasted red peppers (can you hear the music yet?) and does the garlic-butter-toasted bread. The steak get the peppers on top, then a few slices of provolone. He throws a lid on top to give it a steam bath to melt the cheese and assembles the sandwich. He had me at hello. Nice crunch, the peppers make it, a little bit of cheese, and the garlic bread. The bread is homemade, just like the ricotta cheese that Sammy makes every day. That ricotta is best right out of a pan, though . . . and they put it in cannoli and lasagna, blueberry pancakes, too. Creamy, salty, and rich.

Sammy's the real deal.

Sausage Sandwich

ADAPTED FROM A RECIPE COURTESY OF SAMMY AMATO OF AMATO'S CAFE

When I get to learn something like homemade sausage ground fresh from a dude who's been doing it since he was a kid, it's like meeting my favorite football player.

Kitchen note: The sausage mixture needs to rest in the fridge overnight, so start this recipe a day in advance.

MAKES 3 POUNDS SAUSAGE AND 6 TO 8 SANDWICHES WITH EXTRA GARLIC BUTTER SAUCE

Pork sausage

3 pounds boneless Boston butt, cut into 1-inch chunks

1 cup water

¼ cup fennel seeds

2½ tablespoons crushed red chile flakes

2½ tablespoons fine sea salt

2 tablespoons freshly ground black pepper

34- to 36-millimeter hog sausage casing

Pepper sauce

1 (12-ounce jar) roasted red peppers, whole or strips, rinsed

1 cup marinara sauce

1½ tablespoons olive oil

Garlic butter sauce

8 ounces (2 sticks) unsalted butter

1 teaspoon garlic salt

½ teaspoon freshly ground black pepper

½ teaspoon red chile flakes

1 teaspoon chopped fresh Italian (flat-leaf) parsley leaves

2 tablespoons olive oil

6 to 8 hoagie rolls, split with 1 side still attached, for serving

1. **FOR THE SAUSAGE**: Toss the pork with the water, fennel seeds, chile flakes, salt, and black pepper. Cover and refrigerate overnight.

2. Rinse the sausage casing. Attach the casing to the meat grinder and run the meat through on the coarse setting. Make 1 large coil or tie off 6 to 8 individual sausages.

3. **FOR THE PEPPER SAUCE**: Chop the peppers into 1-inch pieces. When you are ready to make the sandwiches, bring the marinara sauce, peppers, and olive oil to a low simmer; keep warm.

4. **FOR THE GARLIC BUTTER SAUCE**: In a small saucepan melt the butter with the garlic salt, pepper, chile flakes, and parsley. Keep warm while you grill the sausages.

5. Preheat a griddle or skillet over medium-high heat. Add the olive oil and heat. Fry the sausages in oil until they are crusty and cooked through, about 15 minutes.

6. Heat another skillet over medium heat, or wipe the griddle clean and reduce the heat a bit. Brush the hoagie rolls with some garlic butter sauce and toast them cut side down until golden brown. Put the sausages in the hoagie rolls and top with a few tablespoons of warm pepper sauce.

AT 12:38 THEY JUST START STARING.

CALIFORNIA TACOS & MORE

EST. 1996 ★ AN INSPIRED TAQUERIA, ALIVE AND WELL IN OMAHA

This one's a great family story. In 1914 a Belgian immigrant built this building and opened up a pharmacy. He later passed it on to his son. Decades later the son retires, and it looks like the Bogart family legacy is going to end on this corner. That is, until the grandson steps up and says he'll take a shot, moves back from Miami, and reopens the place his way, as a taqueria.

★ TRACK IT DOWN ★

3235 California Street
Omaha, Nebraska 68131
402-342-0212
www.californiatacosandmore.com

Brad Bogart is serving all of the classics—chimichangas, enchiladas—but the heavy hitter is something he calls a California taco, even though he discovered it on a trip to the Caribbean. It's a puffy shell taco. When he opened this place he'd never worked in the restaurant business before in his life. He went down to the Mexican grocery store and the staff would point at stuff for him to use. He scratch-makes the dough, and he's self-taught! He has a crazy 1931-patented bun divider to portion the taco dough balls or buns; then he rolls them out by hand to order. That's right; he could make them and stack them with wax paper, but no. He wants the customers' tacos to taste like he wants his tacos. So he rolls them, stuffs them with steak, chicken, or ground beef, and fries them fresh. His carne asada (steak) is seasoned with black pepper, sea salt, onion salt, cayenne, and oregano, then grilled over an open flame to medium rare. He cools it, slices it, and stuffs it in the taco, then into the fryer basket. Add cheese and lettuce and bite in. Outstanding. The meat has great flavor; it's juicy and killer.

He makes a red and a green salsa—with fresh jalapeños. That's money. His beef chimichanga is made with ground beef with ancho chili powder, chipotle, sea salt, and onion salt cooked way down for two hours with a little water. It's like beef sauce. He sorts dried beans by hand, looking for rocks (a tip from the Mexican grocery store guys), cooks them, and mixes a few into the beef. To assemble, he steams the tortilla to make it pliable, then puts some refried beans, onions, and cheese in there with a good amount of beef. Then it's into the deep-fryer. Nice crunch, awesome flavor; and my favorite part is the little bit of onion he puts in there.

It's great food made fresh. And Brad just keeps on frying. His chicken enchiladas (check out the recipe on page 160) require a lot of care and preparation.

So what's the future of California Tacos? Brad thinks there is something to be said for staying small; being able to make these personal connections with his customers is where it's at.

[GUY ASIDE]

If I'm going to a place called California Tacos in Omaha, Nebraska, you know I'm going to be a little suspicious. But I really enjoyed the place—I'd never gone anywhere on Triple D that made their own flour tortillas fresh. When you believe in what you're doing and make it your own, that's having your own style. That's definitely what Brad did—the place is so much fun. And the dude's a really cool cat; he's proud to take over the building for his family. He's a bit of a one-man show, crazy funny—we had the best time. We went out after we'd been shooting, and Brad set us up with tickets to the college world series going on at that time. When I was getting ready to leave right from California Tacos to be the grand marshal at the NASCAR race in California, he said, "Oh, I'm a NASCAR fan!" So I get to the race at Infernian raceway in Sonoma, California, and who comes rolling in? Brad Bogart. Dude's a riot.

SO WHADDAYA SAY, DOES IT LOOK LIKE ME?

Chicken Enchiladas

ADAPTED FROM A RECIPE COURTESY OF BRAD BOGART OF CALIFORNIA TACOS & MORE

The tortilla soaking up the sauce gives this some fantastic flavor.

MAKES 8 LARGE ENCHILADAS

Sauce

4 cups tomato sauce

2 cups water

1 teaspoon onion salt

1 teaspoon sea salt

3 tablespoons ancho chile powder

3 garlic cloves, minced

1 tablespoon diced chipotle en adobo

Filling

2 quarts (8 cups) water

1½ teaspoons sea salt

3 boneless, skinless chicken breast halves

1½ teaspoons ground cumin

1½ teaspoons cayenne pepper

1½ teaspoons paprika

2 cups canola oil

8 medium flour tortillas

3 to 4 cups shredded Cheddar cheese

1. **FOR THE SAUCE**: Combine all of the ingredients in a medium saucepan and simmer for 10 minutes. Set aside.

2. **FOR THE FILLING**: Mix the water and salt in a large skillet or pot and bring to a boil. Add the chicken; if it isn't covered by water, add a bit more. Reduce the heat and cook at a gentle simmer for 15 minutes, or until just cooked through. Remove the chicken from the water and cool slightly. Shred the chicken and dust it with the cumin, cayenne, and paprika, tossing to coat each piece.

3. Heat the oil in a large pan over medium-high heat. Dip a tortilla in the red sauce, then carefully place it in the hot oil; it should sizzle. Flip it after about 10 to 15 seconds, then remove it about 5 seconds after that. This seals the sauce into the tortilla. Repeat with the remaining tortillas. If you don't use the tortillas immediately, stack them with plastic wrap between each layer.

4. Preheat the broiler. Put ½ cup chicken on each tortilla and top with ¼ cup shredded Cheddar cheese. Place it under a broiler just to melt the cheese, then roll the tortilla and place it seam side down in a baking dish. Repeat with the remaining tortillas. Top with more cheese and broil until the cheese melts.

THEY MEET EVERY DAY TO TAKE THEIR VITAMIN SHOTS. RIGHT ON!

DIXIE QUICKS MAGNOLIA ROOM

EST. 1995 ★ THE GREAT MELTING POT OF HANDMADE FOOD

....

One of the things you've learned, no doubt, on Triple D is to slow it down and keep your eyes peeled, because you'd never want to cruise by a joint you didn't notice, but you didn't want to miss. Like here on Leavenworth Street.

> ★ TRACK IT DOWN ★
> ....
> **1915 Leavenworth Street**
> **Omaha, Nebraska 68102**
> **402-346-3549**
> **www.dixiequicks.com**

There's no sign, so you've got to be in the know. This is eclectic, real food done by a serious chef, René Orduña, who cooked all across the country before coming back to Omaha, where he started out in his parents' Mexican restaurant. He's got a little Cajun, a little cosmopolitan, a little Latino influence, a little of everything. The Texas chile pepper steak, for example, is a takeoff on steak au poivre, which typically has green peppercorns, but he's taking it further with fresh Anaheim, jalapeño, and poblano chiles. He takes a ten-ounce New York strip—welcome to Omaha; that's like a business card here—trims it, and gets a little sizzle going with butter, s&p, and red onion; sears it on both sides; then throws a little bourbon on there, flames it (where are the marshmallows, René?), then adds a little beef stock. He then removes the steak to the flattop—wouldn't want to boil it and overcook it—and finishes the searing. His sauce reduces down; then he adds some cream. Plated atop mashed potatoes, that's bananas. That pepper trio, the jalapeños are not overpowering, and the whiskey! The cream! I don't know if it's the shamalama that puts it in the ding-dong or the ooh in the mow-mow. Out of the top pepper steaks I've ever had, that's gotta be in the top three.

This guy has cooked in New York, San Francisco, New Orleans, and Kansas City. As he says, each place has its own flavors, and those things all married in his head. Like some Louisiana cooking he learned from a chef in New York: blackened salmon with tomato butter (recipe on page 164). It's not over-blackened; I would order that once a week—and this at a place I almost drove by cuz I couldn't find it, biggest mistake I would've made.

This guy's like the Wizard of Oz. This isn't Kansas, and it's not Mexico either, but after growing up with Mexican cooking, René's doing that his own way, too—like a traditional Mexican chicken tortilla soup. He starts with a pico de gallo–type mixture of fine-diced tomato, onion, zucchini, yellow squash, green pepper; as the summer goes on he adds more and more vegetables and it gets nicer and nicer. Then he adds the pepper trio—poblanos, Anaheims, and jalapeños—and chopped cilantro. The base is chicken stock, the juice from the diced tomatoes, and some V8 juice, to which he adds cubed potatoes and chicken, his pico mixture, more cilantro, and salt and pepper. That simmers for about fifteen minutes. I like the confetti of the onions and squash in there. He serves it with a few chips and some slices of avocado. Wow, that's good. The flavor is so fresh, almost like a hot pico de gallo chicken soup; I mean, it's not one thing, it's multiple. And it's on the menu every day, made fresh, so if you want to win here at Dixie Quicks, you better get here early.

[GUY ASIDE]

We're in steak country, Omaha, and I think I've seen it all. And here I come rolling into this place—a non-descript medical office or apartment-looking place—and the sign in the window is no more than six by twelve inches. This place is packed, there's eclectic artwork, and René is such a cool cat, a nice guy; dude loves food. It's one of those places you'd be proud to know where it is but don't want to tell anybody about because it will be packed. I enjoyed everything we ate. The steak au poivre (Texas chile pepper steak) is ridiculously good, the salmon, too.

Funny thing: in the final scene of the show I'm talking to René about the pico de gallo chicken soup and something happens and the soup pot gets knocked off the stove and falls on me and burns the back of my leg, gets all over my shorts and onto my flip-flops. So I take off, run through the kitchen, and jump into the pot sink; René is following me, I'm getting cold water onto my leg. It blistered, but not bad, right in the middle of the shot. We laughed after that: wear shorts in the kitchen and you can't have anything to say.

I heard the day the show aired they were supposed to open in the evening, but René got a call to get down there, there were 150 people in line! The Triple D tidal wave strikes again!

Blackened Salmon with Tomato Butter

ADAPTED FROM A RECIPE COURTESY OF RENÉ ORDUÑA OF DIXIE QUICKS MAGNOLIA ROOM

He may be from Omaha, but this dude cooks salmon like he's from the Pacific Northwest.

MAKES 4 SERVINGS

Tomato butter

4 ounces (1 stick) unsalted butter

½ cup canned tomato puree

½ teaspoon minced garlic

2 teaspoons chopped fresh flat-leaf parsley leaves

Kosher salt

Freshly ground black pepper

Blackened salmon

¾ cup Cajun seasoning blend

½ cup pickling spice

1½ teaspoons kosher salt

½ teaspoon coarsely ground black pepper

1½ teaspoons garlic powder

1½ teaspoons dried sage

½ teaspoon dried marjoram

½ teaspoon crushed red chile flakes

½ teaspoon ground cumin

**1 (1½ pounds) skinless salmon fillet,
sliced on the bias into 8 pieces**

2 to 3 tablespoons vegetable oil

YOU KNOW HE'S SERIOUS ABOUT CRAZY FOOD WHEN HE'S WEARING SAFETY GOGGLES.

NOW THAT DUDE IS TAKING A SERIOUS TRIPLE D BITE!

1. **FOR THE TOMATO BUTTER**: Put the butter, tomato puree, garlic, parsley, and salt and pepper to taste in a small saucepan. Heat over medium heat just until the butter melts. Remove from the heat and froth with an immersion blender. (Note: René uses the steamer on the cappuccino machine to cook the tomato butter and so can you, if you have one of those!) Keep warm while cooking the salmon.

2. **FOR THE SALMON**: Combine all the spices and herbs in a small bowl. Lightly coat each piece of salmon with the rub; you will have some of it left over.

3. Heat a cast-iron skillet over medium-high heat until very hot. Film the pan lightly with oil. Cook the salmon 1 minute per side, working in batches if necessary. Serve with warm tomato butter.

HAUS MURPHY'S

EST. 1996 ★ THE BIERGARTEN OF MY BAVARIAN BROTHER

Here on Diners, Drive-ins and Dives we know no boundaries, not of region, size, or cuisine. As a matter of fact we've done Italian, Mexican, American, barbecue—heck, you name it, we've done it all, even Chinese-Jamaican fusion. But one we hadn't done is German, and that brought us here to Glendale, Arizona, to Haus Murphy's.

★ TRACK IT DOWN ★

5739 W. Glendale Avenue
Glendale, Arizona 85301
623-939-2480
www.hausmurphys.com

This is hearty food made from scratch, the kind Rose Hoffmann grew up on in Munich, and her husband, Brett, learned from his German grandparents right here in Arizona. Brett's favorite thing on the menu is his sauerbraten. He trims a big top round with a knife that looks like he should wear it in a sheath and jog through the forest, then bathes it in vinegar and buttermilk—that's the sour part. Then he adds in a mirepoix and seasonings and marinates it for four or five days, yes, *days* (recipe on page 168). He rolls the moisture out and browns it, deglazes with wine, then cooks it down with the marinade. He then strains it and makes a gravy. Grab a beer; it's like a three-hour deal. There's a seriously good sweet and sour contrast.

In Germany you sit and socialize and eat for hours, so they encourage people to sit, enjoy, and stay, says Brett. He does bratwurst with sauerkraut; beef rouladen stuffed with onion, bacon, and pickles; house-made spaetzle; and schnitzel done seven different ways. The paprika schnitzel starts with making the gravy. He renders chopped bacon with onion and chicken base, adds Hungarian paprika and water, and lets that simmer. He thickens it up with a fifty-fifty butter and flour roux. Then the white pepper and yellow curry go in (common in German food, he says; who knew?). He flattens the pork in a perforating machine and gives it a dunk in seasoned flour, egg wash, and bread crumbs. Pan-fried in butter and served with the gravy, it's delicious and has a killer crunch. I've had schnitzel, but this is some-a-da-best. Whatever you're having, this is the undo-your-belt on your lederhosen.

FAKERS—THEY'RE ALL EMPTY! (MUST BE PRACTICING FOR THE BIG DAY!)

[GUY ASIDE]

I'm still asking my parents if there's something I need to know. I've never felt as much like twins, in the tradition of Schwarzenegger and DeVito, as I did with Brett at Haus Murphy's. The crew were telling me, wait till you meet this guy. He could dwarf me; he has the same goatee, bleached hair, and outgoing personality. It was the funniest thing in the world. We have a time limit because I have to catch flights, but the timeline wasn't being followed; he was wrangling me in. Brett is the nicest guy.

If you think you don't like German food, and you think it's all hot dogs and bratwurst, then you're missing it by a mile. They're doing it right, and it's popular. They've got spaetzle, German potato salad; I was eating the whole time I was there, reaching into pots, opening refrigerators, way beyond what we were doing and eating in front of the camera! The next time Oktoberfest hits, I want to go down there: it's party central, from beer to atmosphere, music, the whole deal.

Sauerbraten

ADAPTED FROM A RECIPE COURTESY OF BRETT AND ROSE HOFFMANN, OWNERS OF HAUS MURPHY'S

This is slow food; the meat has to marinate for three to five days. Enjoy the process and you'll be even more happy with the delicious sweet-and-sour result.

MAKES 4 TO 6 SERVINGS

3 cups buttermilk

1½ cups distilled white vinegar

1½ cups water

8 bay leaves

8 whole cloves

6 celery ribs, chopped

6 carrots, chopped

3 onions, quartered, plus 1½ cups chopped onions

1 tablespoon kosher salt, plus more for seasoning the meat

1 tablespoon black peppercorns

1 teaspoon freshly ground white pepper, plus more to taste

½ teaspoon freshly grated nutmeg

2½ to 3 pounds beef shoulder

Freshly ground black pepper

½ cup olive oil

1½ cups red wine

2 ounces (½ stick) unsalted butter

¼ cup all-purpose flour

2 tablespoons gravy flavoring

2 to 3 tablespoons brown sugar

⅓ cup raisins

1. Combine the buttermilk, vinegar, water, bay leaves, cloves, celery, carrots, quartered onions, 1 tablespoon salt, peppercorns, white pepper, and nutmeg in large plastic container. Add the meat and refrigerate, covered, for at least 3 and up to 5 days, turning occasionally.

2. Heat a heavy pot just large enough to hold the meat over medium-high heat. Add the oil. Remove the meat from the marinade, reserving the marinade. Pat the meat dry and season well with salt and black pepper. Add the meat and brown well on all sides. When the meat is well browned, transfer it to a platter. Turn the heat down to medium and cook the onions in the drippings, stirring occasionally, until they start to brown, about 3 minutes.

3. Deglaze the pan with the red wine, letting it bubble for a minute or two and stirring with a wooden spoon to scrape up the brown bits. Return the beef to the pot, pour in the reserved marinade, cover, and simmer until tender, 1½ to 2 hours.

4. Remove the meat from the pot. Strain the marinade and set aside. Discard the vegetables.

5. Add the butter to the pot over low heat, and when melted, add the flour. Whisk until it comes together and bubbles. Slowly whisk in the strained marinade and simmer until thickened. Stir in the gravy flavoring for color. Add the brown sugar a little at a time until the gravy is sweet and sour, and then stir in the raisins. Season to taste with salt and white pepper. Slice the meat and heat it for a few minutes in the simmering gravy. *Guten Appetit!*

DUDE ROCKS "WELCOME TO THE JUNGLE" ON THAT THING!

MATT'S BIG BREAKFAST

EST. 2004 ★ THE SIGN SAYS IT ALL

....

When you're in downtown Phoenix, Arizona, you've just got to check out this little joint. This dude digs breakfast so much he devoted an entire restaurant to it. I had to meet this cat Matt.

★ TRACK IT DOWN ★

....

801 N. 1st Street
Phoenix, Arizona 85004
602-254-1074
www.mattsbigbreakfast.com

Matt Pool's got breakfast basics done the right way, totally from scratch and made with the best ingredients. He doesn't own a freezer, a microwave, or a mixer. And Matt is making fresh batter three times a day for his waffles; that's a lot of whisking. His batter's practically like cake batter, and the waffles come out of the iron like a hiking boot that's just walked on a pancake: a real hot Frisbee of fun. Matt then picks up Granny's tea kettle off the flattop to pour you some hot maple syrup. The waffle has a really nice crust to it, and the center's nice and light and airy; I'd eat it again in a heartbeat.

....

OWNER'S NOTE: We loved the piece. I really think it captured the spirit of our place. We've been crazy since it aired; Guy wasn't lying. I thought we were busy before, but seriously, every day is like a Saturday or Sunday now. The newspaper here also wrote a big story about it so people who don't watch Food Network found out about it. I knew it was a popular show, but it seriously has almost like a cult following—people come to our place straight from the airport now. I just saw that it's airing a bunch of times in May, so we'll just keep riding the wave. By the way, I was in the San Francisco area recently and drove down to Pescadero to eat at Duarte's, the place with the artichoke soup; it was a great place. —Matt Pool

Matt converts non–breakfast eaters with his food—and they wait up to an hour and a half to get into the little spot. He figured that people around there would appreciate a mom-and-pop-style restaurant. He had plenty of memories of going to diners with his dad and just sitting at the counter. So a few years ago he and his wife got a counter of their own, and it filled up quick. Everything has something special about it, like the bacon: he gets it from a local butcher shop, but they don't deliver, and he pays retail. It's as thick as a ham steak and has great texture to it. And for the toast: Matt doesn't like uniformity in bread slices, so he gets the loaf whole, slices it himself, and serves it with some local preserves. As he says, it's like an open-faced jelly doughnut. And Matt puts fresh rosemary in his home fries, which are cooked in tons of butter—just like the killer hash browns. The salami scramble is made with sopressata that's brought in special from San Francisco, and he's even making fresh pesto for his breakfast pork chops (see recipe on page 172).

WELL, MOM, I'LL TELL YA, WE HAVE TO WORK ON YOUR PORTIONING . . . I'M JUST A KID.

[GUY ASIDE]

If it's going to be a breakfast joint it *better be a good one*, because I don't like getting up early to cook *or* eat breakfast. There are a lot of components about breakfast that I'm not a fan of. However, when I do get to find a breakfast joint that's doing things like green pesto pork chops, it changes my mind. I even mentioned in the show *The Best Thing I Ever Ate* that the pork chop was one of my favorites. So if you can take me from zero to hero on a breakfast thing, that's a pretty big deal to me.

Funny thing is, it should've been called Big Matt's Breakfast, because he looks six-foot-twelve and he's as nice as he is big.

Prank: They tell me the mayor of Phoenix, Phil Gordon, likes to go there, and I'm like, far out! And even the mayor has to wait. So he's sitting at the counter, his security detail all out front. He's got his mayoral car sitting there. I start talking to his security, and the next thing I know I've swindled the driver and head of security into letting me sit in the mayor's car, with them in my car. (Have you ever seen the movie *Super Troopers,* where the cop acting like a bad guy thinks he's stealing the cop car and takes the three guys for a ride and says, "You boys ever been to Mexico?") Anyway, the mayor comes out with a camera following him, and it was perfectly timed. When he gets back into the car, I'm in the front seat and say, "So, on our next stop for *Diners, Drive-ins and Dives,* where do you want to go?" He turned four shades of white; it was hysterical.

Chop and Chick

ADAPTED FROM A RECIPE COURTESY OF MATT POOL OF MATT'S BIG BREAKFAST

They serve each chop with two cage-free eggs cooked any style, a choice of hash browns or home fries, and hand-cut toast (sourdough, white, or wheat) with local preserves.

MAKES 4 SERVINGS

4 garlic cloves

1 good handful of local organic fresh basil

2 tablespoons organic pine nuts

¾ cup extra-virgin olive oil, plus more for frying

½ teaspoon coarse-grain sea salt, plus more to taste

¼ teaspoon freshly ground black pepper, plus more to taste

4 boneless pork rib chops, 1 inch thick (about 7 ounces each)

THE LITTLE DUDE RUNS THE WHOLE SHOW!

1. Put the garlic cloves, basil, pine nuts, ½ cup of the olive oil, and ½ teaspoon salt and ¼ teaspoon pepper into the bowl of a food processor or blender. Pulse intermittently until all the ingredients are combined. Slowly add the remaining ¼ cup olive oil with the processor running or as you increase the blender speed. Process or puree until smooth, about 25 seconds.

2. Pour the marinade over the chops and toss to coat. Refrigerate the chops for at least 3 to 4 hours.

3. The next step is to remove the chops from the marinade. Wipe off excess marinade and season the chops with more salt and pepper to taste (discard the marinade). Cook them on a lightly oiled, preheated flattop (or pan-fry for the home cook), flipping once or twice, until just cooked through, about 3 minutes per side.

SALSA BRAVA

EST. 1988 ★ DOING THE NAVAJO TACO HUNCH

....

You've got to love a road trip, and there's nothing better than a Route 66 tour. In Flagstaff, Arizona, you've got to stop at Salsa Brava, where this dude's scratch-making just about everything.

★ TRACK IT DOWN ★
....
**2220 E. Route 66 (Santa Fe Avenue)
Flagstaff, Arizona 86004
928-779-5293
www.salsabravaflagstaff.com**

It's all done by hand, and that's the way native Arizonian John Conley's been rolling for years. When he was twenty-one he decide to drop out of school and open his own little taqueria. Mexican was his first choice; he loves the culture, people, and food. And folks around here love the way he's making the food, from classics like burritos, to something called the Maui Taco with pineapple (see page 175), to a Southwestern favorite, sopapilla.

He makes the dough for the sopapilla out of flour, salt, and baking powder with water, works it for five minutes, then covers it and lets it sit for an hour and a half. For the marinated chicken he starts with lemon-lime soda (I've never seen this move before), cool water, fresh lime juice, red wine vinegar, soy sauce, black pepper, chile powder, and garlic. The chicken marinates in

....

OWNER'S NOTE: To Anthony "Chico" Rodriguez, director of photography.

Unbelievable! Not that we ever want this to stop—but what the heck! I never would have thought the response would be so huge and have such an impact on so many lives. Our food servers are grateful—cooks, host, managers, dishwashers—they've *all* been able to share in the prosperity that's come as a result of this show. Last week everyone (without exception) got raises! When does it slow down? People traveling in excess of 1,000 miles solely to eat at Salsa Brava . . . the website has exceeded the one million mark and crashed multiple times—and we haven't aired in weeks! What an unbelievably beautiful thing you've all created. Thanks again. —John Conley

[GUY ASIDE]

John makes this killer taco called the Navajo taco. The thing was really cool, everything was made to order. You're supposed to eat it on the plate with a fork and knife. But I was running around confiscating silverware and making everybody eat it like a taco, with the hunch. This requires a full Philly Hunch (see the diagram on page 28).

John's gotten a lot of acclaim; he's a sharp chef, and he just came out with a cookbook. Just because an eatery is a funky joint doesn't mean it doesn't have a high-quality chef. He used to have multiple locations and he brought it down to just one in order to focus on execution and quality. It's a hands-on location.

the fridge for twenty-four hours, covered. He then grills it and finishes it in the oven. Back to the dough: he takes about a four-ounce ball, rolls it out (this is to order every time), trims the circle (about as big as my head), and layers some beans, marinated chicken, and shredded Jack and Cheddar cheese. He folds it up, pinches the edges, and it's bye-bye, you go fly—about a minute and a half weighted down in the deep-fryer, then he takes the weight off and flips it. This is where King Kong meets the popover. He then hits it with a little cilantro cream sauce—heavy cream, milk, cilantro, garlic salt, and butter—and plates it with beans and rice and a little cheese, melts that down, and garnishes with chopped cilantro, chopped onion, and their avocado cream. Wow, everything is rockin' inside. What's neat about that chicken is that it's been cooked, then cooked again in the fryer, and it's not dried out. It's nice and tender, and the cilantro cream sauce is outta bounds.

John says great Mexican food is made simple and fresh, and you've got to get the best ingredients for everything. Like for his salsa; they serve five kinds every day, and they tastes like he just picked the ingredients out of his garden. His Roasted Pineapple Habañero Salsa (recipe on page 177) gives you a nice little sugar right in the beginning and then smack, that's hot! I'd buy an ice cube for twenty bucks. One regular said he'd put that on anything, and eat a couple bowls of just that. But as long as you're there, you've got fajitas, quesadillas, and a dish some folks call the state dish of Arizona: the Navajo taco, made from the same dough as the sopapilla and topped open-face with beef, chicken, or pork. For his slow-roasted pork he dusts cubed chunks of pork loin with a mixture of granulated garlic, salt, cracked pepper, Spanish paprika, mild red chile, and sugar. Then he puts the meat on a rack in a roasting pan with two ounces of liquid smoke in the bottom, covers it, and slow roasts it for five hours. After he shreds it, he puts it on the grill with a little bit of fresh orange juice and paprika, then layers it on the fried dough with beans, the meat, and Jack and Cheddar cheeses, then it's back in a 450°F oven for about two minutes and topped with lettuce, salsa fresca, cilantro and onions, cotija cheese, a dollop of sour cream, and a little avocado cream. I recommend short sleeves, a bib, and a drop cloth.

ADAPTED FROM A RECIPE COURTESY OF JOHN CONLEY OF SALSA BRAVA

Note from John: What started out as a mistake has turned into one of our best sellers. One day we were blackening the pineapple for our Seared Pineapple Salsa, and as we pulled the roasting pineapple from the grill a small amount fell onto the flattop and got mixed in with an order of carne adovada. I threw it into a flour tortilla, and the lightbulb went off!

Make no mistake . . . this is not for those with tender palates. The heat from the chile de árbol can be intense. Enough said! Decrease the heat by eliminating a portion of the chile de árbol.

MAKES 8 LARGE OR 16 SMALL TACOS

1 cup packed chile de árbol, stems removed

2 to 3 tablespoons water

3 to 4 tablespoons canola oil, divided

2 pounds pork loin, cut into ½-inch cubes

¼ cup mild red chile powder

5 garlic cloves, chopped

1 tablespoon garlic salt

2 teaspoons kosher salt

1 ½ teaspoons ground cumin

2 tablespoons canola oil

½ cup chopped Maui or other sweet onion

1 cup diced fresh pineapple

8 large or 16 small flour tortillas, warmed

Chopped fresh cilantro leaves, for garnish

Crumbled cotija cheese, for garnish

Roasted Pineapple Habañero Salsa (recipe follows)

THIS IS JUST WRONG . . . WHO TOOK THIS PIC?

1. Place the chile de árbol, 2 tablespoons of the water, and 1 tablespoon of the canola oil in a blender and blend on high to make a paste. Add additional water by the teaspoon if needed.

2. Put the pork in a shallow bowl and pour the marinade on top. Add the chile powder, garlic, garlic salt, kosher salt, and cumin. Cover, and marinate in the refrigerator for 4 hours or overnight.

3. Remove the pork from the marinade (discard the marinade) and pat the pork dry with paper towels. Heat a heavy skillet over medium-high heat. Heat 2 tablespoons of the canola oil. Add half of the pork, onion, and pineapple and cook, stirring occasionally, until the meat is browned and the pineapple and onion have caramelized, 5 to 7 minutes. Remove with a slotted spoon and repeat with the remaining pork, onion, and pineapple, adding more oil if necessary. Serve in the flour tortillas, with chopped cilantro, cotija cheese, and Roasted Pineapple Habañero Salsa.

"SO, WHEN YOU DISSECT THE BURRITO, YOU START WITH . . . COME ON, STUDENTS, FOLLOW ALONG!"

Roasted Pineapple Habañero Salsa

ADAPTED FROM A RECIPE COURTESY OF JOHN CONLEY OF SALSA BRAVA

Note from John: We tried to have this recipe duplicated by a major manufacturer, and the result was a disaster—not even close to our house-made salsa. It's hard to duplicate the same roasted flavor and texture provided by the slow roasting of the tomatoes and jalapeños and the sting of freshly blended habañeros. This salsa can be very hot, so adjust the heat by decreasing the habañero. Start with a small amount and increase accordingly. The habañero will be at its hottest as soon as you blend it, then will mellow to a certain point and maintain this heat level. So when adjusting for heat, keep this in mind. The current recipe is designed to be a hot salsa; however, this is truly dictated by the individual chile—the time of year it was grown, the location where it was grown, and the amount of stress the chile was exposed to while growing.

[CREW ASIDE]

KareBear: "Best thing I've eaten? The pineapple habañero salsa at Salsa Brava in Flagstaff, Arizona, was downright addicting. I'm not usually a fan of pineapple anything, but this salsa was a perfect combo of sweet and heat."

MAKES 6 CUPS

3 medium tomatoes

4 jalapeño chiles, stems removed

¼ medium Maui or other sweet onion, sliced ¼ inch thick

1 to 2 habañero chiles

1 (20-ounce) can pineapple tidbits, with juice

½ cup water, divided

½ cup loosely packed cilantro leaves, chopped

Kosher salt

1. Heat the broiler to high. Put the tomatoes, jalapeños, and onion on a broiler pan or baking sheet. Broil 4 inches from the heat until darkly roasted and even blackened in spots on one side (the tomato skins will split and curl in places), about 6 minutes. Flip the vegetables and broil the other side for another 6 minutes or so. The goal is to char all the vegetables but also to caramelize and cook them through to bring out the rich, smoky, sweet flavors. Cool for 10 minutes, reserving all the juices.

2. Put half of the roasted vegetables, the habañeros, the pineapple and juice, and half of the water in a food processor or blender and pulse; John prefers this salsa to be evenly chopped but not pureed. Add the rest of the roasted vegetables and the cilantro and pulse again.

3. Taste, season with salt, and adjust the consistency with water if necessary. The salsa will thicken as it cools, so take this into account as you add water. It will be hotter at first, then begin to mellow. Use right away or cover and refrigerate for up to 4 days.

GORILLA BARBEQUE

EST. 2006 ★ BIG BBQ FLAVORS AND A BIG CHEESE

So I had picked the wrong day to wear shorts or drive the convertible, but I found myself in Pacifica, California, to check out Gorilla Barbeque . . . served out of this orange train car.

★ TRACK IT DOWN ★

**2145 Coast Highway
Pacifica, California 94044
650-359-7427
www.gorillabbq.com**

Where did the Gorilla name come from? Well, the guy it's named after says his dad came up with it: "You see how I'm a little bigger than normal?" (I just thought it was my TV!) This all started as a hobby for Gorilla, aka Rich Bacchi, who had this vision for years, so along with his old high school buddy, Jeff Greathouse, he made it a reality. After years of cooking for friends, they started catering, then acquired the train car. They start with a "rub-a-dub-dub" of his own concoction—ground cumin, oregano, garlic powder, granulated onion, sea salt, paprika, brown sugar,

GORILLA'S VEGETARIAN CONVERSION PROGRAM.

TWO BBQ BAD BOYS! "ALL ABOARD."

and black pepper—and give it a "mixy-mix" in the "magic mixer." They call this the super-combo spice rub mix, and after a "tasty-taste" I gave it a thumbs-up. They're putting it on everything from ribs to pulled pork to a heavy-hitting Texas-style brisket. You can never put enough spice rub on the brisket, says Gorilla—"the flavors are rendered through the fat on the top"—well, *ahem*! This guy even has a tiny light installed on the ceiling to shine light into his smoker. The brisket cooks on the top rack for sixteen hours; then he lets it rest for thirty minutes. It's tender and good, and here's one you don't see: he's using the brisket in a Philly cheesesteak. Some of that magic rub is even used in the pepper and onions, American Swiss is melted on top, and it's given a squirt of Carolina-style barbecue sauce. There's an explosive Southwestern flavor. (I felt like I needed to shampoo my goatee afterward; as one regular says, you need a spork to eat that bomb.)

Sides are not ignored here: their mac and cheese is engineered like none other. It's a four-cheese wonder, and the cheese outweighs the pasta, with a crusty Goldfish topping that's classic. Check it out on page 180; good is good, but Gorilla BBQ is great!

Gorilla Mac and Cheese

ADAPTED FROM A RECIPE COURTESY OF RICH BACCHI AND JEFF GREATHOUSE OF GORILLA BARBEQUE

Now, this is my kind of cheese-to-pasta ratio, cheesy good. Be forewarned, it takes some serious, constant whisking to get the cheese sauce right — quite a workout, but worth it.

MAKES 8 SERVINGS

Kosher salt, for the pasta water

5 cups shredded sharp Cheddar cheese

3½ cups shredded Asiago cheese

3½ cups shredded four-cheese blend

8 cups large ribbed elbow macaroni

1 Spanish onion, peeled and cut into chunks

10 garlic cloves

4 ounces (1 stick) unsalted butter

1½ tablespoons ground oregano

1½ tablespoons paprika

1½ tablespoons kosher salt

1 tablespoon freshly ground black pepper

2 cups milk

1½ cups heavy cream

1 cup sour cream

2 eggs, beaten lightly

2½ cups Cheddar-flavor Goldfish crackers, pulverized

1. Preheat the oven to 350°F. Bring a large pot of salted water to a boil over high heat.

2. Toss the cheeses together in a large bowl.

3. Boil the macaroni until it is about two-thirds cooked; drain, and transfer to a large bowl. Toss the hot pasta with 4 cups of the cheese mixture.

4. Puree the onion and garlic in a food processor. Melt the butter in a large pot over medium heat until the foam subsides. Scrape the pureed vegetables into the pot; it should sizzle. Reduce the heat to low and whisk in the oregano, paprika, salt, and pepper.

5. Whisk in the milk, heavy cream, and sour cream and continue whisking until everything comes back to a low simmer. Whisk in about 6 more cups of the cheese mixture and keep whisking until the cheese melts; the mixture will stop simmering. Whisk in the eggs.

6. Pour the hot cheese sauce over the pasta, mix well, and transfer it into a 10 by 15-inch baking dish. Scatter the remaining cheese over the macaroni, and top with the pulverized crackers. Cover the dish with plastic wrap and then aluminum foil and bake for 30 minutes.

AT GORILLA, THEY'LL SPELL IT OUT FOR YA . . . P-O-R-K R-I-B-S.

HANK'S CREEKSIDE RESTAURANT

EST. 1992 ★ OUTTA-BOUNDS BREAKFAST IN MY OWN BACKYARD

. . . .

In my hometown, Santa Rosa, California, in the heart of the wine country, it's about real people serving up real food like at Hank's Creekside. One of the things I love about the place is Hank Vance himself, a father of six who cooks the show in the center of the dining room.

> ★ TRACK IT DOWN ★
> . . . .
> **2800 4th Street**
> **Santa Rosa, California 95405**
> **707-575-8839**
> **www.sterba.com/sro/creekside**

Normally when we shoot the show, the person I'm interviewing or talking to doesn't dwarf me completely, but at six-foot-six, Hank has a massive wingspan. I should've had a little orange flag: where's Guido behind the Hank? This big guy has been cranking out big food here for over fifteen years—the breakfast basics, from eggs Benedict to blintzes—and people just keep coming back. As one local puts it, "You don't have to look for other places when you have Hank's."

Let's just let the cat out of the bag: this is one of my favorite places to come, and I can't even get a reservation—because they don't take any reservations. The wait can get over forty-five minutes or longer on Sundays. When I come here I order the hash as an appetizer to my breakfast. The ratio of meat to potato in that recipe is like eight to one; they call the potato the "hash helper." Holy hash, Batman; there's definitely more beef in it than normal. It's basic and simple but it's so killer.

Of course not everything's simple here. When it comes to the eggs Benedict you've got to make a choice: traditional, Florentine with fresh spinach, the Benedict Arnold with smoked salmon, homemade crab cake Benedict, or California style with avocado and tomato. It's a family affair: Hank's wife, Linda, and all six kids have worked here at one point or another. And it's hard work, even for something as simple as pancakes: they grind the whole wheat themselves to make the flour, and I'm not kidding. You see, it loses a lot of nutritional value, says Hank, if you get it already ground. He does blueberry, strawberry, and banana. That's a good pancake—nice crunch on the outside, tastes like dessert.

[GUY ASIDE]

This is "my brotha from another motha," Hank. When I first moved up here, Hank and his family would come into my restaurant; he was well known because he has one of the number one breakfast joints in the area, and he's like six-foot-six. All his kids are good lookin' and tall. Now, I am not a big breakfast man, but he won me over: 1) He had killer corned beef hash. 2) He had grits, and I love grits. 3) It's a show, with the whole family working and Hank on the grill. Hank's was one of the first places I wanted to do for DD&D, not because he needed the business, but to honor my buddy and recognize the mom-and-pop places in my own backyard.

QUESTION IS . . . CAN HE LAND IT? COME AND SEE!

But if that's dessert, what's the cinnamon-walnut French toast? The bread's dense and rich, dipped in egg wash and flipped on the flattop, and it gets dusted with confectioners' sugar. I would be scraping my son Hunter off the ceiling if he ate that.

That's the essence of Hank's: everything's made fresh, all of it made well, served by a family at a place that feels like home.

Corned Beef Hash

ADAPTED FROM A RECIPE COURTESY OF HANK VANCE OF HANK'S CREEKSIDE RESTAURANT

I think running the beef through the meat grinder makes it mix with the potatoes better than cubing it. At Hank's, they cook the hash by the handful on a well-seasoned flattop. You can do that too, using a bit less butter if need be.

MAKES 2 (10-INCH) CAKES

½ pound corned beef, coarsely chopped

2 large russet potatoes, peeled and coarsely shredded

2 ounces (½ stick) unsalted butter

1 large onion, finely chopped

1 teaspoon kosher salt

½ teaspoon freshly ground black pepper

1. Pulse the corned beef in a food processor until it looks like coarsely ground beef, or run it through a meat grinder. Toss the meat with the shredded potatoes.

2. Heat a 10-inch nonstick skillet over medium-high heat. Melt 1 ounce (2 tablespoons) of the butter and add half of the onion; cook and stir for 5 minutes. Add half the corned beef and potatoes; season with ½ teaspoon salt and ¼ teaspoon pepper and toss to mix well. Press the mixture down with a spatula to flatten it into a compact layer.

3. Reduce the heat to low. Cook the hash for 10 to 15 minutes, until the bottom is nicely browned. Flip with a spatula, pat down, and continue cooking another 10 to 15 minutes or until the bottom is well browned. Remove, and repeat with the remaining ingredients. Serve immediately.

Whole Wheat Pancakes

ADAPTED FROM A RECIPE COURTESY OF HANK VANCE OF HANK'S CREEKSIDE RESTAURANT

Remember, Hank grinds his own whole wheat to make the flour so that all the nutrients are preserved . . . but no pressure.

MAKES 14 PANCAKES

2 cups whole wheat flour

1 teaspoon fine salt

1 tablespoon baking powder

2 large eggs

1¾ cups milk

¼ cup vegetable oil

Melted butter or oil, for the griddle

**Blueberries, strawberries, or banana
  slices (optional)**

Real maple syrup, for serving

HANK'S CREEKSIDE DANCE TROUPE!

1. Whisk the dry ingredients together in a medium bowl. In another bowl, beat the eggs well, then add the milk and oil. Stir the wet ingredients into the dry just until combined.

2. Heat a griddle or skillet over medium heat. Brush lightly with butter or oil. Pour on batter by ¼ cupfuls. Drop in berries or banana slices, as you like. When the batter bubbles on the surface and the underside is golden brown, flip over to finish. Serve with maple syrup.

HOB NOB HILL

EST. 1944 ★ COME HOME TO THE 1940S

Something I've always said since we started Triple D is that a classic diner on the East Coast is just like a coffee shop in Cali, without the stainless steel and all. You know it's one of those places that you always want to go to—good food, good prices, and it feels like it's been there forever, like this joint in San Diego. They opened the doors on this place back in the forties.

★ TRACK IT DOWN ★

**2271 1st Avenue
San Diego, California 92101
619-239-8176
www.hobnobhill.com**

When the original owners were considering selling Hob Nob Hill to current owners Tania and Jeff Kacha, they asked the Kachas what they'd do with it if they got it, and Jeff responded, "We wouldn't change a thing." And that's why they were chosen to buy it. They've got regulars who've been coming for forty years, with standing reservations sitting at the same table at the same time of day. It's all as it always was—the French toast, the short ribs, and that childhood favorite, chicken and dumplings.

When I was a kid we used to pack on the horses up into the mountains. It was cold, and my dad said he was going to make something that would warm me up. It was chicken and dumplings, and it was the greatest thing in the world. Man, I couldn't wait to try theirs. Get out. It's massive flavor—the dumpling being done in the steam, the whole giddy-up; it's the definition of chicken and dumplings.

Tania and Jeff do a monster lamb shank served up with mint jelly, and they're making their own corned beef, too. They don't trim the big old briskets because they want all the fat for the flavor. The meat cures for seven days in the pickling-spiced brine, and they make a new batch every day. Pretty cool, huh? Then they put it in a pot with more pickling spice, brown sugar, and water, then it simmers. When that's sliced, it's so tender it's falling apart, and they serve it on a hunk of steamed cabbage with a side of steamed carrots and mustard. It's super tender, and the fat just melts in your mouth like butter. Yep, just like "buttah."

YOU CAN'T TRY JUST ONE! TRUST ME!

HOB NOB BOWLING TEAM.

Hob Nob Hill Old-Fashioned Chicken 'n' Dumplings

ADAPTED FROM A RECIPE COURTESY OF TANIA AND JEFF KACHA OF HOB NOB HILL

This recipe will take you back, and it just might be better than your mom used to make it.

MAKES 4 TO 6 SERVINGS

Chicken and gravy

1 (4-pound) chicken, cut into 10 pieces, plus the backbone

4 celery ribs, roughly chopped

1 carrot, roughly chopped

1 onion, peeled and quartered

2 quarts (8 cups) water

½ teaspoon seasoned salt

½ teaspoon garlic salt

½ teaspoon freshly ground black pepper

4 ounces (1 stick) unsalted butter

½ cup all-purpose flour

Kosher salt, to taste

Cooked peas and diced carrots (optional)

Dumplings

2 cups all-purpose flour

1 teaspoon salt

1 teaspoon baking powder

1 egg

1 tablespoon vegetable oil

1 cup milk

1. **FOR THE CHICKEN AND GRAVY:** Put the chicken, celery, carrot, onion, water, seasoned and garlic salts, and pepper in a small pot. Bring to a simmer, skimming the surface occasionally, and cook, uncovered, until the chicken is just cooked through, about 30 minutes. Let the chicken cool in the broth for 15 minutes.

2. **WHILE THE CHICKEN SIMMERS, MAKE THE ROUX:** In a medium skillet, melt the butter over medium heat. Dump in the flour and cook, stirring, for about 5 minutes. Set aside.

3. Take the chicken out of the broth, pull the skin and meat from the bones, and set the meat aside. Discard the skin, bones, and backbone. Strain the broth into a clean saucepan.

4. **MAKE THE DUMPLINGS:** Bring water to a hard boil in a pot that can hold a perforated steamer, but the water should not rise into the steamer. Whisk the flour with the salt and baking powder in a medium bowl. In another bowl, beat the egg and the oil with a fork, then stir in the milk. Stir the wet ingredients into the dry ingredients until just combined. Drop 8 equal portions of dough onto the steamer insert (about ¼ cup each), cover tightly, and steam for 15 minutes, until the dumplings are firm to the touch.

5. **WHILE THE DUMPLINGS STEAM, MAKE THE GRAVY:** Bring the broth back to a simmer. Whisk in about three quarters of the roux, let it simmer a few minutes, and then add more until the gravy is thickened to your liking. Season to taste.

6. Add the chicken (and peas and carrots, if you are using them) to the gravy, season to taste, and heat through. To serve, place 2 dumplings in a bowl and ladle over chicken and gravy.

[GUY ASIDE]

We were in San Diego, and we'd shot Pizzeria Luigi while we were there, and we pulled up to this place. I'd been past there many times; my buddy used to live down the street. So I'm thinking, by the looks of it, here's some country club food: club sandwiches, chowders on Friday. I go inside and it's circa-1970s decor, there are thirty-year employees, wooden booths—but, again, don't get caught thinking you can stereotype. These guys are making their own corned beef; it's made in such volume nowadays that people can buy good prepackaged corned beef, but no, these guys do it old-school, like the chicken and dumplings. I get jealous that it's not in my town. This is a great town: fly into San Diego and have a full experience of food in a weekend.

PIZZERIA LUIGI

EST. 2004 ★ TRIPPIN' TO ITALY IN SOUTHERN CALIFORNIA

I'm down here in San Diego. Now, Mexican food in this area is on point, but I'm not feeling like Mexican food, I'm feeling like pizza, and I hear this is the joint. Eighteen-inch, thin crust, hand-tossed New York–style pie in Southern California? I had to check this out.

★ TRACK IT DOWN ★

**1137 25th Street
San Diego, California 92102
619-233-3309
www.pizzerialuigi.com**

This place is doing pizza up to twenty different ways, made entirely by hand, like back in northern Milan, Italy, where owner and chef Luigi Agostini was raised. He came to the States in 1994, worked in a couple of pizza joints, and then took a chance and opened his own. He says making good pizza is all about really paying attention to the details, and he means it. He uses bottled water for his pizza dough because it tastes better. And water, he says, affects the way the pizza tastes in Naples versus northern Milan. The chlorine in some water affects the whole deal. He starts the dough with the water at room temperature and adds a little sugar to get the yeast going (as well as using his arm to stir it in and warm up the water a bit—old-school). He then adds the salt and the high-gluten flour; the gluten is what adds the elasticity and chew to the dough. Luigi does eventually use the mixer attachment, and it goes for fifteen minutes. Seriously, even uncooked this dough is delicious. Each ball of dough is formed at eighteen ounces, and he lets it proof a little bit more. He forms the round, then throws his dough, spinning on the back of his hand. That's beautiful—

I'm not gonna play that game! I can throw it, but not at eighteen inches on the back of the hand. My bling will snag it!

His Capone is a meat lover's pizza. I sauced one and told Luigi my theory that if you run the sauce heavier on the outside, it goes back into the middle while cooking and ends up even. He said I could fill out an application and we'll see how it goes. (So there's a future!) He then lays on the freshly grated mozzarella, then the sausage, pepperoni, and ground meatball. His oven's at 525°F or 550°F at all times, and the pizza comes out smokin' hot. That is really great pizza, ridiculous. The Mona Lisa has sausage, pepperoni, mushrooms, red onion, green bell pepper, and black olives. It is some of the best pie; the crust is perfect. I would move into this guy's house and live in the kitchen.

Luigi's red sauce is made with ground tomatoes, red pepper flakes, Greek oregano, salt, black pepper, granulated garlic, Parmesan cheese, and basil. There's a nice bright flavor, good tomato and herbs. But he's also got pesto and barbecue sauce for his barbecue chicken pizza, or no sauce at all. The white pizza has fresh mozzarella, Parmesan, fresh spinach, fresh garlic, and hunks of creamy ricotta cheese. Biting that salty mozzarella and that little bit of spinach, and then that sweet ricotta—awesome.

If I lived in San Diego I would have a signature account here.

SMILE, SON, THEY'LL LEAVE US ALONE SOON.

Pizzeria Luigi Mona Lisa Pizza

ADAPTED FROM A RECIPE COURTESY OF LUIGI AGOSTINI, CHEF AND OWNER OF PIZZERIA LUIGI

You may not be able to throw it like Luigi, but you can aspire; just keep the dough thin and keep the ~~oven hot~~.

Pizza dough

MAKES ENOUGH DOUGH FOR TWO 16- TO 18-INCH PIZZAS

Oil, for the bowls

1½ cups warm water

Pinch of sugar

½ ounce active dry yeast

Pinch of salt

3½ to 3¾ cups all-purpose flour

Pizza

MAKES ONE 16- TO 18-INCH

Flour, for dusting the work surface and the pizza peel, if using

Oil for a pizza pan, if using

1 piece pizza dough (½ of recipe above)

14 ounces pizza sauce

12 ounces whole-milk mozzarella cheese, shredded

4 ounces Italian sausage, cooked

4 ounces sliced pepperoni

4 ounces mushrooms, sliced

1 small red onion, sliced

1 small green bell pepper, sliced

¾ cup sliced black olives

> ## [CReW ASIDe]
>
> *Chico:* "My favorite thing—the food that is the 'if you were trapped on a desert island and only had one food, what would it be' food—is pizza, and possibly the best pizza I've *ever* had is at Pizzeria Luigi in San Diego. This coming from a guy raised in Brooklyn, New York. But Luigi's is the thinnest, crispiest crusted, most delicious pizza you may ever have . . . classic true Italian–New York thin-crust pizza."

1. FOR THE DOUGH: Lightly oil 2 large bowls. Put the warm water and sugar in a medium bowl, sprinkle over the yeast, and stir until the yeast dissolves. Let the yeast activate for 2 to 5 minutes. Add the salt and 2 cups of the flour and stir until blended. Stir in another 1½ to 1¾ cups flour until the dough is too stiff to stir with a spoon.

2. Divide the dough in half. Knead each half about 7 times; don't knead too hard or the dough will rip at the top. Shape the dough into rounds and put in the oiled bowls. Cover the bowls with plastic wrap and let sit in a warm place until doubled in size, 30 to 60 minutes. Put the dough in the refrigerator for 1 hour after it rises to gain elasticity.

3. Preheat the oven to 500°F. If you have a pizza stone, heat that too. If not, lightly oil a pizza pan or baking sheet.

4. FOR THE PIZZA: Put 1 piece of dough on a floured surface and push down on it with your fingertips to get rid of any bubbles. Use a rolling pin to flatten the dough to the size and thickness you choose (16 to 18 inches). Transfer the dough to the pizza pan, if using. If using a stone, sprinkle a wooden pizza peel with flour and place the dough on top.

5. Spread on the sauce, then sprinkle on the cheese and toppings, leaving a 1-inch border. Put the pan in the oven or slip the pizza off the peel directly onto the stone. Cook the pizza for approximately 15 minutes or until the crust is golden brown.

WINDOW-SHOPPING HERE IS DANGEROUS.

SCHOONER OR LATER

EST. 1985 ★ DIVE INTO SCHULTZIE'S MESS

I cruise in—let me correct myself, I boat in to a place called Schooner or Later. Now, a schooner could be a sailing vessel or it could be a nice cold chalice of fermented hops, but in my world Schooner or Later is an off-the-hook eatery in Long Beach.

★ TRACK IT DOWN ★

**241 N. Marina Drive
Long Beach, California 90803
562-430-3495
www.schoonerorlater.com**

It's a big experience. There's a big line, but also a big group of fans who say it's worth the wait. Then you sit outside by the big boats, with big plates of food. Owner Denny Lund and his sister Denise grew up coming here, then bought the place from the original owners, Earl and Helen Schultz, whose signature item, Schultzie's Mess, is still on the menu. As one regular stated, it's everything you want in breakfast thrown on a plate and ready to roll. Head chef Tony Galope has been making the Mess for twenty years, up to sixty in one day. He starts with potatoes, then adds in a mix of bell pepper, ham, and onion, then two eggs are mixed in, and some shredded cheese is melted on top (recipe on page 196). That is good stuff; I like the crust on it, and the onions, and the bell peppers still have a little crunch to them. I can see why they call it the Mess. They also do a crab omelet, eggs Benedict, and an Italian omelet with marinara sauce and sausage.

People come from all over to eat at this place—Oregon, Kansas, Florida. Between the visitors and the regulars they can serve up to a thousand people on an average Sunday. A whole lot of them go for the Belgian waffles with bananas, strawberries, and blueberries and whipped cream on the top. Tony's like the Energizer waffle bunny. It's all real, fresh-cooked, and even more important, what you want the way you want it. Egg whites and spinach? Sure. They're even roasting fresh turkeys, stacking them high with ham, turkey, cheese, and tomato, and serving a massive turkey club melt. The fresh turkey makes all the difference; you don't need any mustard or mayo.

If he won the lottery tomorrow, Denny says he wouldn't change a thing about this place. It's a piece of him and Denise and they truly enjoy it—no pretending. Over time they've become an institution. Denise notes, "People come for the day and stay."

This place is so busy . . . you can get a *schooner* and get seated *later*.

[GUY ASIDE]

My first job out of college at UNLV was at Parker's Lighthouse in Long Beach; it was a big seafood restaurant, and I worked night shifts. So in the morning my buddies and I would get up and go to this breakfast joint, wait two hours to get in there, and get some mimosas or schooners (frozen glass mugs of beer). I wasn't there for the breakfast, so I'd order the club sandwich or the French dip, whatever, and sit on the cement tables. I'd take my rottweilers Rocky and Sierra over there in my big four-wheel-drive lifted truck. Sunday morning tailgating at its finest.

The highlight of this place is Denny and his sister Denise. Denny's the nicest guy, could be my brother; he let me drive his boat for the intro of the show. It was a really awesome time. And I *still* wait in line. Ha ha ha.

....

OWNER'S NOTE: A little history.

When we bought this café, the name was not Schooner or Later; it was called the Little Ships Galley, owned by Earl and Helen Schultz. Our most famous dish is called Schultzie's Mess, created by Helen and Schultzie (Earl's nickname). Schultzie continued to be very much a part of Schooner or Later. He made chili from scratch for us every week until he was eighty years old and we got too busy for him to keep up. He was here every day, enhancing the lives of the old and the new. The Schultzes owned the Galley for twenty years, and customers still sometimes come in and ask about them. Helen lives in Oklahoma since Schultzie passed away in 1989. —Denny Lund

WHERE DID I PARK MY YACHT . . . ? (HAPPENS ALL DA TIME.)

Schultzie's Mess

ADAPTED FROM A RECIPE COURTESY OF DENNY LUND OF SCHOONER OR LATER

Keep in mind, at Schooner or Later this might be one serving.

MAKES 2 GENEROUS SERVINGS

2 tablespoons vegetable oil

1½ cups plain frozen shredded hash browns

Kosher salt

Freshly ground black pepper

½ cup finely chopped cooked ham

¼ cup finely chopped green bell pepper

¼ cup finely chopped onion

3 large eggs

¾ cup shredded Cheddar cheese

2 slices sourdough toast

Chili, fresh salsa, avocado slices, and sour
    cream, for serving

THEY'VE ONLY HAD TO USE THIS A COUPLE TIMES.

1. Heat a griddle or large skillet over medium-high heat. Heat the oil and then add the hash browns, season with salt and pepper, and cook, tossing occasionally, until brown and crisp.

2. Scatter the ham, bell pepper, and onion over the hash browns. Toss the mixture with spatulas—go "Benihana" with it, spreading the whole mixture out thin so it can cook.

3. Break the eggs over the potatoes and toss and scramble them into the mixture. Once the eggs are cooked, scatter the cheese on top of the whole mixture and cover it to speed up the melting process. When the cheese is melted, serve with the sourdough toast, chili, salsa, sliced avocado, and sour cream.

STUDIO DINER

EST. 2003 ★ STU'S EAST COAST ON THE WEST COAST

....

When I'm thinking 24/7, I'm thinking diners. You know, whatever you want, whenever you want it. Like the Studio Diner—they're handling the dinner crowd, getting ready for the overnight crowd, and waiting for those who want breakfast, well, any time at all.

> **★ TRACK IT DOWN ★**
> ....
> **4701 Ruffin Road**
> **San Diego, California 92123**
> **858-715-6400**
> **www.studiodiner.com**

Owner Stu Segall is an original. This former Bostonian and TV and film producer missed the diners he grew up with back east (and was looking for some good grub between shoots), so he built one here in San Diego. He was looking to buy a twenty-stool place and it "turned into a monster." Everything he has in the place is top-notch; Stu says that's the "Stu didn't know when to stop" kinda thing, and there's also the "Stu didn't know how to cook" kinda thing, so he went and found a veteran diner chef: John San Nicolas. He knows how to make everything. John was born in Guam, learned the restaurant business in the mainland United States, and now he's East Coast cooking for a West Coast crowd, rolling out Philly cheesesteaks, a pastrami Reuben, huge fish and chips, and a turkey, ham, and cheese sandwich called a Monte Cristo that's battered, deep-fried, and dusted with powdered sugar. It was like a sandwich fell into my French toast, and frying it opens all the flavor of the ham and turkey and cheese.

John does Maine lobster rolls the real way, with celery and just a little mayonnaise. But that's just the start of Stu's New England thing. He's got whole belly Ipswich clam rolls. Ipswich is in Massachusetts, where these clams come from and where Stu grew up. He has them flown in three times a week. They are really somethin'. Unleash the clam! John drains and rinses them, soaks them in buttermilk for thirty minutes, then drains them and tosses them in corn flour for a light dredge. Then it's hot and fast in the fryer and served with tartar sauce, full belly and all. It's sweet and has a mild flavor; it's a good clam.

In the SamSon steak sandwich, Philly cheesesteak meets teriyaki—see the recipe on page 199 and the Tom Kenny on page 300. It's crazy. I mean, stir-fry meets Philly cheesesteak is a funky good combination; I'd order that fifteen more times.

Whether they're ordering New England seafood or eggs after dark, all kinds of folks have adopted this joint as the place to hang out—military personnel, pilots, musicians, policemen; at any hour it's the food they're coming for.

AT STUDIO YOU CAN ARM WRESTLE FOR YOUR DINNER . . . JUST TRY 'EM.

SamSon Steak Sandwich

ADAPTED FROM A RECIPE COURTESY OF STU SEGALL OF STUDIO DINER

The steak needs to marinate overnight, so start this recipe a day in advance.

MAKES 6 SANDWICHES

Marinade
½ cup pineapple juice
¼ cup soy sauce
1 tablespoon toasted sesame oil
1 tablespoon dark brown sugar
1½ teaspoons minced garlic
½ teaspoon ground black pepper

3 pounds boneless rib-eye steak, sliced about ⅛ inch thick

½ cup olive oil, divided
1 Spanish onion, diced
8 ounces bean sprouts
4 ounces mushrooms, thinly sliced
4 ounces spinach, chopped
Kosher salt and freshly ground black pepper
8 French bread rolls
1 pound shredded mozzarella cheese

1. Whisk the pineapple juice, soy sauce, sesame oil, brown sugar, garlic, and black pepper in a baking dish until the sugar dissolves. Put the meat in a large zip-top bag, pour the marinade over the meat, seal the bag, and knead a bit with your hands to work the marinade into the beef. Refrigerate overnight.

2. Preheat the broiler on low.

THIS? YEAH, THIS IS MAGIC BATTER.

3. Heat ¼ cup of the olive oil in a large skillet over medium-high heat. Add the onion, bean sprouts, mushrooms, spinach, and salt and pepper to taste and cook, tossing, until the mushrooms are just cooked through and the spinach wilts.

4. Heat another large skillet over medium-high heat. Heat the remaining ¼ cup olive oil. Add the meat, in batches if necessary, to make a single layer; cook, pressing with a spatula and stirring occasionally, until the meat reaches the desired degree of doneness; medium-rare is best.

5. Slice the rolls, leaving them attached on one side. Put them open-faced on a baking sheet and top with some of the meat. Add a layer of sautéed vegetables and top with some mozzarella. Broil just until the cheese melts, and serve hot.

....

A short story about the SamSon Steak Sandwich:

The owner of Studio Diner, Stu Segall, lived in Los Angeles and was producing TV shows in the 1980s. He used to eat at a little diner up there and fell in love with this sandwich. So he moved to San Diego in 1991, and in 2003 decided to build Studio Diner and said, "Man, I have to get that sandwich on the menu."

He sent somebody to the restaurant in L.A. to see if he could get the recipe—but the restaurant had closed! Stu *really* wanted that sandwich, so he hired a private detective to track down the old restaurant owner. A few weeks later the detective found the owner and got the recipe. Soooo the diner was getting ready to open, and the cooks were making everything on the menu in order to get the kinks out. They made the SamSon, and it didn't taste like Stu remembered it back in L.A.!

He got back in touch with the guy and said, "Hey, what's going on here . . . it's not the same!" The owner, who was Chinese, said with a thick accent, "Oh, you don't have secret marinade sauce, that's why. Only my wife knows that part of recipe. We divorced now, I not know where she lives." *Oy!* So the detective was hired again, and they finally got the complete recipe!

It's called the SamSon because Stu's father's name was Sam and he is Sam's son. So, there you are . . . the SamSon Steak Sandwich! —*Jim Phillips, general manager*

TOMMY'S JOYNT

EST. 1947 ★ STEP UP, STEP IN—COME IN AND WIN AT THIS LONGTIME LEGEND

When I roll into San Fran for a concert or a game or to just hang out with the krew, one of my favorite places to go is Tommy's Joynt. It's been a local neighborhood favorite for more than sixty years, definitely one of mine, and you're so gonna dig this.

★ TRACK IT DOWN ★

**1101 Geary Boulevard
San Francisco, California 94109
415-775-4216
www.tommysjoynt.com**

Pastrami, brisket, ham, corned beef, turkey—you can have an à la carte sandwich or a dinner plate. Tommy Harris was a radio star and wanted to be in the restaurant business, so he opened this joint, and a few years later his cousin Billy and his cousin's wife, Tootsie Veprin, joined. It's been in the family for more than sixty years. Now Tootsie's daughter Susie's keeping the tradition and rolling with her two sons—Zach behind the bar and Sam behind the meat counter. Everything has stayed the same—same beef, turkey, stews; that's what the Joynt is all about.

The meat's roasted fresh every day down in the basement. (I wondered where this food came from.) It's been done by kitchen manager Eliseo Orozco and his crew for thirty-five years. The corned beef comes brined, but Eliseo adds some more juniper berries and bay leaves and boils the beef for three and a half hours. It's got great marbling, it's not too salty, and it's super-melt-in-your-mouth tender.

Eliseo and his crew go through three steamship rounds a day for their roast beef. He salts and peppers it before popping it in the oven. There are times I like roast beef better than prime rib, and this is one of them; it's so juicy and flavorful and tasty. And they do fresh-roasted turkey sliced in front of you and served on a sourdough roll for $5.50. Crazy! The turkeys are twenty-eight-pounders—you could work out with those guys. They're seasoned with salt and black pepper and roasted, plain and simple. That's a big bird bonanza. Tommy's Joynt is known for good food and good beer at a good price, like corned beef and cabbage over potatoes, meatball subs, and chili done their way. The chili starts with buffalo meat, then Eliseo seasons it with granulated onion, garlic, white pepper, chili powder, cumin, salt, cayenne pepper, Worcestershire sauce, sherry wine, hot sauce, and ketchup boiled together. He adds the beans and serves it up. It's thick, not too spicy, with a great texture to the meat; that's good chili.

The lamb shanks are savory, roasted down with tons of flavor; check out the recipe on page 203 if you can't get to San Fran pronto.

[GUY ASIDE]

One of things about *Diners* is that I always like to show places close to home. We're in a food mecca here in Northern California. Before or after concerts I like to go to Tommy's and get a killer thick-cut hot pastrami sandwich, so I thought, why don't we do that? Tommy's is the capital of funk and great food. Sometimes I don't want to poke a hole in local joints for fear of disappointment, but you've gotta believe it, these guys really are making everything. Every walk of life comes in there, and the cats are knocking it out with sliced roasted meats. It's a bunch of characters in the center of San Francisco—you can't miss it.

WOW, SIAMESE TURKEYS—ONLY AT TOMMY'S JOYNT.

Tommy's Joynt Lamb Shanks

ADAPTED FROM A RECIPE COURTESY OF TOMMY'S JOYNT

They always serve the same specials here for each day of the week. Sundays and Thursdays are lamb shank days.

SERVES 2 HUNGRY PEOPLE OR 4 PEOPLE WITH A NORMAL APPETITE

1 cup water

½ cup red wine

1 tablespoon granulated garlic

1 tablespoon onion powder

1 teaspoon beef concentrate, such as Better Than Bouillon

½ teaspoon kosher salt

½ teaspoon freshly ground black pepper

4 large lamb shanks

2 to 3 cups beef or turkey stock, or low-sodium broth

¼ cup tomato paste

2 tablespoons all-purpose flour

Cooked potatoes and carrots, for serving

1. Preheat the oven to 350°F. Stir together the water, red wine, granulated garlic, onion powder, beef concentrate, salt, and pepper in a roasting pan just large enough to hold the shanks. Turn the shanks in the mixture to coat. Cover the pan with foil and roast for 2 hours.

2. Take the shanks out of the roasting pan and set aside. Scrape the drippings in the roasting pan in order to loosen the brown bits on the bottom of the pan, and pour them into a saucepan. Add 2 cups of the stock, bring to a simmer over medium heat, and then whisk in the tomato paste. Take some of the remaining stock and mix it with the flour in a separate bowl to make a paste. Whisk it into the simmering gravy to thicken. If the gravy seems too thick, add more stock.

3. Put the shanks and the gravy back in the roasting pan. Roast, uncovered, for another 2 hours or so, until the shanks are brown and tender. Make sure to turn the shanks frequently during cooking so that they brown on all sides. Serve with potatoes and carrots.

HARRY'S ROADHOUSE

EST. 1992 ★ THE CULINARY CHAPEL OF SCRAPPLE

....

The show's called Diners, Drive-ins and Dives, but we've got room for all kinds of funky joints, like a roadhouse. Now, the last roadhouse we'd been at was Patrick's Roadhouse on the southern Pacific Coast Highway. This one was off I-25 in Santa Fe, and they were serving up all kinds of breakfast and—believe it or not—homemade scrapple.

> **★ TRACK IT DOWN ★**
> ....
> **96-B Old Las Vegas Highway**
> **Santa Fe, New Mexico 87505**
> **505-989-4629**

When I had scrapple in Philly, no one could tell me what part of the pig it came from. The owner here tells me it's everything but the oink. It's a breakfast staple back in Philly, where Harry Shapiro grew up, hanging out at some classic East Coast diners.

They were places where they served good food at reasonable prices, where you could hang out—and that's exactly what he's doing here. "It's crazy," says Harry. "I'm this Jewish kid in Philadelphia, and I fall in love with Mexican food. I say, that's it, I'm moving to Santa Fe." And with his wife he bought an old gas-station-turned-restaurant on Route 66. They're running an all-day roadhouse, serving comfort diner and Southwestern fare for all sorts of folks from all around Santa Fe—including Oscar-winning actor Gene Hackman, who happened to be there when we were. He says he loves it; he cruises in and nobody bothers him—until we come dragging our cameras in, of course.

So back to the scrapple. Harry says Pennsylvania Dutch scrapple has a lot of pork liver in it, but Harry's doing it different. His scrapple uses pork butt (I'm a little bit more at ease; see the recipe on page 207). I got to be part of the scrapple nation—the flavor and the crunch; his was awesome, and I didn't *want* to like it. Trust me, you'll like it too.

He does lemon ricotta pancakes with strawberries, massive cinnamon rolls, and blue corn waffles done Harry's way, with a couple strips of bacon cooked in (recipe on page 206). That's what I'm talking about, the sugar with the salty, and so moist.

Of the Southwestern dishes, one favorite is an egg, bean, and tortilla dish with a salsa he's making himself. He starts by sautéing whole peppercorns and cinnamon, cumin, and anise in a dry pan to toast and open up their flavor. Then he grinds them up. Next he blends together roasted tomato and onion and grilled garlic, pours in fresh orange and lime juice, and a little veggie stock and salt. The spice mixture is added into the pool; then he cuts an habañero, sticks a toothpick in it (that way he can retrieve the hot little devil easily and it won't accidentally end up on someone's dish!), and lets the pepper sit in there overnight to release its heat. This fabulous sauce is served over tortillas that are lightly fried, then stacked with refried beans and topped with an egg cooked as you like it, with a garnish of some cubed ham, peas, queso fresco, and fried plantain slices.

Great job, Harry, you get to go to the next round.

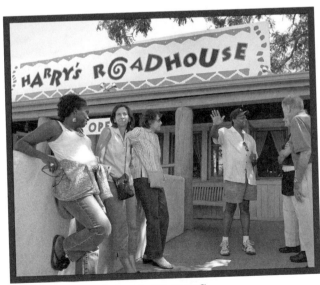

FOLKS . . . SORRY, YA GOTTA GET IN LINE!

Blue Cornmeal Waffles

ADAPTED FROM A RECIPE COURTESY OF HARRY SHAPIRO OF HARRY'S ROADHOUSE

Harry's Note: We serve the waffles with honey butter and sliced bananas, and make them really special by putting two or three strips of cooked bacon to the waffle iron after adding the batter.

MAKES 12 (3 BY 4-INCH) WAFFLES

1½ cups blue cornmeal

1½ cups all-purpose flour

¼ cup sugar

1½ teaspoons baking powder

½ teaspoon baking soda

½ teaspoon fine salt

2 cups buttermilk

4 large eggs

⅓ cup (5½ tablespoons) unsalted butter, melted

I WON AT TIC-TAC-TOE AND NOW I EAT YOUR FLAPJACKS! DEAL WITH IT!

1. Preheat a nonstick waffle iron. Whisk the cornmeal, flour, sugar, baking powder, baking soda, and salt in a medium bowl. In another bowl, beat the buttermilk, eggs, and butter with a fork. Stir the wet ingredients into the dry.

2. Pour a generous ¼ cup batter per waffle into the waffle iron. Cover and cook until the waffles are fragrant and golden brown, and the steam slows, about 4 minutes.

Scrapple

ADAPTED FROM A RECIPE COURTESY OF HARRY SHAPIRO OF HARRY'S ROADHOUSE

Harry's Note: You can make your own pork stock from pork neck bones, boiling them with chopped onions, carrots, and celery.

SERVES 10

1 ½ pounds boneless pork butt, cut into 2-inch cubes

6 cups pork or chicken stock, or low-sodium broth

1 cup polenta

1 ½ teaspoons kosher salt, plus more for seasoning

1 teaspoon freshly ground black pepper, plus more for seasoning

1 teaspoon dried sage

¾ teaspoon dried marjoram

½ teaspoon dried thyme

Nonstick spray

All-purpose flour, for dredging

Vegetable oil, for frying

Poached eggs, for serving, if desired

1. Simmer the pork in the stock until tender, about 45 minutes. Remove the pork, reserving the stock. Grind the pork coarsely with a meat grinder. Stir the ground pork into the stock. Bring the mixture back to a simmer, then whisk in the polenta, salt, pepper, sage, marjoram, and thyme. Simmer, stirring occasionally, until you leave a track when you pull a spoon through it, about 45 minutes. Taste and season again if necessary.

2. Spray a 10 by 5-inch loaf pan with nonstick spray and pour in the pork mixture. Refrigerate overnight.

3. WHEN READY TO SERVE: Put some flour in a shallow dish. Turn the scrapple out of the loaf pan and cut it into ½-inch-thick slices. Heat up about ¼ inch of vegetable oil in a sauté pan over medium-high heat. Coat the scrapple slices with flour. Cook the scrapple until it is crispy on both sides, about a minute or two per side. Sprinkle with salt and serve immediately with poached eggs, if desired.

TUNE-UP CAFÉ

EST. 2008 ★ HOME OF THE FLAVORTOWN VOLCANO

I'm rolling through Santa Fe, New Mexico, and I'm taking you now to a little joint that's probably a perfect example of what we're looking for here on Triple D. It's owned by a husband-and-wife team, they're scratch-cooking just about everything, the place is full of character, and the neighborhood totally digs it.

★ TRACK IT DOWN ★

1115 Hickox Street
Santa Fe, New Mexico 87505
505-983-7060
tuneupcafe.com

This place is run by a couple from the neighborhood. El Salvador native Jesus Rivera and his wife, Charlotte, bought it in 2008. Jesus was working at two restaurants at the same time, and Charlotte thought if he's working that hard, he should have his own place. So now he's cranking out comfort food, like stuffed French toast, and Southwestern favorites like chiles rellenos—along with a Salvadoran dish that Jesus grew up with, beef pupusa (see the recipe on page 210). That's crazy good: if the meat weren't good enough just by itself, the crispy, crunchy masa with all that corn and cheese oozing out of it would be. He completely train-wrecked me, man.

And the locals just can't get enough. Banana leaf tacos, fish tacos, crazy tasty. Even the classics get a Tune-Up twist. He takes the Anaheims and throws them on the grill, roasts and sweats them, then removes the skin. Then he makes a little pocket and pulls the seeds out. He mixes shredded Monterey Jack cheese and chopped onion, forming little cheese torpedos that he stuffs into each pepper. They go into the freezer for twenty minutes so they're firm, then they're coated lightly in flour and dipped into a batter that's made by whisking egg whites till fluffy, then adding the yolks and flour in—makes for a really nice light batter. They fry up fast and are served with roasted tomato salsa; the cheese oozes out like a lava from a Flavortown volcano. I've never been that much of a chile relleno fan, typically because the batter is too eggy for me, but Jesus makes 'em light and creamy and tender and on point.

This is the American dream, and I gotta tell you something, this guy is a working machine—they've got to think about expanding.

"HEY, LOOK, MOMMY, A FIREFLY PARADE . . . KEWL."

El Salvadoran Beef Pupusas

ADAPTED FROM A RECIPE COURTESY OF JESUS RIVERA OF TUNE-UP CAFÉ

At the Tune-Up Café, they use chile pasado, a dried chile, not the Anaheim chiles used in this version of the recipe. If you can find the chiles pasados, just simmer two of them in boiling water for ten minutes, then strain, chop, and dice—and leave the seeds in.

MAKES 6 PUPUSAS

Masa

2¾ cups masa harina (available at Latin markets)

1 tablespoon plus 1 teaspoon olive oil

1½ teaspoons kosher salt

2 cups water, plus more as needed

Filling

½ pound flank steak

1 tablespoon olive oil

¼ cup finely chopped Spanish onion

1 large ripe tomato, diced

2 Anaheim chiles, roasted, peeled, seeded, and chopped

Kosher salt

Freshly ground black pepper

½ cup corn kernels, fresh or defrosted frozen

1 cup shredded Monterey Jack cheese

Nonstick cooking spray, for assembly

Olive oil, for frying

Cortido, for serving (recipe follows)

Roasted Tomato Salsa, for serving (recipe follows)

1. **FOR THE MASA:** Mix the masa harina, 1 tablespoon olive oil, and salt in a big bowl. Add 2 cups of water and mix thoroughly; by hand is best. Add more water a little at a time until the masa has the consistency of Play-Doh. Cover with plastic wrap.

2. **FOR THE FILLING:** Slice the flank steak across the grain into ½-inch-thick slices. Pound the meat on both sides with a meat mallet to tenderize, then rough chop into small pieces.

3. Heat the olive oil in a large skillet over medium-high heat. Add the meat and sauté to get a nice brown sear, about 5 minutes. Stir in the onion and sauté, stirring occasionally, for 5 more minutes. Add the tomato and cook, stirring a few times, for 10 minutes. Finally, add the chiles and simmer for 20 minutes. Add a bit of water if the mixture seems too dry or close to scorching; it should be wet but not too saucy. Season with salt and pepper to taste.

4. **TO ASSEMBLE:** Cut some parchment or wax paper into a 6 by 18-inch strip. Lay the strip on a work surface and spray well with nonstick spray. Form the masa into twelve 2-inch balls (like golf balls). Place a ball at either end of the parchment strip.

5. Cover with plastic wrap and flatten each ball with something flat, like the back of a sauté pan, to make a tortilla about ¼ inch thick and 5 to 6 inches across. Remove the plastic.

6. Put 2 heaping tablespoons meat, 1 heaping tablespoon corn, and some cheese in the center of one tortilla. Now fold the paper at the center to flip the other tortilla on top and pinch around the edges to seal. It is important to seal the seam well, so take your time. Repeat with the remaining masa and filling.

7. Heat about 2 tablespoons olive oil in a small skillet. Brown the pupusas on both sides, 3 to 5 minutes. Serve hot with the Cortido on the side and Roasted Tomato Salsa over the top.

POWER LUNCH!

Cortido

RECIPE COURTESY OF JESUS RIVERA OF TUNE-UP CAFÉ

MAKES ABOUT 2 QUARTS

¼ small green cabbage, cored and thinly sliced

1 medium beet, roasted, peeled, and julienned

1 carrot, peeled and julienned

1 jalapeño chile, stemmed and thinly sliced

2 teaspoons dried oregano

½ cup white vinegar

1 quart (4 cups) water

Kosher salt

Freshly ground black pepper

A TASTY BOWL OF CHIMNEY SWEEP SOUP.

Combine the cabbage, beet, carrot, jalapeño, oregano, vinegar, and water in a large nonreactive container. Season with salt and pepper to taste. Cover the container and chill overnight. Shake off the excess marinade when serving.

Roasted Tomato Salsa

RECIPE COURTESY OF JESUS RIVERA OF TUNE-UP CAFÉ

MAKES ABOUT 1 QUART

3 ripe tomatoes

1 jalapeño chile, stemmed and halved

¼ large peeled onion

1 garlic clove

½ cup water

¼ cup chopped fresh cilantro leaves

1. Preheat the oven to 400°F. Put the tomatoes, jalapeño, onion, and garlic on a rimmed baking sheet and roast until slightly charred, about 1 hour. Blend the roasted vegetables in a deep container with an immersion blender or in a blender.

2. Put the salsa in a small pot, add the water, and simmer for about 25 minutes. Season to taste, stir in the cilantro, and serve warm.

THEY SERVE FAMILY PORTIONS, TOO! (GET IT? HA HA.)

MAGNOLIA CAFE

EST. 1988 ★ SORRY, WE'RE OPEN

If you've ever been to Austin, Texas, then you know about the Congress Avenue bridge—it's where all the bats live underneath. At night about a zillion bats fly outta there; it's really cool. And a little farther down the street is something else that's cool, a little 24/7 joint called Magnolia Cafe.

Nachos, tacos, chicken stir-fry, pancakes, polenta, omelets, Benedicts—they've been doing it all since they opened this joint twenty years ago, but they weren't always open all the time. That started when people came knocking on the door while they were mopping up. So they took the place 24/7. Owner Eric Westphal says he calls it 24/8 because that's what it feels like, and the place is packed. He started cooking here ten years ago, and he makes it fresh with dozens of specials. The blackened salmon is a ride in itself. He starts with paprika, then cayenne, black pepper, white pepper, granulated garlic, onion powder, thyme, and basil. He then sprinkles a little kosher salt on the salmon, then does the dry rub with the spice mixture—the classic way, but the cooking method sure ain't classic. Eric turns a cast-iron skillet upside down on the burner to get it even more insanely hot. (Do not try this at home; you'd need a NASCAR hazmat suit.) He throws a little oil on the pan bottom and it bursts into flames. The fish goes on next, sitting among the flames. He does it pretty rare, and it happens quick, because the thing has got to be up in the 700-degree range. That is just optimum: the spice isn't overdone, the fish is medium rare, and it's a great technique for firefighters. And check out what they're serving it with: jambalaya stuffed in red bell peppers.

For the jambalaya he starts with a dark roux of oil and flour, then adds garlic, green bell peppers, jalapeños, shallots, green onion, andouille sausage, rice, tomato, Cajun seasoning, and stock that he makes from shrimp shells and chicken stock. Then the crab and crawfish go in, he covers it, and it cooks for 30 to 45 minutes. There's the perfect amount of spice, not too heavy on the seafood overtone. I didn't know how jambalaya could get much better, but some bread crumbs toasted on top added some great crunch, and the red bell pepper flavor really does make it.

The fans keep coming in here for the food and the funk. The Texas Benedict comes with grilled sausage and homemade chipotle hollandaise, and the pancakes come in cornmeal, whole wheat, or buttermilk, however you like them. Their gingerbread pancake recipe starts with coffee (recipe on page 216). Another dish you won't find at other places is the polenta topped with ragu. This guy's making his own preserved lemons for his polenta; it's a Moroccan thing, Eric says. He's in it to win it.

IT'S MAGIC INVISIBLE SYRUP—ZERO CALORIES.

[GUY ASIDE]

Austin is a phenomenal food town. We had a blast there—great food, great people, great music. Even before we shot at Magnolia I told my wife this is going to be an interesting one. They've got a quirky sense of humor and an enormous menu, like a small phone book, and they're open 24/7. The place is an institution. I think one of the funny things about cooking with this cat Eric is that he uses the measure-free method—he's so in touch with all the food he's doing. I come from the same school—you've got to feel comfortable and know where you're at with your food to make those maneuvers. They could make the electricity for Austin the way this place was humming along. On my filing cabinet in my office is a "Sorry, We're Open" magnet from Magnolia. Talking about tchotchkes from locations: every time we go somewhere the crew grabs me some T-shirts. We rotate them through in my restaurants to show people where we've been.

Magnolia Cafe Gingerbread Pancakes

ADAPTED FROM A RECIPE COURTESY OF MAGNOLIA CAFE

At Magnolia Cafe, they add banana slices to the batter right before flipping. And as you know, "bananas iu good.

MAKES 12 TO 14 PANCAKES

2½ cups unbleached all-purpose flour

1 tablespoon ground cinnamon

1 tablespoon ground ginger

1 tablespoon ground nutmeg

1 teaspoon ground cloves

½ teaspoon fine salt

½ teaspoon baking powder

¼ teaspoon baking soda

3 large eggs

¼ cup light brown sugar

1 cup buttermilk

½ cup water

¼ cup brewed coffee, cooled

2 ounces (4 tablespoons; ½ stick) butter, melted, plus more for the griddle

1. Sift the flour, cinnamon, ginger, nutmeg, cloves, salt, baking powder, and baking soda into a large bowl.

2. Beat the eggs with the brown sugar in another bowl. Whisk in the buttermilk, water, and coffee. Stir the wet ingredients into the dry just until combined. Stir in the 4 tablespoons melted butter.

3. Heat a griddle or heavy skillet over medium-high heat and butter lightly. Pour on the batter by 2-ounce ladlefuls. Cook until little bubbles appear around the edges of the pancakes, and then flip. Cook on the second side until golden brown and cooked through in the middle.

Eric Westphal's Ragu with Polenta with Gorgonzola

ADAPTED FROM A RECIPE COURTESY OF ERIC WESTPHAL OF MAGNOLIA CAFE

Note that unlike on the show, this polenta version uses Gorgonzola and forgoes the preserved lemon; but feel free to get funky with your own versions.

MAKES 12 SERVINGS, WITH LEFTOVER RAGU

3 tablespoons olive oil or bacon fat

3 pounds loose Italian sausage, hot or sweet

2 Spanish onions, diced

7 garlic cloves, minced

1 red bell pepper, stemmed, seeded, and chopped

1 green bell pepper, stemmed, seeded, and chopped

2 teaspoons dried oregano

1 ½ teaspoons dried basil

1 ½ teaspoons dried thyme

1 to 2 teaspoons crushed red chile flakes (optional)

1 cup white wine

1 (6-pound 6-ounce) can crushed tomatoes

1 tablespoon kosher salt

1 tablespoon freshly ground black pepper

Polenta with Gorgonzola, for serving (recipe follows)

Olive oil, for sautéing

Grated Parmesan cheese, for serving

Fresh basil leaves, torn, for serving

1. Heat the olive oil or bacon fat in a heavy pot over medium-high heat. Brown the sausage and transfer to a plate. Sauté the onions, garlic, and bell peppers in the drippings until softened, about 5 minutes.

2. Add the oregano, basil, thyme, and red chile flakes and cook, stirring, for 1 minute. Add the wine and let it bubble for a minute or two. Add the crushed tomatoes, salt, and pepper and bring to a boil. Reduce the heat to low and simmer for at least 1 hour or, ideally, 5 hours.

3. When ready to serve, slice the polenta into twelve 3-inch squares. Heat a little olive oil in a nonstick skillet over medium-high heat. Add some polenta slices without crowding the pan and cook until nicely browned, about 2 minutes. Turn carefully and brown the second side.

4. Spoon some ragu over the polenta, and garnish with Parmesan cheese and basil.

I KNOW YOU KNOW I KNOW THAT I KNOW YER WATCHING ME.

Polenta with Gorgonzola

ADAPTED FROM A RECIPE COURTESY OF ERIC WESTPHAL OF MAGNOLIA CAFE

The polenta needs to chill overnight, so make it a day or even two ahead.

MAKES 12 SERVINGS

Olive oil, for oiling the baking dish
6 cups water
1 cup chopped oil-packed sun-dried tomatoes, drained and patted dry
2 cups fine or coarse cornmeal
1 cup crumbled Gorgonzola cheese

Lightly oil a 9 by 13-inch baking dish. Bring the water to a boil in a heavy pot over medium heat. Stir the sun-dried tomatoes into the boiling water. Slowly sprinkle in the cornmeal, stirring constantly. When the mixture thickens, stir in the Gorgonzola. Cook, stirring, until it reaches the consistency of thick porridge. Pour the polenta into the baking dish. Chill overnight.

The Cove

EST. 1998 ★ **WHERE YOUR CLOTHES, YOUR CAR, AND YOUR TASTE BUDS COME CLEAN**

I travel all over the country, so it's nice sometimes to stop and wash down the '67. So here I am in San Antonio, and the only food I've ever gotten at a car wash has come out of a vending machine, so you've got to know I was totally blown away to find out that connected to this car wash is a totally legit restaurant called the Cove.

> ★ **TRACK IT DOWN** ★
>
> **606 W. Cypress Street**
> **San Antonio, Texas 78212**
> **210-227-2683**
> **thecove.us**

It's a car wash and, oh yeah, a Laundromat. Crammed in the middle is a full-blown restaurant. Lisa Asvestas and her husband, Sam, started out doing sandwiches, but Lisa kept asking for more—"Can I have a grill? a griddle?"—then they started having cooks, and they ended up with a CIA-trained chef, Michael Sohocki, who was looking to build a menu he could have some fun with. Before they knew it they had a full restaurant heavy on fresh, organic, and homemade, from scratch-made Moroccan sweet potato salad to fancy quesadillas with portobello mushrooms and organic spinach. A crowd favorite is the lamb burger. It's like a meat milkshake in a bun—so juicy I needed a blanket. Some of the best lamb burger I've ever had—and at a car wash?

The first out-of-the-box item on the menu was Lisa's original fish taco, with homemade coleslaw and poblano sauce. For her portobello spinach quesadilla, Lisa marinates

A FISH PLAYIN A GUITAR . . . YEAH, RIGHT . . . MAYBE A BASS ON A BASS!

JOE, HURRY UP WITH YER SOLO—FOOD'S GETTING COLD.

her mushrooms with balsamic vinegar, extra-virgin olive oil (emulsified), fresh-ground peppercorns, fresh garlic, salt, and herbes de Provence. They go on the grill for about twenty minutes. Then for her poblano sauce she roasts and seeds the peppers and blends them with yogurt, mayonnaise, sour cream, salt, and fresh ground pepper. Next she takes a locally made whole grain tortilla and toasts it on the grill, slices up the portobello, and sautés it with red onion and spinach (wilting the spinach by covering it with a lid), spreads some shredded cheese on half of the tortilla, then puts the whole deal together, folds it, slices it, and serves the poblano sauce for dipping. The sauce fits it perfectly; the only thing I didn't like about it is that I finished. And I felt healthier just eating it. Forget the car—I'm going to walk the States.

I would have the cleanest car and laundry in San Antonio if I lived there.

[GUY ASIDE]

When I'm on the road shooting a show, there are seven segments on each show, and I do two and a half full shows in four days. (The crews take much longer.) It's tiring getting up at six, shooting four to six hours on locations, traveling up to an hour to the next one, and doing it all over again. It's kinda like *Groundhog Day.* So between shoots, when I have a chance to sit down and chill, I try to e-mail the family, have something to drink. Anyhow, at the Cove a gentleman walks up to me and says, "How are you doing?" I say hello, and he says, "Hi, I'm Gary. I'm a fan of the show, and my wife really likes the show—could you sign something?" I'm beat tired, but I get up, 'cuz the fans are the heartbeat of the show. I talk to his family, and I notice when I shake his hand that he has on a championship ring. Well, he happens to be one of the investors in the San Antonio Spurs, and he ends up inviting the entire krew to the Spurs game. He picks us up in a limo bus, takes us down to the locker room, sets us up in a suite—the whole enchilada. It was the best time in the world. A big shout-out to Gary and his family, and a big thank you—one of those doors that gets opened by the wonderful world of Triple D.

Latin-Spiced Lamb Burgers

ADAPTED FROM A RECIPE COURTESY OF MICHAEL SOHOCKI OF THE COVE

This is something good and juicy; I dove into it, then headed to the car wash to hose myself down

MAKES 6 BURGERS

Sauce
2 pasilla chiles, stems removed

1 each ancho and guajillo or pulla chile, stems removed

1 cup water

¼ cup extra-virgin olive oil

2 to 3 tablespoons freshly squeezed lime juice

1 tablespoon sour cream

1 garlic clove, chopped

1½ teaspoons kosher salt

2 to 3 tablespoons heavy cream

Lamb burgers
1½ teaspoons black peppercorns

½ teaspoon coriander seeds

½ teaspoon cumin seeds

2 pounds ground grass-fed lamb

2 garlic cloves, minced

1 teaspoon kosher salt

¼ to ½ teaspoon cayenne pepper

To assemble
6 ciabatta buns, split horizontally and grilled

3 ounces cotija cheese, crumbled

4 large ripe tomatoes, thinly sliced

1 red onion, thinly sliced

Lettuce

1. FOR THE SAUCE: Tear the chiles open to shake out the seeds (if a few seeds are left in, that's fine). Throw the chiles in a saucepan with the water, bring to a boil over medium heat, and cook, uncovered, until only ¼ cup of liquid remains at the bottom.

2. Put the chiles with their cooking liquid, the oil, lime juice, sour cream, and garlic in a blender, and puree until very smooth. Scrape down the sides of the blender, add the salt, and blend again. Add 2 tablespoons of the cream and pulse a few times just to incorporate and get a saucy, squirtable consistency. Add up to 1 tablespoon more cream if necessary. Taste and adjust seasonings.

3. FOR THE BURGERS: Toast the peppercorns, coriander, and cumin in a dry pan over medium-high heat, shaking the pan constantly, until they crackle and pop. They should be light brown and smell smoky, or like toast or popcorn. Then grind them to a fine powder in a spice grinder. Add them to the lamb with the garlic, salt, and cayenne and use your hands to combine thoroughly. Gently form the meat into 6 equal size patties.

4. Heat a grill or grill pan over medium-high heat. Grill the burgers until they have nice, dark grill marks, about 3 minutes per side for medium-rare (130°F). Let the burgers rest for a few minutes before serving. Spread some sauce on both halves of the buns, and top with the burgers, some crumbled cotija, and plenty of tomato, onion, and lettuce.

LONE STAR TAQUERIA

EST. 1994 ★ FLAVORTOWN'S FOUR DEGREES OF SEPARATION IN A REAL-DEAL TAQUERIA

Usually on Triple D you see me cruising the convertible '67, but when I find a joint that's got a car as sick as the one they've got parked outside, well, I just got to check it out. The thing is covered in bumper stickers, and it has a shark's fin on the roof. And it's not just the car that's unique here; they're doing Mexican the real-deal way.

★ TRACK IT DOWN ★

**2265 Fort Union Boulevard
Salt Lake City, Utah 84121
801-944-2300**

I felt like I walked into a fiesta, the place is so wild. Everybody's happy, because this ain't Susan Harries' first rodeo. After being in the restaurant biz since she was thirteen, running all kinds of joints, she wanted to open a Mexican place. So she brought in an old friend, Manuel Valdez, and his brothers (Fernando, Enrique, and Gustavo) to do the food they grew up with. Cousins Efren, Francisco, and Indalcio work part-time.

To make their carne adovada, Manuel trims the pork butt of the silver skin, then slices it real thin. He's a butchering machine. His spice marinade is made of cumin, cayenne, garlic, California chile powder, New Mexican chile powder, whole cloves, bay leaves, and salt. Then he adds oil, mixes it all up, and lets it sit overnight. He then puts it in the oven, covered, and cooks it for a couple of hours to get it really soft. It's tender and killer. To make the taco, he throws some of the chopped meat on the flattop to get more of a crust on it, heats up the tortillas, then builds the taco with cilantro, chopped onion, and lime juice. That's it; you don't mess with it. The flavor is so amazing.

Some of the other favorites here are seafood—in Utah? They get fresh fish in every day, sometimes salmon, halibut, cod, sole, sea bass, mahi mahi, red snapper, ahi . . . even shark. It's a good kind of fish roulette. The shrimp burrito is on the menu every day. For that he uses green and red bell pepper and red onion, sliced. They go into a pot with cayenne, garlic, ground pepper, California chile powder, New Mexican chile powder, salt, and a little bit of soybean oil. This cooks down for about two hours—whew, there's some heat on that, too. The shrimp are quickly sautéed with a little bit of garlic and oil, then some of the pepper mixture is added to the pan. On a big warm tortilla he layers some rice, beans, shredded cheese, the shrimp, cilantro, chopped onion, tomatoes, and shredded lettuce. A little sour cream spread on and you're ready to roll. That's what I'm talking about. It should be called the killer burrito. Nice and tender shrimp, the distinct flavor of the pepper; I've got nothing but happy on that.

AERODYNAMIC FIN . . . WICKED!

[GUY ASIDE]

There may generally be six degrees of separation between people, but in Flavortown I believe there are four degrees. At Lone Star Taqueria, the owner, Susan, happens to own this property in Mexico in the same little village where I own property. We're not more than a quarter mile apart on the beach. We were sitting there talking about Mexico, how much we love it. "What? No! Where? You know who? You gotta be kidding me!"— and sure enough, when I go down there the following winter they all know her. Crazy.

If I'm not in Cali or Mexico I question Mexican food, but talk about the real-deal taqueria in Salt Lake City! We always dig a taco joint that makes its own tortillas, but Susan uses them to make her own chips, too! We'd never seen that before on Triple D. And they go through a hundred pounds of fish a day. I don't like to see concepts go chain, but if they could do this on a national level it would be an awesome restaurant. People love this place—there's a line out the door. I tell people, if you live witin 250 miles of this place, it's worth a road trip.

When you're visiting some funky joint, always ask, "What do the owner and staff eat?" At Lone Star they have a crazy dish called What the Boys Eat—it's not on the menu, but it's featured on the board. The kitchen guys saute pork and sirloin adovada with the vegetariano ingredients, mix it up, and serve it with white corn tortillas. Coming from the restaurant business, so many great ideas come from my culinary team!

About that car: one of her cooks' cars broke down in front of the restaurant one day, so they left it there and went crazy with stickers!

Carne Adovada Tacos

ADAPTED FROM A RECIPE COURTESY OF SUSAN HARRIES OF LONE STAR TAQUERIA

Why even have the tortilla? Just serve it in my hand, or my shoe, or my pocket.

MAKES 10 TACOS

2 tablespoons ground cumin

2 tablespoons California chile powder

2 tablespoons New Mexican chile powder

1 tablespoon cayenne pepper

1 tablespoon kosher salt, plus more to taste

1 teaspoon freshly ground black pepper

1 teaspoon garlic powder

3 pounds pork butt, trimmed and sliced ¼ inch thick

2 cups vegetable oil

5 whole cloves

2 bay leaves

20 (6-inch) white corn tortillas, heated

Diced white onion, for serving

Coarsely chopped fresh cilantro leaves, for serving

Lime wedges, for serving

IT'S A PATIO PARTY, PEOPLE.

THEY WON'T TOW YOUR CAR, JUST DECORATE IT FOR YOU.

1. Mix the cumin, chile powders, cayenne, 1 tablespoon salt, pepper, and garlic powder in a 9 by 13-inch baking dish. Toss the meat with the spice mixture to coat completely. Stir in the oil, cloves, and bay leaves. Cover with foil and refrigerate for at least 6 hours or overnight.

2. Remove the meat from the refrigerator and let sit at room temperature for 30 minutes. Preheat the oven to 350°F. Bake the meat, covered, for 1 hour or until it is tender. Allow the meat to cool slightly, then remove it from the liquid with a slotted spoon and chop into bite-size pieces. Spoon off some of the oil floating on top of the cooking liquid, and reserve.

3. Heat a griddle or skillet over medium-high heat. Spoon a bit of the reserved oil onto the griddle, add some of the meat (mix up the leaner and fattier pieces so everyone gets some of both), season with salt, and cook, tossing, until hot and starting to crisp.

4. To serve, overlap 2 tortillas on each plate, top with ½ cup meat, some onions, and a sprinkle of chopped cilantro. Squeeze lime juice over all.

MOOCHIE'S MEATBALLS AND MORE

EST. 2003 ★ SALT LAKE'S BIG BITE OF PHILLY

So I'm cruising Salt Lake City, Utah, and I've got a hankering for some Philly food. You know, cheesesteaks, meatball subs. The only problem is that I'm 2,100 miles away from Philly. People around here say, don't worry about that, all you have to do is check out Moochie's.

★ TRACK IT DOWN ★

232 E. 800 South
Salt Lake City, Utah 84111
801-596-1350
www.moochiesmeatballs.com

The Philly infusion comes from Philly native Joanna Rendi, nicknamed Moochie by her dad and raised on Philly classics. When she moved to Salt Lake City, she couldn't find a good sandwich shop, so she opened one in her husband Don MacDonald's pottery shop. Anything she ate as a kid she put on the menu, and the pottery is still for sale, but the sandwich business has taken off.

For the Philly cheesesteak they put some oil down on the griddle, some sliced onions and salt, then very-thin-sliced rib-eye steak. After that some red and green bell pepper gets sautéed with some mushrooms. Then the processed American cheese slices top the meat to melt. Top that with a crispy roll and the heat steams that bread on top: this deal's legit. The meat is super tender, the peppers are cooked a bit so they're broken down, and the juiciness is all there. You can have it any way you like it—even with Moochie's homemade marinara sauce on top. You'd be surprised how that can pull it all together.

To make the sauce, she starts with a little olive oil in the pan, adds garlic and onions, and sweats them with a little salt and pepper and fresh roasted red peppers. She freezes some fresh herbs to make it easier to chop them up (her mom taught her that trick), so she's got parsley and basil, then some dried parsley, basil, and oregano for good measure. A little bit of water goes into the mix to hydrate the spices; then she adds the tomato sauce and a secret spice ingredient. It cooks down for three hours. The sauce is also a key ingredient in her meatball sandwich. For her meatballs she uses a mixture of hot and mild Italian pork sausage, eggs, garlic, salt, pepper, parsley, bread crumbs, oatmeal, and extra-lean ground beef. She makes the balls the size of her hand, but she ends up cutting them in half. Why not just make smaller meatballs? Because that's how everybody else does it. Those bad boys hang out simmering in marinara sauce all day. She then takes warm bread, lays down the provolone, then the sauced meatballs (down flat, another reason to cut them in half). Okay, arms out, keep away your predators, take a big bite: that was so worth the burn, subtle and delicious.

[GUY ASIDE]

I know meatballs, and when a place claims to be doing real-deal meatballs or Philly cheesesteaks I start to ask questions. That all changed with Moochie's, and we're back to one of my fave food cities in the country, Salt Lake City. They got it going on. I had never heard of it being a foodie place—I just thought of skiing, the Tabernacle Choir, Olympics, Donny and Marie Osmond—but we found some killer places. Blue Plate, Lone Star—good times.

The other thing I dig about this place: I grew up in Ferndale, California, a little tourist town where my parents were leather artists, making belts, purses, and vests. We had a lot of friends who were pottery throwers, so we had a lot of pottery in my house as a kid. So when I go into this place and we have these killer meatballs, and we're waiting in line for a meatball sandwich and see funky pottery, I'm naturally drawn to it, checking it out. Joanna's husband is an artist who teaches pottery-making. I'm like, I'm home; I end up buying a pottery pitcher for my mom for Mother's Day by the end of the show. It goes back to the whole thing about the feeling and connection that goes on with these people and these locations.

GET YOUR TICKETS TO ARNIE'S GUN SHOW . . . YAH!

Eggplant Parmigiana Sandwich

ADAPTED FROM A RECIPE COURTESY OF JOANNA RENDI MACDONALD OF MOOCHIE'S MEATBALLS AND MORE!

If you don't think you like eggplant, this will convert you.

MAKES 6 SERVINGS

¼ cup kosher salt, plus 1 teaspoon

1 large firm eggplant

3 large eggs

1 teaspoon freshly ground black pepper

4 cups Italian seasoned bread crumbs

½ to 1 cup olive oil

6 Italian style hoagie rolls, split

1 cup part-skim mozzarella, shredded

2 cups prepared marinara sauce, warm

1. Preheat the oven to 350°F.

2. Fill a large bowl with warm water and stir in the salt until it dissolves. Slice the eggplant crosswise about ¼-inch thick, making sure that the slices are as consistent as possible. If the base of the eggplant is very large, cut those slices in half lengthwise. Add the eggplant slices to the salt water and let stand for 1 hour. Make sure the eggplant is completely submerged.

3. Remove the eggplant slices from the salt bath and shake off excess moisture. In a shallow dish, whisk together the eggs, 1 teaspoon salt, and the pepper to make an egg wash. Spread the bread crumbs in another shallow dish. Dip the eggplant in the egg wash, then the bread crumbs, covering all surfaces.

4. Line a large plate or baking sheet with paper towels. Lightly coat a large heavy frying pan with olive oil and allow it to heat up over medium-high heat. Add some eggplant slices to the pan, cover and cook until you see the eggplant begin to be translucent, about 5 minutes. If the eggplant becomes too dark, lower the heat and allow it to cook slowly. Using a large spatula, turn the eggplant onto the other side and cook until it is completely tender, about 1 to 2 minutes more. When eggplant is completely cooked, transfer it to the paper towels to blot any excess oil. Repeat with the remaining eggplant.

5. Place the hoagie rolls in the oven until warm, about 5 minutes. Divide the eggplant evenly among the rolls and top with shredded mozzarella cheese and warm marinara sauce. Enjoy!

I DON'T KNOW WHAT TO SAY 'BOUT THIS ONE. (SOMETIMES YOU JUST TURN THE PAGE QUICKLY . . . HA HA HA.)

PAT'S BARBECUE

EST. 2003 ★ A CIRCUS OF SMOKIN' FLAVOR

When you're thinking barbecue, you're probably thinking Texas, Memphis, the Carolinas—you're not thinking Utah and the Wasatch Mountains. When you put down your snowboard and you're heading back from Park City, on your way back through to Salt Lake, stop by this joint, run by a competition barbecue dude named Pat.

> **★ TRACK IT DOWN ★**
>
> 155 W. Commonwealth Avenue
> South Salt Lake, Utah 84115
> 801-484-5963
> www.patsbbq.com

It all started out as a hobby for Pat Barber. You see, you're at a barbecue competition, and you get to a point where you say, if I win big, I'm doing this. Pat said to himself, if I come in tenth place in any category, I'm quitting my day job. A bunch of blue ribbons and six years later, it's like the circus came to town. Pat and his crew are cranking out two thousand meals a week, all from a smoker parked outside on a trailer—this is a culinary gangster right here, this guy rolls it out big time.

OWNER'S NOTE: Since the show aired, our business has exploded and hasn't fallen off. We've gone from three hundred meals a day to twelve hundred and had to buy a smoker that's twice as big. The new smoker can hold twenty-one hundred pounds of meat at once! —Pat Barber

He's smoking up the same recipes that got him those ribbons, but there's a one-of-a-kind, once-a-week specialty that's got them lining up an hour before he opens and waiting till they're ready. Hunks of brisket, double rubbed and smoked twice: they're called burnt ends, and you're lucky if you get them, they go so fast. He doesn't trim any of the hunk of meat he starts with: fat's flavor and fat's moisture. He rubs it down with a product called Butt Rub (that product's put out by a very famous barbecue team; this is the goods) and he adds steak seasoning, chile powder, and his signature secret ingredient that's from out of the country. He lets it sit overnight to let all the spices marry into that meat. They roll down a big long hallway and out to the smoker for ten hours; then he pulls them, cuts the ends off, rubs them again, and puts them back in the smoker for another ten hours. That's what BBQ heaven looks like right there. There's just enough marbling in there; it's savory and crunchy enough—he's not doing this wrong at all.

[ROAD TIP]

One of the identifiers I'll always teach: when you're on the road and you can't find a place to eat, pull into the local fire department and ask those cats what they eat. They're great chefs, and they pride themselves on it. So if you want a good recommendation, call them. When I find a fireman eating in a joint, I'm usually impressed. Big props to the South Salt Lake City Fire Department for the ride in the fire engine. You say cops and doughnut shops? I don't know about doughnuts, but firemen and BBQ makes sense.

And he's making pulled pork and ribs, and fresh smoked chicken and sausage for New Orleans jambalaya (that's a lot of big flavor, and great sausage; I could hear it snap when I bit into it), plus classic sides like coleslaw and honey-sweetened cornbread.

Pat will smoke just about anything, like meatloaf (recipe on page 234); it's got just the right smoked flavor, not too sweet. It's down-home comfort food at its best. Come check it out and you'll know why they're lined up.

THE SAUCE IS SOOO GOOD, YOU MIGHT EAT YOUR HAND . . .

Smoked Barbecue Meatloaf

ADAPTED FROM A RECIPE COURTESY OF PAT BARBER OF PAT'S BBQ

This just in: Pat reports that they've been topping this with biscuits and country gravy, in addition to the onion and barbecue sauce option, and it's gone ballistic!

MAKES 10 SERVINGS

5 pounds 80/20 ground beef

3 large eggs

2½ cups dried seasoned bread crumbs

2½ cups milk

1 cup barbecue sauce, plus more for serving

1 box (2 packets) Lipton onion soup mix

Grilled onions, for garnish

1. Heat a smoker to 225°F.

2. Combine the meat, eggs, bread crumbs, milk, barbecue sauce, and soup mix. Shape the mixture into a tube or loaf and place it inside a tin baking pan. Place the pan inside the smoker for 4 hours. Pat uses cured applewood in the smoker.

3. Serve with a ribbon of your favorite barbecue sauce with grilled onions on top.

[GUY ASIDE]

Pat and I knew some similar people from the barbecue circuit world. Just like at Wilson's, we'd been at the same Houston barbecue school. The barbecue circle is tight—a lot of respect and camaraderie.

Pat's restaurant is in the middle of nowhere, and he's telling me it will fill up. Well, it opened to fifty or sixty people in line—a cavalcade (big word for me) of people. Pat's got a great logo, delivery with golf carts, lots of live music, and happy people, and he embraces the eclectic nature of the city. An eclectic place like Salt Lake brings out eclectic food.

RED IGUANA

EST. 1985 ★ THE KILLER HOLY MOLE

My first job in the restaurant business was at a Mexican restaurant in Ferndale, California. Now, I live in California, so you know I love Mexican food, but especially places that are doing it right—like this place in Salt Lake City, where they're making seven different kinds of mole. Holy mole!

★ TRACK IT DOWN ★

736 W. North Temple
Salt Lake City, Utah 84116
801-322-1489
www.rediguana.com

"Mole" means sauce, and it's a favorite in Mexico for parties and celebrations. They've been doing moles here since 1985, when Lucy Cardenas's parents, Maria and Ramón, opened the place. The Cardenases originally came to Salt Lake from San Francisco in 1965 to open the Casa Grande restaurant. Lucy and her husband, Bill Coker, took over Red Iguana a few years ago, and yes, they're doing seven or eight moles every day, with nuts, herbs, chiles, spices, and more.

The mole negro is the king of moles, says Lucy, and she makes it in fifteen-gallon batches, with a list of ingredients (recipe on page 237) that will blow your mind—even avocado leaves. (That's it, we had now entered the boundaries of "I've never cooked with avocado leaves—next we'll be cooking with my sock.") It's a heck of a family recipe. She served it to me on a bean-filled corn tortilla, and you get this sweet and heat . . . my taste buds rocked! And remember, that's just one of her moles: the green mole is great on the chicken enchiladas; there's Suizas, mole poblano with chiles, fruit, nuts, and a touch of chocolate; and there's an almond mole served with another Red Iguana specialty, puntas de filete a la norteña, which is chopped sirloin tips served with bacon, jalapeño, onion, and tomato. Wow, that's hot, and it's like a creamy soup.

Lucy's even making her own chorizo, which she serves in her tacos Don Ramón. She starts with granulated garlic, onion, pepper, powdered oregano, thyme, marjoram, allspice, cinnamon, cayenne, paprika, New Mexican red chile powder, salt, bay leaves, and vinegar. (At least this won't be lacking in flavor; it would be good on Styrofoam peanuts.) Then she adds coarse-ground pork and leaves it in the refrigerator for about a day. For the tacos she starts with some chopped sirloin seared in a bit of oil on the grill. She sprinkles on some New Mexico powder (garlic and salt) and then adds the chorizo on top. She puts on her tortillas to heat (after dipping them in oil to make them more pliable) and puts some of the chorizo oil in the tortillas to give them a shot of color and seasoning. She puts some shredded lettuce and queso atop the meat in the tacos, with some avocado salsa and pico de gallo on the side. *Love, peace, and taco grease—delicious.* The chorizo's fantastic, the meat is nice and tender, and I didn't get anything on my wardrobe—that was a miracle.

FIFTY GALLONS OF MOLE . . . FOR MY CAMARO. LEMME THINK ABOUT IT . . .

Mole Negro with Chicken

ADAPTED FROM A RECIPE COURTESY OF LUCY CARDENAS AND BILL COKER OF THE RED IGUANA

Spend some time with the king of moles.

MAKES 6 SERVINGS

Chicken with Mole Negro

3 tablespoons vegetable oil

6 boneless, skinless chicken breast halves

Kosher salt to taste

3 to 4 cups Mole Negro (recipe follows)

12 (8-inch) flour tortillas, warm

1. Heat a medium skillet over medium heat. Add the oil. Season the chicken breasts with salt and cook until golden brown on both sides, about 3 minutes per side.

2. Add enough mole to just about cover the chicken and simmer 12 minutes. Serve with warm flour tortillas.

Mole Negro

7 pasilla negro chiles

6 mulatto chiles

1 quart (4 cups) hot water

½ cup vegetable oil, plus more for cooking the chicken

1 (8-inch) flour tortilla, roughly torn, plus more for serving

1 overripe plantain or banana, roughly chopped

1 small poblano chile, stemmed and roughly chopped, seeds removed

5 cherry tomatoes, halved

4 garlic cloves

¼ yellow onion

½ cup raisins

6 whole sprigs of fresh epazote

3 whole sprigs of cilantro

⅓ cup roughly chopped walnuts, toasted

⅓ cup salted peanuts, toasted

2 ounces Mexican chocolate, roughly chopped

1 bay leaf

1 avocado leaf

½ teaspoon black peppercorns

½ teaspoon coriander seeds

¼ teaspoon cumin seeds

¼ teaspoon anise seed

¾ teaspoon dried marjoram

¾ teaspoon dried thyme

1 whole clove

½ cinnamon stick

¼ cup sugar

Kosher salt

1. Remove the stems and seeds from the pasilla and mulatto chiles, then let them soak in the hot water for 20 minutes.

2. Heat ¼ cup of the vegetable oil in a large saucepan over medium-high heat. Toast the tortilla in the hot oil until golden brown. Add the plantain or banana, poblano, tomatoes, garlic, onion, raisins, epazote, and cilantro and sauté until the poblano and onion soften.

Add all the nuts, the chiles with their soaking water, the chocolate, bay and avocado leaves, peppercorns, coriander, cumin, and anise seeds, marjoram, thyme, clove, and cinnamon stick. Simmer for 10 minutes.

3. Remove the bay leaf and the clove and cinnamon stick. Transfer the mole to a blender and puree (carefully, it's hot) until smooth. If the mixture is too thick, add some hot water to thin; it should be the consistency of tomato sauce.

4. Heat ¼ cup oil in a deep skillet over high heat. Pour in the mole, being careful not to spatter yourself with the hot oil. Stir in the sugar and some salt, reduce the heat slightly, and let simmer for 15 minutes.

THE BEGINNING OF "HOLY MOLE." YEAH!

Acknowledgments

Just like the show, they're a ton of people who play a role in the creation of this book:

First and foremost, huge thanks to my wife, Lori, and sons, Hunter and Ryder.

My Knuckle Sandwich team: Tom Nelson (consigliere), Korina McAlister (culinary handler), Roni Brown (chief of staff), Kleetus Cox (right-hand man), Dirty P. Thompson (left-hand man), and the rest of "da krew!"

Many thanks to the unbelievably great Page Production crew: creator and executive producer, David "Klinger" Page, Roberta Brackman, the horse jumping Hannah, Maria Carrera, Kat Higgins, Ryan Dodge, Drew Sondeland, Brad Keely, Kathryn Browning, Wade Barry, Ian Logan, Jeff Mandell, Erin Halden, Elizabeth Winter, Jamie Vincent, Rick Berland, Kris Ausan, David Canada, Bryna Levin, Jeremy Green, Kari Kloster, Neil Martin, Ron Gabaldon, Jeff Assell, Matt Giovinetti, Mark Farrell, Mike Morris, Anthony Rodriguez, Kate Gibson, and Craig Alreck.

My agents: Jason "Mcguire" Hodes, Jeff "Hack" Google, Michelle "Michi" Bernstein, and assistants Brittney and Meg. And thanks to my literary agent, Dorian Karchmar.

From the Food Network: production executives Brian Lando and Jordan Harman, as well as Susan Stockton, Danielle LaRosa, and Ashley Archer from the Culinary Department. Miriam Garron who wrote, translated, or edited much of the recipe material that crossed her desk and managed a sterling team of Food Network recipe testers: Morgan Haas, Jay P. Brooks, Vincent Camillo, Santos Loo, Young Sun Huh, and Brook Herrit, along with Maryann Pomeranz, Enrique S. Gatchalian, and Theresa Lee.

From HarperCollins: many thanks to editor Cassie ("the Machine") Jones and editorial assistant, Jessica Deputato, as well as Liate Stehlik, Mary Ellen O'Neill, Lynn Grady, Tavia Kowalchuk, Brianne Halverson, Joyce Wong, Paula Szafranski, Kris Tobiassen, and Karen Lumley. And many thanks to Emeril Lagasse, "the Man."

My "sista from anotha mista" Ann Volkwein. Every once in a while you get a chance to meet and work with someone that really gets your attitude, energy, and focus. I am so fortunate to have Ann on my team. I really appreciate all that she can capture in my wild style.

To Chevrolet, for makin the sooooo money '67 Camaro. . . . What a great ride.

And finally, thanks to all the great chefs, staff, and restaurant owners that make Triple D off da hook!

Recipe Index

List of Restaurants

Here's a list of all the terrific restaurants that have been shown on Diners, Drive-ins and Dives. The restaurants in red are featured in this book and the restaurants with an asterisk were in the first book. But you gotta visit 'em all!

❏ **A1 DINER***
3 Bridge Street
Gardiner, ME 04345
207-582-4804
www.a1diner.com/menus

❏ **ALCENIA'S**
317 N. Main Street
Memphis, TN 38103
901-523-0200

❏ **ALPINE STEAKHOUSE**
4520 S. Tamiami Trail
Sarasota, FL 34231
941-922-3797
www.alpinesteak.com

❏ **AL'S BREAKFAST***
413 14th Avenue S.E.
Minneapolis, MN 55414
612-331-9991

❏ **AMATO'S CAFE**
6405 Center Street
Omaha, NE 68016
402-558-5010

❏ **BABY BLUES BBQ***
444 Lincoln Boulevard
Venice, CA 90291
310-396-7675
www.bluesvenice.com

❏ **BACKROAD PIZZA**
1807 2nd Street
Santa Fe, NM 87505
505-955-9055
www.backroadpizza.com

❏ **BAR GERNIKA**
202 South Capitol Boulevard
Boise, ID 83714
208-344-2175
www.bargernika.com

❏ **BAR-B-Q KING**
2900 Wilkinson Boulevard
Charlotte, NC 28208
704-399-8344
www.barbaking.com

❏ **BAYWAY DINER***
2019 S. Wood Avenue
Linden, NJ 07036
908-862-3207

❏ **BBQ SHACK**
1613 E. Peoria Street
Paola, KS 66071
913-294-5908
www.thebbqshack.com

❏ **BEACON DRIVE-IN**
255 John B. White Sr.
  Boulevard
Spartanburg, SC 29306
864-585-9387
www.beacondrivein.com

❏ **BENNY'S SEAFOOD***
2500 SW 107th Avenue
Miami, FL 33165
305-227-1232

❏ **BERT'S BURGER BAR**
235 N. Guadalupe Street
Santa Fe, NM 87501
505-982-0215

❏ **BIG JIM'S IN THE RUN**
201 Saline Street
Pittsburgh, PA 15207
412-421-0532
www.bigjimsrestaurant.com

❏ **BIG MAMA'S KITCHEN
  & CATERING**
3223 N. 45th Street
Turning Point Campus, Building A
Omaha, NE 68104
402-455-6262
www.bigmamaskitchen.com

❏ **BIG STAR DINER**
305 Madison Avenue North
Bainbridge Island, WA 98110
206-842-5786

❏ **BIZZARRO**
1307 N. 46th Street
Seattle, WA 98103
206-632-7277
www.bizzarroitaliancafe.com

❏ **BLOW FLY INN**
1201 Washington Avenue
Gulfport, MS 39507
228-896-9812
www.blowflyinn.com

❏ **BLUE MOON CAFÉ***
1621 Aliceanna Street
Baltimore, MD 21231
410-522-3940

❏ **BLUE PLATE DINER**
2041 S. 2100 Street East
Salt Lake City, UT 84108
801-463-1151

❏ **BLUE WATER
  SEAFOOD MARKET
  AND GRILL**
3667 India Street
San Diego, CA 92103
619-497-0914

❏ **BOBBY'S HAWAIIAN
  STYLE RESTAURANT***
1011 Hewitt Avenue West
Everett, WA 98201
425-259-1338
www.bobbyshawaiianstyle
  restaurant.com

❏ **BOBO DRIVE-IN**
2300 S.W. 10th Avenue
Topeka, KS 66604
785-234-4511

❏ **BRANDY'S
  RESTAURANT AND
  BAKERY**
1500 E. Cedar Avenue
Flagstaff, AZ 86004
928-779-2187
www.brandysrestaurant.com

❏ **BREWBURGER'S**
4629 S. 108th Street
Omaha, NE
402-614-7644
www.brewburgersomaha.com

❑ **BRICK OVEN PIZZA**
800 S. Broadway
Baltimore, MD 21231
410-563-1600
www.boppizza.com

❑ **BRINT'S DINER**
4834 E. Lincoln Street
Wichita, KS 67218
316-684-0290

❑ **BROADWAY DINER**
6501 Eastern Avenue
Baltimore, MD 21224
410-631-5666
www.broadwaydiner1.com

❑ **BROWNSTONE DINER
AND PANCAKE
FACTORY***
426 Jersey Avenue
Jersey City, NJ 07302
201-433-0471
www.brownstonediner.com

❑ **BRYANT-LAKE BOWL**
801 W. Lake Street
Minneapolis, MN 55408
612-825-3737
www.bryantlakebowl.com

❑ **BYWAYS CAFE**
1212 NW Glisan Street
Portland, OR 97209
503-221-0011
www.bywayscafe.com

❑ **CABBAGETOWN
MARKET**
198 Carroll Street
Atlanta, GA 30312
404-221-9186
www.cabbagetownmarkt.com

❑ **CAFE ON THE ROUTE**
1101 Military Avenue
Baxter Springs, KS 66713
620-856-5646
www.cafeontheroute.com

❑ **CAFE ROLLE**
5737 H Street
Sacramento, CA 95819
916-455-9140
www.caferolle.com

❑ **CALIFORNIA TACOS &
MORE**
3235 California Street
Omaha, NE 68131
402-342-0212
www.californiatacosandmore
.com

❑ **CAPTAIN CHUCK-A-
MUCK'S**
21088 Marina Road
Rescue, VA 23424
757-356-1005
www.captainchuck-a-mucks
.com

❑ **CASAMENTO'S
RESTAURANT**
4330 Magazine Street
New Orleans, LA 70115
504-895-9761
www.casamentosrestaurant
.com

❑ **CASINO EL CAMINO**
517 E. 6th Street
Austin, TX 78701
512-469-9330
www.casinoelcamino.net

❑ **CECILIA'S CAFE**
230 6th Street S.W.
Albuquerque, NM 87102
505-243-7070

❑ **CEMITAS PUEBLA**
3619 W. North Avenue
Chicago, IL 60647
773-772-8435
www.cemitaspuebla.com

❑ **CENTRAL CITY CAFÉ**
529 14th Street West
Huntington, WV 25704
304-522-6142

❑ **CHAP'S PIT BEEF***
5801 Pulaski Highway
Baltimore, MD 21205
410-483-2379
www.chapspitbeef.com

❑ **CHARLIE PARKER'S**
700 North Street
Springfield, IL 62704
217-241-2104

❑ **CHARLIE'S DINER**
32 W. Main Street
Spencer, MA 01562
508-885-4033

❑ **CHEF POINT CAFÉ**
5901 Watauga Road
Wautaga, TX 76148
817-656-0080
www.chefpointcafe.org

❑ **CHINO BANDIDO***
15414 N. 19th Avenue,
Suite K
Phoenix, AZ 85023
602-375-3639
www.chinobandido.com

❑ **THE COFFEE CUP**
512 Nevada Way
Boulder City, NV 89005
702-294-0517
www.worldfamouscoffeecup
.com

❑ **COLONNADE**
1879 Cheshire Bridge Road
N.E.
Atlanta, GA 30324
404-874-5642
www.colonnadeatl.com

❑ **THE COVE**
606 W. Cypress Street
San Antonio, TX 78212
210-227-2683
www.thecove.us

❑ **COZY CORNER**
745 N. Parkway
Memphis, TN 38105
901-527-9158
www.cozycornerbbq.com

❑ **CREOLE CREAMERY**
4924 Prytania Street
New Orleans, LA 70115
504-894-8680
www.creolecreamery.com

❑ **CRYSTAL
RESTAURANT**
1211 Penn Avenue
Pittsburgh, PA 15222
412-434-0480

❑ **DADDYPOPS DINER**
232 N. York Road
Hatboro, PA 19040
215-675-9717

❑ **DARI-ETTE DRIVE-IN**
1440 Minnehaha Avenue East
St. Paul, MN 55106
651-776-3470

❑ **DARWELL'S CAFE**
127 E. First Street
Long Beach, MS 39560
228-868-8946
www.darwellscafe.com

❑ **DELL RHEA'S CHICKEN
BASKET**
645 Joliet Road
Willowbrook, IL 60527
630-325-0780
www.chickenbasket.com

DEWESE'S TIP TOP CAFE*
2814 Fredericksburg Road
San Antonio, TX 78201
210-732-0191
www.tiptopcafe.com

THE DINING CAR*
8826 Frankford Avenue
Philadelphia, PA 19136
215-338-5113
www.thediningcar.com

DI PASQUALE'S
3700 Gough Street
Baltimore, MD 21224
410-276-6787
www.dipasquales.com

DIXIE QUICKS MAGNOLIA ROOM
1915 Leavenworth Street
Omaha, NE 68012
402-346-3549
www.dixiequicks.com

DONATELLI'S
2692 East County Road E
White Bear Lake, MN 55110
651-777-9199
www.donatellis.com

DOR-STOP RESTAURANT
1430 Potomac Avenue
Pittsburgh, PA 15216
412-561-9320
www.dor-stoprestaurant.com

DOT'S BACK INN*
4030 Macarthur Avenue
Richmond, VA 23227
804-266-3167

DOUMAR'S
1919 Monticello Avenue
Norfolk, VA 23517
757-627-4163
www.doumars.com

DUARTE'S TAVERN*
202 Stage Road
Pescadero, CA 94060
650-879-0464
www.duartestavern.com

EL INDIO MEXICAN RESTAURANT*
3695 India Street
San Diego, CA 92103
619-299-0333
www.el-indio.com

11TH STREET DINER
1065 Washington Avenue
Miami Beach, FL 33139
305-534-6373
www.eleventhstreetdiner.com

EMILY'S LEBANESE DELI
641 University Avenue N.E.
Minneapolis, MN 55416
612-379-4069
www.emilyslebanesedeli.com

EMMA JEAN'S HOLLAND BURGER CAFÉ*
17143 D Street (Route 66)
Victorville, CA 92394
760-243-9938
www.hollandburger.com

EVELYN'S DRIVE-IN*
2335 Main Road (Route 77)
Tiverton, RI 02878
401-624-3100
www.evelynsdrivein.com

EVEREADY DINER*
4189 Albany Post Road
(Route 9 North)
Hyde Park, NY 12538
845-229-8100
www.theevereadydiner.com

THE FLY TRAP*
22950 Woodward Avenue
Ferndale, MI 48220
248-399-5150
www.theflytrapferndale.com

FOUR KEGS SPORTS PUB*
267 N. Jones Boulevard
Las Vegas, NV 89107
702-870-0255
www.fourkegs.com

FRANKS DINER*
508 58th Street
Kenosha, WI 53140
262-657-1017
www.franksdinerkenosha.com

G & A RESTAURANT
3802 Eastern Avenue
Baltimore, MD 21224
410-276-9422
www.gandarestaurant.com

GAFFEY STREET DINER
247 N. Gaffey Street
San Pedro, CA 90731
310-548-6964
www.gaffeystreetdiner.com

GALEWOOD COOKSHACK
Various locations
Chicago, IL
773-470-8334
www.galewoodcookshack.com

GIUSTI'S
14743 Walnut Grove-Thornton Road
Walnut Grove, CA 95960
916-776-1808
www.giustis.com

GLENN'S DINER
1820 W. Montrose Avenue
Chicago, IL 60613
773-506-1720
www.glennsdiner.com

GORILLA BARBEQUE
2145 Coast Highway
Pacifica, CA 94044
650-359-7427
www.gorillabbq.com

GRAMPA'S BAKERY AND RESTAURANT
17 SW First Street
Dania Beach, FL 33004
954-923-2163
www.grampasbakery.com

GREEN MESQUITE
1400 Barton Springs Road
Austin, TX 78704
512-479-0485
www.greenmesquite.net

GRUBSTAKE
1525 Pine Street
San Francisco, CA 94109
415-673-8268
www.sfgrubstake.com

GUMBO SHACK
212 ½ Fairhope Avenue
Fairhope, AL 36532
251-928-4100
www.guysgumbo.com

HACKNEY'S ON HARMS*
1241 Harms Road
Glenview, IL 60025
847-724-5577
www.hackneys.net

❑ **HANK'S CREEKSIDE RESTAURANT**
2800 4th Street
Santa Rosa, CA 95405
707-575-8839
www.sterba.com/sro/creek
side

❑ **HAROLD'S RESTAURANT***
608 N. Limestone Street
Gaffney, SC 29340
864-489-9153
www.haroldsrestaurant.com

❑ **HARRY'S ROADHOUSE**
96-B Old Las Vegas Highway
Santa Fe, NM 87505
505-989-4629

❑ **HAUS MURPHY'S**
5739 W. Glendale Avenue
Glendale, AZ 85301
623-939-2480
www.hausmurphys.com

❑ **HAVANA HIDEOUT**
509 Lake Avenue
Lake Worth, FL 33460
561-585-8444
www.havanahideout.com

❑ **THE HIGHLANDER**
931 Monroe Drive NE
Atlanta, GA 30308
404-872-0060
www.thehighlanderatlanta
.com

❑ **HIGHSTOWN DINER**
151 Mercer Street
Highstown, NJ 08520
609-443-4600

❑ **HILLBILLY HOT DOGS***
6591 Ohio River Road
Lesage, WV 25537
304-762-2458
www.hillbillyhotdogs.com

❑ **HOB NOB HILL**
2271 1st Avenue
San Diego, CA 92101
619-239-8176
www.hobnobhill.com

❑ **HODAD'S***
5010 Newport Avenue
Ocean Beach, CA 92107
619-224-4623

❑ **HULLABALOO DINER**
15045 FM 2154
Wellborn, TX 77845
979-690-3002
www.hullaboodiner.com

❑ **IRON BARLEY***
5510 Virginia Avenue
St. Louis, MO 63111
314-351-4500
www.ironbarley.com

❑ **JAMAICA KITCHEN**
8736 Sunset Drive
Kendall Lakes, FL 33173
305-596-2585
www.jamaicakitchen.com

❑ **JAMIE'S BROADWAY GRILLE**
427 Broadway
Sacramento, CA 95818
916-442-4044
www.jamiesbroadwaygrille
.com

❑ **JAY BEE'S**
15911 Avalon Boulevard
Gardena, CA 90247
310-532-1064
www.jaybeesbbq.com

❑ **JEFFERSON DINER**
5 Bowling Green Parkway
Lake Hopatcong, NJ 07849
973-663-0233
www.jeffersondiner.com

❑ **JOE'S CABLE CAR**
4320 Mission Street
San Francisco, CA 94112
415-334-6699
www.joescablecarrestaurant
.com

❑ **JOE'S FARM GRILL***
3000 E. Ray Road
Gilbert, AZ 85296
480-821-0596
www.joesfarmgrill.com

❑ **JOE'S GIZZARD CITY***
120 W. Main Street
Potterville, MI 48876
517-645-2120
www.gizzardcity.com

❑ **JOE TESS PLACE**
5424 S. 24th Street
Omaha, NE 68102
402-733-4638
www.joetessplace.com

❑ **JOEY K'S RESTAURANT & BAR**
3001 Magazine Street
New Orleans, LA 70115
504-891-0997
www.joeyksrestaurant.com

❑ **J.T. FARNHAM'S***
88 Eastern Avenue
(Route 133)
South Essex, MA 01929
978-768-6643

❑ **KEEGAN'S SEAFOOD GRILLE***
1519 Gulf Boulevard
Indian Rocks Beach, FL 33785
727-596-2477
www.keegansseafood.com

❑ **KELLY O'S DINER**
1130 Perry Highway # 28
Pittsburgh, PA 15237
412-364-0473
www.kellyos.com

❑ **KELLY'S DINER**
674 Broadway
Somerville, MA 02144
617-623-8102
www.kellysdiner.com

❑ **KRAZY JIM'S BLIMPY BURGER**
551 S. Division Street
Ann Arbor, MI 48104
734-663-4590
www.blimpyburger.com

❑ **KUMA'S CORNER**
2900 W. Belmont Avenue
Chicago, IL 60618
773-604-8769
www.kumascorner.com

❑ **LEONARD'S PIT BARBECUE**
5465 Fox Plaza Drive
Memphis, TN 38115
901-360-1963
www.leonardsbarbecue.com

❑ **LEO'S BBQ**
3631 N. Kelley Avenue
Oklahoma City, OK 73111
405-424-5367

❑ **LO BELLO'S SPAGHETTI HOUSE**
809 5th Avenue
Coraopolis, PA 15108
412-264-9721
www.lobellosspaghettihouse
.com

❑ **LITTLE TEA SHOP**
69 Monroe Avenue
Memphis, TN 38103
901-525-6000

❑ **LONE STAR TAQUERIA**
2265 Fort Union Boulevard
Salt Lake City, UT 84121
801-944-2300

❏ **LOS TAPATIOS**
354 N. White Rd.
San Jose, CA 95127
408-729-6199

❏ **LOUIE MUELLER BARBECUE***
206 W. Second Street
Taylor, TX 76574
512-352-6206
www.louiemuellerbarbecue
.com

❏ **MAC AND ERNIE'S ROADSIDE EATERY***
Williams Creek Depot FM 470
Tarpley, TX 78883
830-562-3250
www.macandernies.com

❏ **MAD GREEK'S DINER**
72112 Baker Boulevard
Baker, CA 92309
760-733-4354

❏ **MAGNOLIA CAFE**
1920 S. Congress Avenue
Austin, TX 78704
512-445-0000

2304 Lake Austin Boulevard
Austin, TX 78703
512-478-8645
www.themagnoliacafe.com

❏ **MAMA'S 39TH STREET DINER**
3906 Waddell Street
Kansas City, MO 64111
816-531-6422

❏ **MANCI'S ANTIQUE CLUB**
1715 Main Street
Daphne, AL 36526
251-626-9917
www.manci.net

❏ **MARIA'S TACO XPRESS***
2529 S. Lamar Boulevard
Austin, TX 78704
512-444-0261
www.tacoxpress.com

❏ **MARIETTA DINER***
306 Cobb Parkway South
Marietta, GA 30060
770-423-9390
www.mariettadiner.net

❏ **MARLOWE'S RIBS**
4381 Elvis Presley Boulevard
Memphis, TN 38116
901-332-4159
www.marlowesmemphis.com

❏ **MASSEY'S RESTAURANT**
1805 8th Avenue
Fort Worth, TX 76110
817-921-5582

❏ **MATTHEWS CAFETERIA**
2229 Main Street
Tucker, GA 30084
770-939-2357
www.matthewscafeteria.com

❏ **MATT'S BIG BREAKFAST**
801 N. 1st Street
Phoenix, AZ 85004
602-254-1074
www.mattsbigbreakfast.com

❏ **MIKE'S CHILI PARLOR***
1447 N.W. Ballard Way
Seattle, WA 98107
206-782-2808
www.mikeschiliparlor.com

❏ **MIKE'S CITY DINER**
1714 Washington Street
Boston, MA 02118
617-267-9393
www.mikescitydiner.com

❏ **THE MODERN**
337 13th Avenue N.E.
Minneapolis, MN 55413
612-378-9882
www.moderncafeminneapo
lis.com

❏ **MOGRIDDER'S***
565 Hunts Point Avenue
Bronx, NY 10474
718-991-3046
www.mogridder.com

❏ **MONTE CARLO STEAKHOUSE***
3916 Central S.W.
Albuquerque, NM 87105
505-836-9886

❏ **MOOCHIE'S MEATBALLS AND MORE**
232 E. 800 South
Salt Lake City, UT 84111
801-596-1350
801-364-0232
www.moochiesmeatballs.com

❏ **MUSTACHE BILL'S DINER**
8th Street and Broadway
Barnegat Light, NJ 08006
609-494-0155

❏ **NADINE'S BAR AND RESTAURANT**
19 S. 27th Street
Pittsburgh, PA 15203
412-481-1793
www.nadinesbar.com

❏ **THE NOOK**
492 Hamline Avenue South
St. Paul, MN 55116
651-698-4347

❏ **O'ROURKE'S DINER**
728 Main Street
Middletown, CT 06457
860-346-6101
www.orourkesdiner.com

❏ **THE ORIGINAL FALAFEL'S DRIVE-IN***
2301 Stevens Creek Boulevard
San Jose, CA 95128
408-294-7886
www.falafeldrivein.com

❏ **THE ORIGINAL VITO & NICK'S PIZZERIA**
8433 S. Pulaski Road
Chicago, IL 60652
773-735-2050
www.vitoandnick.com

❏ **PANINI PETE'S***
42½ S. Section Street
Fairhope, AL 36532
251-929-0122
www.paninipetes.com

❏ **PARADISE PUP**
1724 S. River Road
Des Plaines, IL 60018
847-699-8590

❏ **PARASOL'S**
2533 Constance Street
New Orleans, LA 70130
504-897-5413

❏ **PAT'S BARBECUE**
155 W. Commonwealth Avenue
Salt Lake City, UT 84115
801-484-5963
www.patsbbq.com

❏ **PATRICK'S ROADHOUSE**
106 Entrada Drive
Los Angeles, CA 90402
310-459-4544
www.patricksroadhouse.info

❏ **PENGUIN DRIVE-IN***
1921 Commonwealth Avenue
Charlotte, NC 28205
704-375-6959

PIZZA PALACE*
3132 E. Magnolia Avenue
Knoxville, TN 37914
865-524-4388
www.visitpizzapalace.com

PIZZERIA LUIGI
1137 25th Street
San Diego, CA 92102
619-233-3309
www.pizzerialuigi.com

PSYCHO SUZI'S*
2519 Marshall Street N.E.
Minneapolis, MN 55418
612-788-9069
www.psychosuzis.com

RAMONA CAFE*
628 Main Street
Ramona, CA 92605
760-789-8656
www.ramonacafe.com

RED ARROW DINER*
61 Lowell Street
Manchester, NH 03101
603-626-1118
www.redarrowdiner.com

RED IGUANA
736 W. North Temple
Salt Lake City, UT 84116
801-322-1489
www.rediguana.com

RITZ DINER
72 E. Mount Pleasant Avenue
Livingston, NJ 07039
973-533-1213

RIVERSHACK TAVERN*
3449 River Road
Jefferson, LA 70121
504-834-4938
www.therivershacktavern.com

ROBERTO'S
675 W. Union Hills Drive
Phoenix, AZ 85027
602-439-7279

THE ROCK CAFÉ
114 W. Main Street
Stroud, OK 74079
918-968-3990

ROSIE'S DINER
4500 14 Mile Road N.E.
Rockford, MI 49341
616-866-3663
www.rosiesdiner.com

RUSSIAN RIVER PUB
11829 River Road
Forestville, CA 95436
707-887-7932
www.russianriverpub.com

RUTH'S DINER
2100 Emigration Canyon
Salt Lake City, UT 84108
801-582-5807
www.ruthsdiner.com

SALSA BRAVA
2220 E. Route 66 (Santa Fe
Avenue)
Flagstaff, AZ 86004
928-779-5293
www.salsabravaflagstaff.com

SCHOONER OR LATER
241 N. Marina Drive
Long Beach, CA 90803
562-430-3495
www.schoonerorlater.com

SCULLY'S TAVERN*
9809 Sunset Drive
Miami, FL 33173
305-271-7404
www.scullystavern.net

SILK CITY PHILLY*
435 Spring Garden Street
Philadelphia, PA 19123
215-592-8838
www.silkcityphilly.com

THE SILVER SKILLET
200 14th Street N.W.
Atlanta, GA 30318
404-874-1388
www.thesilverskillet.com

**THE SKYLARK FINE
DINING AND LOUNGE**
Route 1 and Wooding Avenue
Edison, NJ 08817
732-777-7878
www.skylarkdiner.com

**SLIM'S LAST CHANCE
CHILI SHACK**
5606 1st Avenue South
Seattle, WA 98108
206-762-7900
www.slimslastchance.com

**SMOKEY VALLEY
TRUCK STOP**
40 Bond Court
Olive Hill, KY 41164
606-286-5001

SMOQUE*
3800 N. Pulaski Road
Chicago, IL 60641
773-545-7427
www.smoquebbq.com

SOPHIA'S PLACE
6313 4th Street N.W.
Albuquerque, NM 87107
505-345-3935

**SOUTH SIDE SODA
SHOP AND DINER***
1122 S. Main Street
Goshen, IN 46526
574-534-3790
www.southsidesodashop-
diner.com

SQUEEZE INN*
7916 Fruitridge Road
Sacramento, CA 95820
916-386-8599
www.thesqueezeinn.com

STANDARD DINER
320 Central Avenue S.E.
Albuquerque, NM 87102
505-243-1440
www.standarddiner.com

STARLITE LOUNGE
364 Freeport Road
Blawnox, PA 15238
412-828-9842

STONEY CREEK INN
8238 Fort Smallwood Road
Baltimore, MD 21226
410-439-3123
www.stoneycreekinnrestau
rant.com

STUDIO DINER
4701 Ruffin Road
San Diego, CA 92123
858-715-6400
www.studiodiner.com

**SUPER DUPER
WEENIE**
306 Black Rock Turnpike
P.O. Box 320487
Fairfield, CT 06825
203-334-3647
www.superduperweenie.com

**SURREY'S CAFE AND
JUICE BAR**
1418 Magazine Street
New Orleans, LA 70130
504-524-3828
www.surreyscafeandjuicebar
.com

SWEETIE PIE'S
4270 Manchester Avenue
St. Louis, MO 63110
314-371-0304

❏ **TAYLOR'S AUTOMATIC REFRESHER***
933 Main Street
St. Helena, CA 94574
707-963-3486
www.taylorsrefresher.com

❏ **TECOLOTE CAFÉ**
1203 Cerrillos Road
Santa Fe, NM 87505
505-988-1362
www.tecolotecafe.com

❏ **TED PETERS***
1350 Pasadena Avenue South
South Pasadena, FL 33707
727-381-7931

❏ **THEE PITTS AGAIN***
5558 W. Bell Road
Glendale, AZ 85308
602-996-7488
www.theepittsagain.com

❏ **TICK TOCK DINER***
281 Allwood Road
Clifton, NJ 07012
973-777-0511
www.ticktockdiner.com

❏ **TIOLI'S CRAZEE BURGER**
4201 30th Street (near El
 Cajon Boulevard)
San Diego, CA 92104
619-282-6044
www.tioliscrazeeburger.com

❏ **TOM'S BAR-B-Q***
4087 New Getwell Road
Memphis, TN 38118
901-365-6690
www.tomsbarbq.com

❏ **TOMMY'S JOYNT**
1101 Geary Boulevard
San Francisco, CA 94109
415-775-4216
www.tommysjoynt.com

❏ **TOWN TALK DINER**
2707 ½ E. Lake Street
Minneapolis, MN 55406
612-722-1312
www.towntalkdiner.com

❏ **TRIPLE XXX FAMILY RESTAURANT***
2 N. Salisbury Street
West Lafayette, IN 47906
765-743-5373
www.triplexxxfamilyrestau
rant.com

❏ **TUFANO'S VERNON PARK TAP**
1073 W. Vernon Park Place
Chicago, IL 60607
312-733-3393

❏ **TUNE-UP CAFÉ**
1115 Hickox Street
Santa Fe, NM 87505
505-983-7060
www.tuneupcafe.com

❏ **TWISTED ROOT BURGER CO.**
2615 Commerce Street
Dallas, TX 75226
214-741-7668
www.twistedrootburgerco
.com

❏ **UNCLE LOU'S FRIED CHICKEN**
3633 Millbranch Road
Memphis, TN 38116
901-332-2367
www.unclelousfriedchicken
.com

❏ **VALENCIA LUNCHERIA**
172 Main Street
Norwalk, CT 06851
203-846-8009
www.valencialuncheria.com

❏ **VICTOR'S 1959 CAFÉ**
3756 Grand Ave South
Minneapolis, MN 55409
612-827-8948
www.victors1959cafe.com

❏ **VILLAGE CAFÉ**
1001 W. Grace Street
Richmond, VA 23220
804-353-8204
www.villagecafeonline.com

❏ **VIRGINIA DINER***
322 W. Main Street
Wakefield, VA 23888
888-823-4637
www.vadiner.com

❏ **VOULA'S OFFSHORE CAFÉ***
658 N.E. Northlake Way
Seattle, WA 98105
206-634-0183
www.voulasoffshore.com

❏ **WHITE MANNA***
358 River Street
Hackensack, NJ 07601
201-342-0914

❏ **WHITE PALACE GRILL**
1159 S. Canal Street
Chicago, IL 60607
312-939-7167
www.whitepalacegrill.com

❏ **THE WIENERY**
414 Cedar Ave. South
Minneapolis, MN 55467
612-333-5798
www.wienery.com

❏ **WILLIE BIRD'S**
1150 Santa Rosa Avenue
Santa Rosa, CA 95404
707-542-0861
www.williebirdsrestaurant
.com

❏ **WILSON'S BARBEQUE**
1851 Post Road
Fairfield, CT 06824
203-319-7427
www.wilsons-bbq.com

❏ **YJ'S SNACK BAR***
128 W. 18th Street
Kansas City, MO 64108
816-472-5533